The Philosophy of George Berkeley

A FIFTEEN-VOLUME
FACSIMILE SERIES REPRODUCING
CLASSIC STUDIES AND INCLUDING
FOUR NEVER-BEFORE-PUBLISHED TITLES

EDITED BY
George Pitcher
Princeton University

A GARLAND SERIES

Berkeley and Malebranche

A STUDY IN THE ORIGINS OF
BERKELEY'S THOUGHT

A. A. Luce

GARLAND PUBLISHING, INC.
NEW YORK & LONDON 1988.

For a list of the titles in this series, see the final pages of this volume.

This reprint has been authorized by Oxford University Press. Copyright Oxford University Press 1934.

Library of Congress Cataloging-in-Publication Data

Luce, A. A. (Arthur Aston), 1882–
Berkeley and Malebranche: a study in the origins of Berkeley's
    thought / A. A. Luce.
p. cm — (The Philosophy of George Berkeley)
Reprint. Originally published: London: Oxford University
Press, 1934.
Includes index.
ISBN 0–8240–2442–7
1. Berkeley, George, 1685–1753. 2. Malebranche, Nicolas,
1638–1715 — Influence. I. Title. II. Series.
B1348.L8 1988 88–21472 192 — dc19

Printed on acid-free, 250-year-life paper.
Printed on United States of America

BERKELEY
AND
MALEBRANCHE

+ Infinite number why absurd. not rightly [soth'd]
by Locke.

3|1 Qu: how 'tis possible we should see flats or
right lines.

2|1 Qu: why the Moon appears greatest in
the Horizon?

3|1 Qu: why we see things erect when painted
inverted.

S Question put by Mr Deering touching the
[Mises] & paradise.

S Matter tho' allow'd to exist may be no
greater than a pin's head.

+ Motion is proportionable to space described in
given time.

+ Velocity not proportionable to space described
in given time.

M No active power but the will, wherefore motion of [body]
[fools] &c.

BERKELEY'S COMMONPLACE BOOK, page 118

(reduced from 200 mm. × 158 mm.), showing marginal signs (*see p. 180 below*)

BERKELEY

AND

MALEBRANCHE

A STUDY IN THE
ORIGINS OF
BERKELEY'S THOUGHT

BY

A. A. LUCE, D.D.
Berkeley Professor of Metaphysics
in the University of Dublin

OXFORD
AT THE CLARENDON PRESS

Oxford University Press, Ely House, London W.1

GLASGOW NEW YORK TORONTO MELBOURNE WELLINGTON
CAPE TOWN SALISBURY IBADAN NAIROBI LUSAKA ADDIS ABABA
BOMBAY CALCUTTA MADRAS KARACHI LAHORE DACCA
KUALA LUMPUR HONG KONG TOKYO

FIRST PUBLISHED 1934
REPRINTED LITHOGRAPHICALLY, WITH A NEW PREFACE
IN GREAT BRITAIN
AT THE UNIVERSITY PRESS, OXFORD
BY VIVIAN RIDLER
PRINTER TO THE UNIVERSITY
1967

PREFACE TO THE NEW IMPRESSION

MY *Berkeley and Malebranche* was written more than thirty years ago, when the view that Berkeley owed his 'immaterial hypothesis' to a French monk was a novelty to most readers. If I were covering the same ground today, I should present the evidence with more conviction, and draw my conclusions with full confidence. My main thesis, I think, has been established, and the subsequent discovery of new facts and new documents has confirmed it. I went wrong in a few points of detail, and I make the corrections below in this Preface; but it can hardly be doubted today that Malebranche's *Recherche* set Berkeley's problem, and helped him to seek and find his solution.

I do not see Malebranche, however, and his influence upon Berkeley, quite as I did thirty years ago. Malebranche and the issue he raised must be viewed within the wide context of French scepticism, as the research and writings of Professor R. H. Popkin showed.[1] Malebranche was no sceptic; but his influence, passing through the hands of Bayle, made for scepticism. I have long known that articles in Bayle's *Dictionary* had a strong influence upon Berkeley (see below pp. 53–55); and when in recent years I resumed my studies in Berkeley's notebooks and the making of his *Principles*, I soon saw that the Male-branche–Bayle influence was more subtle and dialectical

[1] See especially his 'The Sceptical Crisis and the Rise of Modern Philosophy' in the *Review of Metaphysics*, September 1953.

than I used to think. On the one hand Bayle produced stronger arguments for immaterialism than Malebranche had done, and introduced Berkeley to Simon Foucher's assimilation of the primary and secondary qualities; but on the other hand he forced Berkeley to see the sceptical tendencies of his 'first arguings'.[1]

No summary statement can do justice to the subtle relationships involved; but it may help readers to appreciate the general situation if I point to my former estimate (which still stands, see p. 7), viz. 'Locke taught him, but Malebranche inspired him', as amplified recently by my addition of the words, 'Bayle alarmed and alerted him'.[2]

Berkeley's contemporaries in France immediately recognized the Malebranche strain in his work. Professor H. M. Bracken[3] quotes from the 'Mémoires de Trévoux' a reviewer's description of Berkeley as 'Malebranchiste de bonne foi'.

David Hume, too, can now be summoned to the witness-box. From his letter to his friend, Michael Ramsey, recently found and published, dated from Orleans, 31 August 1737, we now know on the best possible authority that Berkeley's sources were Hume's sources, too. Hume is returning home with the manuscript of his *Treatise* (published 1740), nearly completed. He tells his friend that on his return he will show him all his 'performance',

---

[1] Note the entry (686*a*), 'On second thoughts I am on t'other extream. I am certain of that wch Malbranch seems to doubt of, viz. the existence of Bodies.'

[2] See my *The Dialectic of Immaterialism*, p. 59.

[3] *The Early Reception of Berkeley's Immaterialism, 1710–1713*, The Hague, 1959.

adding that if Ramsey wishes to understand the metaphysical parts, he should read[1] Malebranche's *Recherche*,
Berkeley's *Principles*, metaphysical articles in Bayle's
Dictionary, and (if he can find a copy) Descartes' *Meditations*.[2]

What I wrote formerly about Berkeley's early essays in
relation to his notebooks and the *Principles* was incomplete, and, in part, mistaken. I have now no doubt that
a draft of the Essay on Vision was more or less complete,
before the notebooks were begun; and instead of saying
(below, p. 29) that the Essay on Vision was 'structurally
dependent' on the notebooks, I should have said that the
opening pages of the notebooks imply that a draft of the
Essay on Vision was already written with a structure much
as it is at present.

I also see now that there were collateral writings on
immaterialism before the notebooks were begun. These
included an essay on time, and a work on aspects of perceptual theory, primary and secondary qualities, the
infinite divisibility of time and space, and the nature of
the soul or person.[3] What I wrote on pp. 70 and 194 about
the marked change in the style of writing the word *idea*,
should be read in the light of Professor Furlong's study,
'Two Notes on Berkeley's Philosophical Commentaries',
Proc. R. I. Acad., vol. 62, C. I. I also owe to him a

[1] Hume names them in this order.
[2] 'So, Hume did read Berkeley', by R. H. Popkin in *Journal
of Philosophy*, vol. lxi, Dec. 1954.
[3] See Ch. III on Berkeley's Early Writings in my *The Dialectic of Immaterialism*, 1963.

confirmation of my theory that the marginal plus sign in the notebooks indicates discarded entries. This is a very important point for students of the notebooks and of the development of Berkeley's thought. I spoke too diffidently about it on page 187 below. In the footnote on p. 105 I have mentioned a possible exception to what I said about Berkeley's scheme of knowledge. Students of the question should consider also Berkeley's reference to relations in the *Principles* (1734), section 142. I do not myself consider it an exception. Berkeley's statement that all relations include an act of mind is ambiguous; it confuses the relation and the relating. The relation or 'habitude' between the cup and its saucer is just as visible, tangible, and passive, as are the cup and saucer separately.

Malebranche's attack on abstraction, though forceful, was limited in scope; and I have wondered whether I overplayed my hand in what I said on pages 143 ff. Professor Furlong, who has kindly read the work with a critical eye *ad hoc*, thinks I have nothing to withdraw on this point. I ought to add, however, that Berkeley's attack on abstract general ideas was in the main a result of his discovery of his New Principle.[1]

I must add a note on the story and the name of the two notebooks on which this whole study is based. Unless readers are clear on the facts, they will find the initials *C. P. B.* and the title *Commonplace Book*, which meet them on every other page very confusing. A. C. Fraser who found the notebooks, found them bound in the

---

[1] See my *The Dialectic of Immaterialism*, pp. 104 ff.

wrong order. He read and published them in the wrong
order. Naturally, he never understood them, and his
name for them, the *Commonplace Book*, is a complete
misnomer. Through the combined efforts of several
scholars, the right order and correct text of the entries
have now been established; and in my *editio diplomatica*
of 1944 I changed the name to *Philosophical Commentaries*
(abbrev. 'P.C.'), which is now accepted. When the following pages were first published, the only available text
was that of Dr. G. A. Johnston, whose numbering of the
entries differs from mine. The Conversion List, which
follows, will enable the reader to track down any entry he
may wish to look up.

A. A. LUCE

Trinity College, Dublin, 1967

CONVERSION LIST

THE numbers of the entries in Berkeley's notebooks, mentioned below in the text, are those assigned by Dr. G. A. Johnston in his edition of 1930. The corresponding numbers in my edition of 1944, given also in volume i of the *Works* (Luce and Jessop), can be found in the following List. I have not included all the entries mentioned in Appendix I, which deals solely with the marginal signs.

Johnston	Luce	Johnston	Luce
1–78	1–78	239–40	230–1
83	82	247	238
87	85b	264	255
88, 89	86, 87	266	257
95	93	272–4	263–5
98	96	277–8	268–9
111	109	283	274–5
113	111	284–7	276–9
123	121	290	282
126–8	124–6	296	288
135–7	133–5	299	290
141	139	300	292
143–6	141–4	302	293
155–6	153–4	303	293a
158–62	156–60	306	296
163–4	161–2	308–10	298–300
168	166	321	310
172	170	323	312
180	177	329–30	318
181	177a	361	348
182	178	363–4	350, 350a
203	197	365	351
208	202	367	353
220	212	369	354
226	217	371	356
231	222	373	358
237	228	378	363

Johnston	Luce	Johnston	Luce
379	362a	566	561
380	363a	569	564
385	365a	571–2	566–7
388	367	574–6	569–71
392	369	581	576
395	377	582	576a
396–7	400–1	583	577
405	409	585–9	579–83
411	415	590–2	584–6
418–20	422–4	594	588
424	427	597–8	591–2
437	440	600	594
441	444	605–6	599–600
444–5	447–8	613	607
447	449	615	609
452	453	626–8	617–19
458	459	631	622
464	465	634	625
471	472	640	631
473	474	646	637
479–80	478, 478a	650–1	641–2
485–6	483–4	653	644
488	486	657–8	648–9
492	490	665	656
495–6	493–4	667	657a
498–9	496–7	668	658
504	501	670	660
510–11	507–8	671	661, 661a
515–17	512–14	686–7	675–6
527–8	523–4	696–7	685–6
532	528	698	686a
536–7	531–2	699	687
541	536	701	689
545	540	704	692
549	544	707	695
552–4	547–9	709–10	697–8
556	551	712–13	700–1
561	556	724	712

Johnston	Luce	Johnston	Luce
727	715	812–15	800–3
731–2	719–20	819	807
736–7	724–5	822	810
739	727, 727a	825	813
740–1	728–9	830	818
747	734	835	823
750–4	737–41	839	827
760–1	747–8	843–4	831–2
763	750	850	838
766	753	855	843
770	757	865	853
788	775	870	858
790	777	872–3	860–1
792–3	779–80	881	869
795	782	884	872
804	792	894	882
807–10	795–8	898	886

PREFACE

Out of a close examination of the *Commonplace Book* sprang my desire to reconstruct the genesis of the Berkeleian philosophy, by following up the clues contained in the two famous note-books. Reading where Berkeley read, using sometimes the volumes he used, I studied the authorities he mentions. Malebranche was to me, at the outset, simply one of a large number of such authorities. The extent of Berkeley's debt to the *Recherche de la Vérité* came to me as an unanticipated discovery. The following pages contain my attempt at detailed verification and show surmise passing into assurance.

As befits a study in origins, the book gives an exposition of its thesis on the basis of empirical fact. I have avoided the *a priori* of history, and have taken no account of logical relationship.

My thesis is somewhat complex. I have tried to show that Berkeley, when he was preparing to write his early books, made a thorough study of the *Recherche*, that the Berkeleian philosophy still bears the specific impress of that study, and, in particular, that the conception of seeing all things in God is at the back of the Berkeleian *idea*. The questions of literary dependence and of doctrinal affinity are closely knit, and I have not found it practicable to treat them separately. The case rests on evidence drawn from several sources, and the evidence, naturally, is not all on the same level of importance or cogency. A few parallels and resemblances have been included, partly because they might be missed, if not mentioned, and partly because, though they are not proof, they may lend support. Some readers will find, I hope, that my main contention is already familiar; to some, I doubt not, it will come as a novelty; all, perhaps, may be glad to have the evidence for the connexion presented with a fullness not hitherto attempted.

This is primarily a book about Berkeley. My task obliged me to sketch the features of *his* metaphysic, but has not required me to deal at equal length with Malebranche's system. I have attempted to prove affinity, but not identity. There are elements in the philosophy of Malebranche that were repugnant to Berkeley and are alien to Berkeleianism. While I have not defined my attitude to either system, I have treated Berkeley's doctrine sympathetically, at times to the extent of illustrating or even defending a tenet of his. I am not without hope that the emphasis here placed upon the Malebranchian factor may help to correct one-sided interpretations which portray Berkeley as a subjective idealist or a solipsist, and to check the habit of treating this distinctive philosophy as a mere link between Locke and Hume.

I have to thank Professor H. S. Macran and Mr. F. La T. Godfrey, my colleagues, and Mr. T. E. Jessop, Ferens Professor of Philosophy in the University College of Hull, for reading the proof-sheets. Their suggestions and criticisms have been of great service to me. My debt to books is not so easy to determine. My first aim, in some measure carried out, has been to read Berkeley himself and all the books he is known to have read before 1710; but I have not neglected recent works on that account, and in particular I recognize my indebtedness to Dr. G. A. Johnston's edition of the *Commonplace Book*. I have had for some months past the advantage of using Professor Jessop's bibliography, before it went to press, and I have drawn from it not only facts, but also encouragement. Many, besides professed Berkeleians, will read with satisfaction its plain record, down the decades, of Berkeley's gathering influence upon European and American thought.

A. A. L.

Trinity College, Dublin, 1934

CONTENTS

LIST OF ABBREVIATIONS

C.P.B. Berkeley's *Commonplace Book*. The number, if given, is that of the entry as numbered in G. A. Johnston's edition.

T.V. Berkeley's *An Essay towards a New Theory of Vision*.

T.V.V. Berkeley's *The Theory of Vision . . . . Vindicated*.

Prin. or *Principles*. Berkeley's *A Treatise concerning the Principles of Human Knowledge*.

Int. or *Intro*. Berkeley's Introduction to the *Principles*.

Hylas. Berkeley's *Three Dialogues between Hylas and Philonous*.

Alc. Berkeley's *Alciphron or the Minute Philosopher*.

Search. De la Recherche de la Vérité, by Père Malebranche (N.B. A. Collier, 1713, uses this abbreviation in his *Clavis Universalis*).

L.L. Life and Letters of George Berkeley, by A. C. Fraser (1871).

Works. The Works of George Berkeley, by A. C. Fraser (1901).

The *Three Dialogues*, unlike the majority of Berkeley's works, has no numbered sections. So in references to it I give the page number in Fraser's (1901) edition of the *Works*, vol. i.

Quotations from Malebranche's *Recherche de la Vérité* are taken from the English translation by T. Taylor, 1st edition, 1694, Oxford and London.

CHRONOLOGICAL LIST OF BERKELEY'S PHILOSOPHICAL WORKS

Date of writing or publication	Abridged titles
c. 1706	*Of Infinites*
c. 1707–8	*Commonplace Book*
1707	*Arithmetica* and *Miscellanea Mathematica*
1709	*Theory of Vision* (first edition, and second edition revised)
Nov.–Dec. 1708	Draft introduction to the *Principles*
May 1710	*Principles* (first edition)
May 1713	*Three Dialogues* (*Hylas*) (first edition)
1721	*De Motu*
1725	*Three Dialogues* (second edition, unchanged)
1732	*Alciphron* (first edition, and second edition revised) with *Theory of Vision* (further revised, appended to both editions)
1733	*Theory of Vision Vindicated*
1734	*Principles* (second edition, revised) with *Three Dialogues* (third edition, revised) appended
1734	*Analyst*
1735	*Defence of Free-Thinking in Mathematics*
1735	*Reasons for not replying*
1744–7	*Siris* (at least six editions in 1744, another in 1747)
1752	*Alciphron* (third edition, further revised)
1752	*De Motu* (reprinted in *Miscellany*)

INTRODUCTION

A STUDY in the origins of Berkeley's philosophy is eminently practicable. The reasons are plain. In the first place, Berkeley completed the main lines of his philosophy in very early manhood, while the creative impulse was strong within him and the external formative influences comparatively few. Again, we possess in the *Commonplace Book* an eyewitness of his book-making. Here, open to our inspection, are the two note-books in which the young author entered systematically the main heads of the philosophy he was struggling to shape and express; note-books in which he records his silent arguments with himself and with his authorities. Thus we know what authorities he consulted and can estimate fairly accurately the degree of respect he paid to each. The reliability of this source of information is unquestioned. The relation between the *Commonplace Book* and the *Theory of Vision* and the *Principles* is very close. The two publications could hardly be in their present shape but for the work done in these two note-books, and certainly the note-books would be to us a sheer mystery if we had not the publications in which they issued. There is scarcely a point in his published philosophy not dealt with in his *Commonplace Book*, except knowledge of other spirits. We might infer that during the period 1707–8 Berkeley could not have consulted an author or book at all extensively without disclosing the fact to us. There is little need to say, as in some studies of origins, 'he must have used this source'; we can say 'he did use this source', and can often point to chapter and verse.

Further, we are fortunately placed for this study in that we possess a group of early subsidiary writings of his, which at certain points throw light on the genesis of his thought. These are, in their probable time-order, the Description of the Cave of Dunmore, the 'Of Infinites', the *Arithmetica* and *Miscellanea Mathematica*, the draft Introduction to the *Principles*, the draft of the *Principles* sect. 85–145, and the letters to Percival.

Berkeley has been so long in the public eye that it would be natural to assume that we already know all there is to know about his sources. But new documents bring new knowledge. The *Commonplace Book* is still, in one sense, a new document. First published by Fraser in 1871, not till G. A. Johnston's edition of 1930 did it become available in a form proper for systematic study. Even yet perhaps, in spite of the studies of Lorenz, Aaron, and others, the higher criticism of the document is not complete. The *Hermathena* article, reprinted as an appendix to this book, is an attempt at a comprehensive solution of the chief problems. Its conclusions about the purpose, structure, and date of the *Commonplace Book* have been here relied upon by the author. It is hoped that they may prove fairly trustworthy. As my study in the origins of Berkeley's thought sprang directly from a critical examination of the *Commonplace Book*, I may perhaps be allowed to assemble here the main results of that examination, referring the reader to the Appendix for the detailed evidence. These are as follows:

(1) The *Commonplace Book* is not a collection of casual 'jottings', but is a definite composition, undertaken by Berkeley as a preparatory study in the argument for immaterialism. It is therefore to be regarded as a preliminary stage in the composition of the *New Theory of Vision* and the *Principles*, and to be viewed in intimate connexion with these two works.

(2) Johnston's text, on the whole, gives the entries in their proper sequence; but the entries, numbered by

him 903–45, should be restored to their manuscript position after 395.[1]

(3) The *Commonplace Book* proper was not begun before December 7, 1706, and was finished before November 1708. There are grounds for holding that it was not begun till after June 9, 1707, and was completed on August 28, 1708.

(4) The apparatus of marginal signs and the change in the orthography of the word 'idea' can throw some light upon the development of Berkeley's thought and the making of his books.

A. J. Balfour opens his essay on Berkeley's life and letters, with the words, 'It is as a descendant in the true line of succession from Locke to the modern schools of thought ... that he is and that he'deserves to be chiefly remembered'. Fraser says, 'Berkeley is the immediate successor of Locke and ... was educated by collision with the *Essay on Human Understanding*'.[2] G. A. Johnston is emphatic to the same effect: 'From Locke only did he really *derive* anything of the first importance. The original impulse and direction of his philosophy came from Locke, and from Locke also the great *Gemeingut* of ideas which makes the continuity between them as remarkable as their differences.'[3]

[1] Dr. Dawes Hicks suggests taking entry No. 70 as the first. I have examined the manuscript *ad hoc* and cannot see in *it* any justification for the suggestion. Sixty-nine and seventy are more or less continuous in subject-matter. Dr. Dawes Hicks does not press the suggestion or build on it. If he did, I think he would find it raises more problems than it settles. His difficulty is solved, I think, by the consideration that Berkeley was, at this stage, taking immaterialism hypothetically, and perhaps arguing with future readers. See G. Dawes Hicks, *Berkeley*, p. 27.

[2] *Works*, vol. i, (1901), p. xi. The same judgement occurs elsewhere in Fraser's writings.

[3] G. A. Johnston, *The Development of Berkeley's Philosophy*, p. 32. cf. pp. 67–73 and 370 for the influence of Malebranche.

My purpose is to try to recall opinion to an earlier and, I believe, a truer view. With the Fraser-Johnston judgement about Berkeley's sources firmly fixed in my mind, when engaged upon a close study of the *Commonplace Book*, I happened on the following entry (274), 'From Malbranch Locke, and my first arguings it can't be prov'd that extension is not in matter.' Pondering the implications of that entry, I studied the other references to and mentions of Malebranche in the *Commonplace Book*. Gradually I became convinced that Berkeley studied the *Recherche de la Vérité* fully and thoroughly. Seeing reason to think that he read it in Taylor's translation,[1] I made a close study of that translation and found the debt to be greater than I had anticipated. Returning to Berkeley's works with the details of the *Search* fresh in my mind I thought that the familiar words and thoughts of the *Principles* took on a new meaning, and the Berkeleian system a new firmness and depth and solidity. Hence this book.

A student who reads Berkeley on the look out for Male-

---

[1] T. Taylor, M.A., of Magd. Coll. in Oxford, 1694. Berkeley probably used the second edition, of 1700, which contains the short tract on Light and Colours 'never before printed in any language', perhaps referred to in *C.P.B.* 932. A copy is in T.C.D. Lib., with 1701 in ink on cover. My reasons for thinking Taylor's translation used are many. I need not give them *seriatim*, as they come out in the body of my work. There are several verbal echoes of Taylor in the *C.P.B.*, notably the term 'illustration' in 812 for *éclaircissement*, Malebranche's technical term for *excursus*. Commentators have missed this meaning of 'illustration', which is found e.g. in Keill's *Exam. Burnet's Theory*, 1698, p. 8, 'The oftner I read his (Malebranche's) long Illustration on this point'. For 'outness' in Taylor's translation of the 'illustration' mentioned in *C.P.B.* 812, *v. infra*, p. 46. Accordingly I quote uniformly from Taylor's translation of the *Recherche* and use his title for the book, the *Search*, the title familiar to Berkeley and to his English contemporaries.

branche, and Malebranche on the look out for Berkeley, is in serious danger of 'reading in' what is not there. I have been alive to the danger, and my consequent attempt to be 'objective' may be my apology for the excessive documentation of the following pages.

My primary aim, then, is to establish on internal evidence the position that Berkeley used the *Search* extensively, and that Malebranche was to him not merely a Cartesian (Malebranche often distinguishes himself from the Cartesians), but at any rate for a time, indeed for the critical time, a master-mind, one of his two primary sources, comparable in importance to Locke and, in some ways, of higher importance.

What difference can the establishment of so narrow and so literary a thesis make? What does it matter to philosophers to-day what Berkeley's sources were? I shall try to suggest in the course of my argument, especially in Chapters V and VI, a full answer to those questions. Here I will only say that if Bergson's remark[1] is just, that every philosophy of recent times has had to take its start by reckoning with the contentions of Berkeley, then the source of Berkeleianism matters to all philosophers to-day; for on the source the spirit of the philosophy will in large measure depend. Fraser wrote (and many moderns would endorse his words): 'Berkeley would be less at home in the "divine vision" of Malebranche than among the "ideas" of Locke'.[2] I should like, I venture to confess, to see that judgement reversed. I believe that Fraser here is wrong in point of fact, and that this and similar judgements of his have led many to misconceive the spirit of the philosophy. Neglect of the Malebranche factor in Berkeleianism takes the heart out of it, reducing its solid reality to flimsy dream,

[1] Quoted with approval by Dawes Hicks, op. cit. p. 285.
[2] *Works*, vol. i, p. 217.

negating Berkeley's claim to stand in the 'Pantheon of god-like figures'. Recent studies, notably Dr. Dawes Hicks's *Berkeley*, have shown that Berkeley is no mere link between Locke and Hume; but Berkeley's right to the rank of Leader of Philosophy will be open to challenge until the lengthening tradition of his sole dependence upon Locke is once and for all broken.

I have not attempted to give a complete presentation here of Berkeleianism. It would be unnecessary to do so while Fraser's edition of the *Works* and the careful and critical studies in the system by Johnston and Dawes Hicks are accessible. But I have tried so to present my primary argument that the *Theory of Vision* and the *Principles* will stand out sharply, in their main positive features, before the reader's eye. I have scarcely noticed Berkeley's important answers to objections and arguments in support. The book may thus serve as an introduction to Berkeleianism. At the same time advanced students will find in it several critical studies in disputed points of Berkeleian exegesis.

I have not even attempted here to survey the whole field of Berkeley's sources. My study then is not open to the charge of underestimating Locke's influence upon Berkeley. I have not tried to give an estimate of it. Others have performed that task. To neglect the Lockian element in Berkeley would be to fly in the face of the facts,[1] and I have no wish to go from one extreme to another. The balanced view surely would be that Malebranche and Locke both exerted a potent influence upon the young Irishman in his plastic days, and that the two influences were so heterogeneous that a comparison of weight and value is futile. Many reflective scholars can remember some schoolmaster of theirs to whom they are indebted for years of solid

[1] Within two years of its publication (1690) Locke's *Essay* was on the course at Trinity College Dublin.

grounding. But they remember too a personality who crossed their path perhaps after school and even after college days, and who was to them an intellectual stimulus of a higher order. Contact may have been brief, but the influence deep and strong. It was so with Berkeley, I submit. Locke taught him, but Malebranche inspired him.

My limited objective should exempt me also from the charge of impugning Berkeley's originality. I would deprecate that charge. Originality, it should be unnecessary to say nowadays, does not stand in thinking the thing all out for oneself *de novo*. The 'original' philosopher is no recluse out of touch with his times, but the philosopher who makes creative, or at least novel, use of the material furnished by the representative thought of his day. Berkeley did so, but it is beside my purpose to show it. Suffice it here to say that Berkeley was original in all his ways. He nearly hanged himself in his college days, as an experiment, no doubt, in trains of ideas. He was original in wishing to give America the episcopate and make her spiritually independent. He was original in his views on Irish government and economics. He was original in his therapy. 'Neminem transcripsi: nullius scrinia expilavi', he wrote in the Preface of his first publication. It is not to be thought that such a man would slavishly copy or re-edit the system of Malebranche or of Locke.

If he found in Malebranche the hint of the heterogeneity of sight and touch, it was of himself to see the connexion with the Molyneux problem, and find there a clue to the nature of things. Thousands read Malebranche without dreaming of immaterialism. Norris and Collier, contemporaries of Berkeley, steeped themselves in Malebranche's philosophy, but originated little. The divine spark was not in them. Berkeley's rejection of abstract ideas, his attempt to turn ideas into things, his account of the sensible world, be they right or wrong, were strokes of genius. And he knew his own originality. 'So far as authority is of any weight with me', he wrote in his draft Introduction to the *Principles*.[1] Twenty-five years later he writes: 'The only advantage I pretend to is that I have always thought and judged for myself.'[2] The entry in the *Commonplace Book* which gave rise to this study in origins brackets his own 'first arguings' with his two other authorities, Malebranche and Locke.

This study is as far then from detraction as from adulation. It is simply an attempt to elicit and weigh the facts about Berkeley's use of the *Search*. Some may think that the thesis, however intended, would, if established, discredit Berkeley by proving him guilty of *suppressio veri*, if not of *suggestio falsi*. Neither charge can, I think, be sustained; nor does my thesis lend colour to either of them. Berkeley's words about Malebranche's system and his silences will be discussed later. Here I will only say that Berkeley nowhere denies his indebtedness to the Oratorian himself. An author is not bound to declare his sources, even if he knows them, and perhaps he ought not to do so, if, as in Berkeley's case, it is clearly against his interest to do so. After all, Berkeley in November 1713, within a week of his first arrival in Paris, secured an introduction to Father Malebranche and made arrangements to visit him.[3] If, when he went, (it may have been to say 'thank you',) he stayed to dispute, perhaps the fault was not all on the side of the younger man.

---

[1] *Works*, vol. iii, p. 363; cf. *C.P.B.* 464.

[2] *Def. of Free-thinking in Math.* § 19.

[3] Rand, *Berkeley and Percival*, p. 129; Fraser, *L.L.*, p. 67; v. Appendix ii, p. 208, for discussion. Locke's own debt to Malebranche was considerable; yet the *Essay* contains no recognition, and his posthumously published *Examination* treats the *Search* with scant respect. *Essay*, bk. iv, c. 19 seems to have Malebranche in view. See Ep. to Reader and *Fam. Letters*, p. 42.

A few representative views upon Berkeley's sources, in
addition to those already quoted, may be collected here.
Clarke and Whiston, the leaders of English thought of that
day, who read the *Principles* a few months after its publication rank its author with Malebranche and Norris.[1]
Bolingbroke writes to Swift, regretting that he had missed
seeing Berkeley, 'I would not by any means lose the opportunity of knowing a man who can espouse in good earnest
the system of Father Malebranche' (July 24, 1725, *L.L.*,
p. 118). The *Acta Eruditorum* (1727, pp. 380–3), after
reviewing the *Three Dialogues*, says: 'De origine, quicquid
Autor dissimulet, sic sentimus, ex Cartesii, Malebranchii et
Spinosae philosophiarum mixtura prognatum hoc λυβικὸν
θηρίον'. Baxter's *Enquiry* (1733, vol. ii. 2) says little of
Berkeley's sources, but suggests that Berkeley may have
learned immaterialism from Descartes. Dr. Clayton's
Essay on Spirit (1750, v. *L.L.*, p. 324 note) opens with the
statement that Spinoza's opinion 'with some few alterations
hath been embraced and cultivated by P. Malbranche and
Bishop Berkeley'. Reid (*Inquiry c.* i, § 5) writes: 'Berkeley's
arguments are founded upon the principles which were
formerly laid down by Descartes, Malebranche and Locke',
and (*Int. Powers*, Essay II, c. 10): 'Berkeley's system follows
from Mr Locke's by very obvious consequence.' On the
whole Reid affiliates Berkeley to Locke, while Hamilton,
according to Graham (*Idealism*, p. 124), finds 'the whole of
Berkeley's philosophy wrapped up in Malebranche's'.
Beattie (*On Truth*, 1770, pt. ii. 2. 1) says: 'The substance, or
at least the foundation, of Berkeley's argument against the
existence of matter may be found in Locke's *Essay*[2] and in

[1] Rand, op. cit., p. 87, with Berkeley's reply, pp. 88–9; cf.
Fraser, *L.L.*, pp. 45–6.
[2] The author of the *Remarks*, p. 41 in the 1776 ed. of the
Principles, categorically denies this statement as regards Locke.

the *Principia* of Des Cartes.' Dr. C. R. Teape, in his preface
to *Berkeleian Philosophy* (1870) quotes one of the authors
of *Essays and Reviews* to the effect that Berkeley 'was not
a closet-thinker, like his master Malebranche'. To come
to more recent times, we have already quoted Fraser and
Johnston. Dr. Dawes Hicks on the whole follows the
English tradition, saying 'Undoubtedly the teachers to
whom Berkeley was chiefly indebted were Descartes and
Locke, above all Locke; and it was from a careful and critical study of their systems that his new principle emerged.'[1]

From this welter of opinion certain things emerge.
Berkeley, in his lifetime, was regarded as a disciple of Malebranche. Subsequently he came to be regarded as a Lockian.
The new opinion was a natural growth. In the course of
time British acquaintance with Malebranche sank, and the
fame of Berkeley rose. National sentiment adopted him as
the English philosopher in succession to Locke. It may
therefore be in place here to mention the danger of over-
estimating the degree to which the young Berkeley was
anglicized. There are two national sentiments to be considered, and to hold the balance is not easy. To speak of
him, without qualification, as an English philosopher cannot
be right. Leslie Stephen's statement[2] 'Berkeley always considered himself an Englishman', is misleading, if not mistaken. Berkeley was born and bred in Ireland. His education was entirely Irish. He speaks of himself as an Irishman
several times in the *Commonplace Book*. Newton to him was
'a philosopher of a neighbouring nation'.[3] As with many

[1] Dawes Hicks, *Berkeley*, p. 70. He adds, however, when dealing with Berkeley's relation to contemporary philosophers (p.
229), 'I cannot help thinking that Berkeley's indebtedness to the
writings of Malebranche is apt to be underrated.'

[2] *Dict. Nat. Biog.* art. 'G. Berkeley'.

[3] *Principles*, § 110, 1st ed. only.

of English descent settled in Ireland, brought up among
kindly men of another faith and race, his sentiments were
necessarily mixed and his loyalties divided. But credit must
go where it is due. Berkeley's system in so far as it forms
part of the heritage of international philosophy was complete before he set foot in England, and in England he
wrote little or no philosophy.[1]

All modern students of Berkeleianism owe a great debt to
A. C. Fraser, and I do not belittle that debt in giving a reason
why Fraser's judgement about the origin of Berkeley's
thought must be received with caution. The fact is that
Fraser misconceived the state of education in Ireland at the
time, and therefore came to his subject with a slight prejudice against the education of the young Fellow of Trinity
College. Holding erroneously that at that time 'Ireland, like
Scotland, was in a state of provincial barbarism',[2] he came
to the mistaken judgement (repeated since by other writers)
implied in his words, 'It does not seem that his scholarship
or philosophical learning was extensive.' This was the time
of Swift and King,[3] writers of European reputation, of the
Molyneuxs, Browne, Gilbert, Palliser, and the scores of
cultured men who founded the Dublin Society. Berkeley,
while still too young to take the degree of Master of Arts,
read Latin, Greek, French, and some Hebrew, had published a work on mathematics in Latin, was versed in contemporary works on theology, philosophy, the higher
mathematics, and physics, and within two years of proceeding M.A. he had written books that are, after two

[1] The *De Motu* was written in France, the *Alciphron* in Rhode
Island, the *Theory of Vision Vindicated* and possibly the *Analyst*
in England, the remainder in Ireland.

[2] *L.L.*, p. 62, *v.* also *Works*, vol. i, p. 351, and vol. i, p. 4.

[3] Swift, like Berkeley, was a product of Kilkenny College and
Trinity College. King was educated at Dungannon Royal School
and Trinity College.

centuries, still considered good literature as well as profound philosophy.

Then, as now, there was direct commerce in ideas between Dublin and the Continent. It was only natural that
a man of Berkeley's breadth of vision should read and
respect the great works then being produced in England,
and should yet take an independent line in their regard, just
because he was in immediate contact with continental
thought. Berkeley read Leibniz as early as 1706. Leibniz
knew of Berkeley's speculations.[1] Two draft Latin letters
by Berkeley to Leclerc are extant, and the *Theory of Vision*
was reviewed at length in the *Bibliothèque Choisie*, Amster-
dam, in 1711. Further, we know that Malebranche was
valued in Berkeley's immediate circle. The *Search* is placed
only second to Locke's *Essay* in the Preface of Molyneux's
Dioptricks.[2] There is, however, no need to concern ourselves with the probabilities of the case. It is certain on the
evidence of the *Commonplace Book* that Berkeley used the
Search extensively. Accordingly this study, basing itself on
clear external evidence, proceeds to investigate the internal
evidence of connexion, and thereby to provide a measure,
it is hoped, of the degree of importance to be attached to
that connexion.

[1] Leibniz to Des Bosses, March 1715, ed. Erdmann, pt. i,
p. 726.
[2] *v.* also Locke's letter to Molyneux of March 28, 1693, *Fam.
Letters*, p. 42. In the T.C.D. copy of Malebranche's *De Inqui-
renda Veritate* from the Palliser gallery there is a statement penned
on the fly-leaf under Palliser's name, to the effect that in the
opinion of Edwards, Stillingfleet, and Burnit 'Malebranche deserves not that mighty esteem he has obtained with some'.

I

THE RULES OF METHOD

FROM his earliest days of authorship Berkeley was conscious of method and critical of method (*C.P.B.* 405, 447). The purpose of this chapter is to show that in his method of setting and solving problems, in his actual writing, and in the spirit of his approach to philosophical questions he was directly influenced by what Malebranche had said on methodology. Book vi of Malebranche's *Search* is devoted to method. Berkeley, as we shall show, gives in his *De Ludo Algebraico* a reference to the central feature of Book vi and speaks of it appreciatively. So there is a solid foundation in fact for our attempt to trace out in detail the connexion between the methods of the two thinkers.

Malebranche in Book vi is attempting a *Novum Organum*. In his own words he wants 'to give the mind all the perfection it can naturally attain to'. He wants to increase the mind's capacity and to perfect its application and attention. In Book vi, Part 1, he investigates the bases of geometry, arithmetic, and algebra. These, he argues, are the disciplines proper to form the philosophic mind. Geometry is the proper discipline for the imagination; for it gives, in simple lines, illustrations of forces and of movements, and so deepens the mind's attention. Arithmetic makes no appeal to the imagination, since it does not work in the concrete. Arithmetic uses abstract symbols, and thus develops the range and capacity of the mind. Algebra is a higher development of the arithmetical method. Algebra is the model science for methodology; for in virtue of its powers of abridgement, it is intellect's short-hand, opening up illimitable expanses of new territory for the mind.

In Book vi, Part 2, Malebranche deals with the actual conduct of the mind in its search for truth. He elaborates a code of rules, modelled largely upon Descartes's rules; he illustrates the working of his rules, and makes them an occasion for an outline study of the logic of Aristotle and the physics of Descartes. Before giving a detailed account of these rules we must trace Berkeley's connexion with them.

The methodology of Malebranche was, in some measure, common property to all adherents of the 'New Learning'. A good deal of it is implicit in Locke's *Essay* and explicit in Locke's *Of the Conduct of the Understanding*. Berkeley might have learned it from Locke or from other writers. In point of fact, at the time his attention was called to method, he came definitely and directly under the influence of the Oratorian. Berkeley's *Arithmetica* and *Miscellanea Mathematica* furnish the evidence as regards method. The *Commonplace Book* supports it, and so, to a lesser extent, do his main publications of the period.

The *Arithmetica* was published early in 1707. The imminent fellowship examination, no doubt, occasioned its publication then. But the work had been on the stocks for two or three years, and was, perhaps, designed originally as a study of and an exercise in method. Berkeley intends to smooth the path of students of elementary mathematics by reducing to principle the network of rules. He writes in the Preface: 'Nempe id mihi imprimis propositum fuerat ut numeros tractandi leges ex ipsis principiis, proprii exercitii et recreationis causa, deducerem. Quod et deinceps horis subsecivis prosecutus sum.' At the conclusion of the preface we find a curious phrase, 'Monstravi porro ad quem collimaverim scopum.' Berkeley is here obeying a general direction given by Malebranche, and the phrase must surely be an echo of Taylor's quaint translation of

that direction 'Still having before your eyes the scope[1]
you aim at'.

The climax of the publication is the *De Ludo Algebraico*,
a piece which, as he says, 'miscuit utile dulci'. From his
game of algebra he passes to an extravagant but quite
serious commendation of the 'mirifica algebrae vis'. He
marshals his authorities—an impressive list— Halley,
Temple, Bacon, Descartes, Malebranche, Locke, quoting
from most of them. Locke comes in for very high praise;
but the thoughts and, not infrequently, the words are
those of Malebranche. Berkeley calls algebra 'universae
matheseos nucleus et clavis'. Malebranche had called it 'an
universal science . . . the key of all other'.[2] Berkeley adds
that some call algebra 'the foundation of all the sciences'—
the very term which Malebranche (bk. vi. 1, 5) applies to
arithmetic and algebra. It is 'difficult to assign the limits of
algebra', says Berkeley; and the unlimited range of knowledge opened up to the mind by the algebraic method is the
theme of several passages in the *Search* (ii. 2. 3, iii. 1. 3, iv.
11, vi. 1. 5).

This adulation of algebra has no intrinsic importance; it
was only a passing phase. I refer to it partly as evidence
of Berkeley's close reading of the *Search* (*n.b.* Berkeley's
'alibique passim'), and partly because it introduces the
following important passage: 'Regulae quidem quas hic in
quaestionum solutione observandas tradit lib. 6 part. 2 cap.
1. quaeque tam sunt eximiae, ut meliores angelum non
fuisse daturum credat auctor quidam ingeniosus; illae,
inquam, regulae angelicae ex algebra desumi videntur.'[3]

[1] Bk. vi, 2. 1. Neither the French nor the Latin translation
(*terme, terminus*) suggests the word 'scope'. The phrase recurs
in the *De Motu*, § 38.

[2] *Search* bk. iv. 11; cf. Collier, *Clavis Universalis*.

[3] *Works*, vol. iv, p. 61.

Berkeley here states the facts correctly; for Malebranche himself (vi. 1. 5, vi. 2. 1) speaks of these rules as originating in algebra, and he mentions the fifth and sixth as especially algebraic.

I must consider in detail these 'angelic rules'; for they express the spirit of his inquiry, and must have influenced the interrogations which the young querist put to the universe. The code of rules is founded upon that of Descartes. Malebranche advances them as a continuation of the mathematical disciplines, as an alternative to the logic of the schools, and therefore as enabling the mind to secure all the perfections it is capable of. He claims that the rules are simple, coherent, and practical. The code forms in fact a system of empiricist method.[1]

The principle upon which they all depend is 'Truth with evidence'. That principle was common to all the empiricists of the day, and was the spear-head of their attack upon obscurantism, dogmatism, and authority. The general rule which results, is expressed in two propositions: (1) We ought only to reason upon such things whereof we have clear and distinct ideas. (2) We must begin with the most easy and simple subjects and insist long upon them before we undertake the inquiry into such as are more composed and difficult. Malebranche devotes five chapters to these two parts of his general rule. He then treats the six derivative rules for resolving questions, styling the truthseeker the 'Querist'. Now Berkeley was a querist all his life,[2] and these six rules for systematic querying were clearly and consciously before him in all his early work.

[1] Leclerc, *Logica* (used by Berkeley, *v. C.P.B.* 361), pt. iii, c. 4, on Method (1692), follows these rules fairly closely; *v.* his note on c. v.

[2] *v.* conclusion of the *Analyst*, of the *Defence of Free-thinking*, and *Querist*.

The first rule is: 'We must very distinctly conceive the state of the question proposed to be resolved: that is, have ideas of the terms so distinct as that we may compare them together, and discover the relations which we look for.'[1] The querist must put his difficulty in question form. Scores of the *Commonplace Book* entries are questions; all the more striking and concrete ones at their first appearance are introduced by *Qu:* or *Quaere*. To put the problem as a query is one way of clarifying the subject under discussion. The query tends to get rid of ambiguity and verbal equivocation, makes for clear and distinct ideas, and releases the issue from the tyranny of words and jargon. The dialectic of question and answer is the characteristic method of the *Commonplace Book*. Berkeley's diligent pursuit of clarity and of distinct ideas is illustrated by the following entries (and there are many others): 25, 27, 30, 226, 367, 545, 549, 585, 597, 640, 650. Malebranche points out that some queries are not in words, and he regards experiments as queries addressed to the author of nature. Berkeley was fond of such practical querying. He experimented in colour composition, and he conducted psychological experiments to find out the effect on the mind of such experiences as hanging, silence, and wearing inverting glasses. Further he followed up in thought experimental conceits such as the blind man made to see, the dumb man, and the solitary man.

The second rule is: 'We must try by an essay of thought to discover one or several intermediate ideas, that may be a means or common measure to know the relations that are betwixt those things.' Two entries in the *Commonplace Book* (444, 709) show him perhaps trying to put this rule into practice. But as his views on abstract ideas clarified,

[1] Malebranche lists the rules in bk. vi, 2, 1, and discusses them *seriatim* in chapters 7–9.

he abandoned the method of intermediate ideas, along with
the doctrine of certainty and demonstration (741).

The third and fourth rules prescribe respectively isola-
tion of subject-matter and analysis. Berkeley has clearly
cultivated the habit of keeping to the point and of excluding
irrelevant issues. His outline of immaterialism (*Prin.* §§ 1–
33) is a model of precision. In dealing with objections and
consequences he is forced to go over the same ground more
than once, but even where redundant he is always relevant.
His formed habit of analysis is seen in the construction of
his books. The *Theory of Vision* and the *Principles* fall into
clearly marked divisions, sections and sub-sections. The
marginal signs in the *Commonplace Book* are part of the
machinery of analysis. To this practice of analysis we may
trace his clear and simple views of things, his perspicuity,
and his limpid style. His *forte* is to see distinctions, con-
cealed by custom and by language.[1]

The fifth and sixth rules are described by Malebranche
as particularly algebraic in spirit. The fifth rule lays down
that we must 'abridge ideas and dispose them in the imagination or write them upon paper, that they may no longer
clog and fill up the capacity of the mind'. This rule is for
very intricate questions, such as require great extent of
mind. The sixth rule prescribes that when 'the ideas of all
the things that necessarily require examination are clear,
familiar, abridged and disposed and ranged in good order
in the imagination or written upon paper, they are all to
be compared by the rules of complication, one with the
other alternately, either by the view of the mind alone,
or by the motion of the imagination, attended with the
view of the mind, or by the calculation of the pen joined
to the attention of the mind and imagination'. Clearly
Malebranche has in his mind's eye, as model, the setting

[1] For instances of analysis see *C.P.B.* 237, 323, 396, 752, 865.

out of some involved mathematical problem in simple algebraic notation.

The *Commonplace Book* is, I think, a result of and, indeed, an embodiment of this pair of rules. 'We have got the Algebra of pure intelligences', he says (*C.P.B.* 926). He means, no doubt, that what is real to man is symbolic nota- tion to the angelic intelligence (cf. *T.V.* § 155). But we may legitimately adapt his phrase and say that the *Commonplace Book* is the algebra of a good human intelligence. In its entries mind, imagination, and pen join to fix as with precise notation the fluid features of his thought. At first sight it is a purposeless compilation, random jottings for Berkeley; for us a fund of quotations. On careful examination it proves to be a definite composition, an algebraic abridge- ment of the material of his books. The brevity and point of the earlier entries is noticeable. Berkeley throughout its pages aims at clear, distinct, and coherent ideas. We might style the *Commonplace Book* a 'Recherche de la Vérité' con- ducted under the auspices of the 'angelic rules' of method. Berkeley began it shortly after he was engaged upon the final pages of the *De Ludo Algebraico*[1] where these rules are commended and where his language is redolent of the *Search*. Malebranche tells his readers how to 'improve the attention and extension of the mind' and make it 'more enlightened, sagacious, and piercing' (bk. vi, 2. 1. cf. *De Lud. Alg.* 'Ingenium sagax, intellectum capacem, judicium acre'). The only way, he says, to enlarge the mind's 'capa- city' is to reduce to scale, i.e. abridge the ideas put into it. This abridgement is to be followed by repeated comparison of ideas. If ever there was a task needing a great extent and capacity of the mind, it was that of the young seeker after truth, when in the opening pages of the *Commonplace Book*,

---

[1] Probably prepared for the press early in 1707 (*v.* Appendix, p. 204). Locke's *Opera Posthuma*, there quoted, appeared in 1706.

he abridges his ideas and outlines the 'immaterial hypothe-sis'. On a small canvas (1–27) he crowds eternity, time, space, primary and secondary qualities, the real world, infinite divisibility with the attendant mathematical prob-lems, the nature of the soul, and the psychology of vision. 'Capacity' must have been his prayer. His consciousness of the duty of comparing ideas appears repeatedly in the *Commonplace Book*, e.g. 47, 51, 309, 873, and notably in the 'demonstration' by comparison (918b–922) which ori-ginally concluded the first note-book.

Malebranche represents the search after truth as an intelli-gent adventure. 'We should always know whither we are going,' he says. Berkeley as he fills his note-books knows whither he is going. He is not jotting down ideas on isolated topics. All his themes are connected, and he is struggling for clear vision and clear expression of that connexion. His writing is for him a great adventure. There lies before him 'much terra incognita to be travel'd over and discovered. A vast field for invention' (561). And Malebranche takes care to promise a reward for persistency with varied effort. He undertakes that the methodical seeker will attain by intuition an 'infallible Principle' which he can use in the furtherance of knowledge. He writes: 'We must above all take care not to satisfy ourselves with some glimpse or likely-hood; but begin anew so often the comparisons that are conducible to discover the truths enquired after, as that we may not withhold our assent to it, without feeling the secret lashes and reproofs of our internal master that answers our questions, that is, the application of our minds, and the desires of our heart. Then will that truth serve as an infal-lible Principle, to proceed in the acquisition of sciences' (bk. vi. 2. 1). One could hardly have a better summary of the method and achievement of Berkeley's first (B) note-book, which culminates in his irrefragable intuitive prin-

ciple formally stated in 923-4 (cf. 287) and demonstrated
in form twice in the previous entries (903-22).[1] Berkeley
thus attains the reward that Malebranche had promised.
He has the deep satisfaction of the explorer who achieves
his aim and sees his method vindicated. As from a Pisgah
peak, Berkeley sees all of a sudden, *par simple vue*, what he
had come to look for. After long analysis and wearisome
study of intricate queries, he frees himself from the lets
and hindrances of jargon and conventional thought. Then
an idea can be like nothing but an idea; abstract general
ideas are ghosts, and infinitesimals are nothings. The mist
of matter thus melts away, and the Promised Land of being
flames in the morning light of young percipience.

It is clear then that Berkeley not only praised these 'rules
angelic' of Malebranche, but practised them. Perhaps they
did not leave a deep specific impress upon his work in other
respects, but it can hardly be doubted that the algebra that
is in them and over them stayed with him, and showed in
his doctrine of sense symbolism.[2] He soon gave up his early
hope of finding in algebra the key of universal knowledge,
but the relation of the algebraic sign to the quantity signified
became to him of decisive importance. Algebra seems to
have cured him of the geometrical method, to which he was
at one time devoted. Demonstration was the fashion of the
hour. Defoe in his *Consolidator* (1705) has some chaff about
the moon-blind understanding, 'furnisht with Hocoscopes,
Microscopes, Tellescopes, Caeliscopes, Money-scopes, and
the D . . .L and all of glasses' making its way by the aid of
'Physics, Politics, Ethics, Astronomy, Mathematics, and
such sort of bewildering things, with vast difficulty to a little

---

[1] See App. p. 198 and, if possible, consult the manuscript.
Editions cannot convey the full significance of these entries.
[2] See *T. V.* § 140. *Int. Prin.* § 19. cf. *Works*, vol. iii, p. 373,
Alc. vii. 12-3.

Minute-spot, call'd Demonstration.'[1] Berkeley began the
Commonplace Book as a demonstrator. He will indeed
demonstrate all his doctrines (592). Certain entries are
marked as axioms (369, 371; cf. 517, 532, 792, 793). At the
end of the first note-book he wrote a double demonstration
of the New Principle *more geometrico* (903-24). This specimen is an interesting relic. It consists of two distinct lines
of proof. The subordinate principles are listed, abridged,
and numbered. Inferences are drawn in form. The first
proof ignores comparison, the second is built on the fact
and act of comparison. The two proofs meet in the same
conclusion, 'Nothing like an idea can be in an unperceiving
thing' (918, 922).

Towards the end of the *Commonplace Book* (870), he
writes: 'I must not pretend to promise much of demonstration. I must cancell all passages that look like that sort of
pride, that raising of expectation in my readers.' We must
connect this change of method with the fact that in the
meantime one of the pivotal principles of the demonstration,
'all significant words stand for ideas' (904), had been completely upset. He writes, 'Some words there are wch do
not stand for ideas' (671). He develops this thought and
makes an important principle of it in connexion with abstract
ideas in his introduction to the *Principles* (§§ 19, 20). He
there says that names are 'for the most part used as letters
are in Algebra, in which . . . it is not requisite that in every
step each letter suggest to your thoughts that particular
quantity it was appointed to stand for.' Thus the algebraic
method is the high-road to symbolism; for the algebraic
sign is negligible in itself, but it can suggest an indef-
initely wide area of reality. Vision is to him, we might
say, the algebraic sense, on account of 'the vast extent,
number, and variety of objects that are at once, with so

[1] *Consolidator*, pp. 58 sqq.

much ease and quickness, and pleasure, suggested by it'
(*T.V.* § 148).

Malebranche does not give separate treatment to algebra,
for he regarded it as a higher extension of arithmetic.
Berkeley appears to have followed his example. In the
Principles, (§§ 121-2) we find no separate study of algebra;
but what he says of arithmetic holds of the sister science.
He attacks the view that arithmetic is a theoretical science
leading to a knowledge of eternal verities. Arithmetic is a
practical science. The primary purpose of numbering is
'ease of memory and help of computation'. So arithmetic
begins by abridging. Strokes, points, roman figures, and
arabic figures are successive developments of the primary
impulse, the figure '5' being simply an arbitrary abridgement of 'IIIII'. Hence 'the great use of the Indian figures
above the Roman shows arithmetic to be about signs not
ideas' (*C.P.B.* 815). Then the subject-matter of arithmetic, and *a fortiori* of algebra, is neither abstract ideas nor
ideas different from the numbers themselves, but signs deri-
ving from particular things and meaning particulars, but by
the nature of signification achieving concrete generality.

Passing from Malebranche's formal rules of method, we
may note in passing that Berkeley in his Introduction to the
Principles, §§ 1-5, seems to have Malebranche in view. He
contrasts his own conception of the task of philosophy with
that of 'the wisest men who have thought our ignorance
incurable', and his phrase 'those lets and difficulties, which
stay and embarrass the mind in its search after truth' all but
names the author of the *Recherche de la Vérité*. These 'lets
and difficulties' form the subject-matter of the first five books
of the *Search*. The words 'darkness and intricacy in the
objects' echo Malebranche's phrase the 'dark, intricate and
confused' effects of Nature (bk. vi. 2. 4). The 'natural defect
in the understanding' is a favourite topic with Malebranche,

who often describes in that way the effect of the Fall and
of the Union with the body.

The contrast between Principles and Faculties, which
dominates this section, derives perhaps from the same
source. The self-partiality which puts the blame on our
faculties is scornfully referred to in the *Commonplace Book*
as 'The Excuse' (300, 363, 364; cf. 760). Berkeley met this
'excuse' in Locke and in the 'mathematicians'; he met it,
much emphasized, in Malebranche's trenchant indictment
of the whole natural man, his sense, imagination, unaided
intellect, passions, and will. Malebranche *qua* monk
was acutely conscious of the defects in our faculties; *qua*
scientist he realized the importance of correct principles.
His study of method culminates in the long and close review
of principles which occupies the greater part of book vi,
part 2. Here he contrasts the true principles of the Cartesian
philosophy with the false principles of the Aristotelian. He
shows that in certain points Descartes himself has been false
to his own principles, and that in the case of cohesion
Descartes's account must be corrected by the True Principles of physics, viz. 'the simple Principles of Extension,
Figure, Motion'. Berkeley's repeated protest against 'learned
dust' and his appeal to common sense are well known. In a
similar vein Malebranche attacks 'the Incomprehensible
Principles of the falsely learned'.

Instruction in method formed the least part of Berkeley's
debt to Malebranche; for the method did not make the doctrine. But the facts given above are important as showing
how seriously and systematically Berkeley took the *Search*.
He was not content to know the more spectacular parts of
Malebranche's system. His contemporaries were prepared
to discuss and criticize the doctrine of seeing all things in
God. But Berkeley went beneath the surface; he dug down
and saw the foundations.

II

THEORIES OF VISION

BERKELEY's first philosophical publication, *An Essay towards a New Theory of Vision*, appeared in 1709, probably not later than May.[1] His second philosophical work, *A Treatise concerning the Principles of Human Knowledge*, was 'in the press' by March 1, 1710, and appeared in May.[2] A good deal of the preparatory work of both books was done concurrently. The Introduction to the *Principles* was in an advanced stage by November 1708, i.e. nearly six months before the issue of the *Theory of Vision*. It seems strange that a young author coming before the world with a daring metaphysic should have weighted his studies with a psychological investigation of great moment, requiring close and technical knowledge. Accordingly the relation between the two books calls for fuller treatment than it has yet received.

Fraser twice speaks of the *Theory of Vision* as a 'tentative juvenile essay'. He recognizes that Berkeley was an immaterialist when he wrote it. He complains of its 'studied reticence', and says that it 'was meant to prepare the way for the exposition and defence of the new theory of the material world'. Dr. Dawes Hicks prefers another explanation. He thinks that Berkeley may have written a good part of it before 1707, 'whilst he was still entertaining the belief that the objects of touch exist independently of being perceived, and that he considered it beside his purpose in finishing the volume to disturb that view, seeing that he was about to do

[1] In the dedication Berkeley speaks of Percival who came to Dublin in Oct. or Nov. 1708 as his friend of 'these few months'; and in appendix to 2nd ed. he says that the operation of June 29, 1709, occurred 'soon after the first edition'.

[2] Rand, op. cit., pp. 73, 86.

so in another treatise which was then on the eve of publication'.[1] There is truth in both accounts; but neither seems
adequate. The *Theory of Vision* is more than the thin end
of the wedge. It is not merely ancillary; yet the *Principles*
has not superseded it. All the evidence indicates that the
Principles was conceived first, and the *Theory of Vision*
second. Berkeley was a master of tactics, and he would
not have disdained to make converts by an economy of
truth, but we cannot think that a work so sustained and
comparatively independent was mainly meant to 'insinuate' his metaphysic.

My view in brief is this: Berkeley's thoughts turned towards a systematic study of vision because, on the received
theory, the facts of vision were an insuperable objection to
immaterialism. His study of Malebranche provided a clue
to a new theory which removed the gravest objections. He
published it separately because there was then a demand for
a theory of vision.

Let us take the last point first. Why should a tract on
vision by an unknown and very junior Fellow of Trinity
College reach a second edition in one year, be answered by
the famous Archbishop King, and be reviewed almost at
once on the Continent? *The Principles of Human Knowledge*
made no such stir. Clearly there was a demand for works on
vision. The demand had existed for some time. In 1682
Dr. William Briggs presented to the Royal Society a small
physiological work entitled *A New Theory of Vision*. Bar-
rows's *Optical Lectures* were well known to the learned, and
Barrow (*T.V.* § 29) called for a new theory. Molyneux's
Dioptricks was published in 1692.[2] The eighteenth century
opened with an outburst of visionism. Newton's *Optics* was
published in English in 1704. Defoe[3] says jestingly, 'A

---

[1] Dawes Hicks, *Berkeley*, pp. 39, 40.
[2] See below p. 38, note.   [3] 1705, *Consolidator*, p. 57.

generation have risen up, who to solve the difficulties of
supernatural systems, imagine a mighty vast Something,
who has no form but what represents him to them as one
Great Eye. This infinite Optick they imagine to be *Natura
Naturans* . . . the soul of man therefore, in the opinion of
these naturallists is one vast Optick Power . . . . From hence
they resolve all Beings to Eyes.'

This general interest was largely practical. Spectacles,
telescopes, and microscopes, had focused attention on
vision, but the theoretical implications were studied too.
Arthur Collier, who was working in the same field as
Berkeley about January 1708,[1] after outlining the Aristotelian theory of vision says (p. 39): 'From the old I proceed to
the hypothesis of vision which is a part of the new philosophy. Everyone, I suppose, has heard of the doctrine of
seeing the Divine Ideas, or (as Mr Malebranche expresses
it) seeing all things in God.' It is noteworthy that Collier's
Part I is related to his Part II much as Berkeley's *Theory
of Vision* is related to his *Principles*. In Part I he proves that
the visible world is not external, and in Part II he proves
that there is no invisible world external.

Now just as Collier knew quite well when he began to
write Part I what the conclusion of Part II would be, so
Berkeley, when he began (probably in the spring of 1708)
to draft the *Theory of Vision*, was familiar with the thesis
of the *Principles*. But in publishing the *Theory of Vision*
separately without an explicit denial of matter, he was just
taking one thing at a time. He had written a good book
which his public would read. It was self-contained, and
yet was a natural stepping-stone to his metaphysic.

There is no antagonism between the two books. They
are complementary. The *Theory of Vision* is not superseded by the *Principles*. In the *Principles* (§ 44) Berkeley

[1] See R. Benson's *Collier*, p. 18.

refers to the earlier work for 'fuller information'. He republished the *Theory of Vision* in 1732, and issued a vindi-
cation and explanation of it in the following year.[1] In
America he wrote of 'the design and connexion' of his
philosophical works, and desired his disciples there to
read them in the order in which he published them, taking
care to send them copies of the '*Principles*, the *Theory*, and
the *Dialogues*'.[2] The psychology of the theory is independent of the metaphysic to which it leads. In both books he
asserts the internality of ideas of sight or the ideality of
objects seen. In the earlier book he allows the reader to
assume the externality of ideas of touch, or the reality of
objects touched, not as an economy of truth, but because it
was foreign to his immediate purpose to carry the argument
further.

On the eve of the publication (March 1, 1710) of the
Principles Berkeley speaks of the two books together. He
tells Percival that the *Principles* will vindicate the usefulness
of the *Theory of Vision* and will make its argument 'appear
subservient to the ends of morality and religion'. But
Percival was not a philosopher, and could not appreciate
the real connexion. We must look rather to Berkeley's
published statements. We have first, in the dedication to
Percival, the vague statement, 'my thoughts concerning
Vision have led me into some notions so far out of the
common road ...'. The words may not refer to immaterialism; if they do, they mean that his study of the Molyneux
problem, &c., helped to establish his new creed. They
could hardly mean that writing his book on vision made him
an immaterialist. The time-factor, if no other reason, bars

---

[1] *The Theory of Vision Vindicated* not only gives a masterly
summary of the earlier work, but adds several new arguments,
e.g. §§ 46, 51, 55-7.

[2] Letter to Johnson, March 24, 1730, *Works*, vol. ii, p. 20.

that explanation. The Preface to the *Principles* mentions a
'long and scrupulous inquiry'. Again, more precisely, 'The
opinion of matter I have entertained some years', he writes
to Percival on September 6, 1710, and he speaks of the time
'long since ... when the conceit was warm in my imagination'. Further the *Commonplace Book* makes it certain, I
think, that he was an immaterialist before he began the
Theory of Vision. That essay is structurally dependent
upon the *Commonplace Book*, and could scarcely have been
begun, was certainly not far advanced, until at least the first
note-book was filled with entries. The earliest possible
date[1] for the opening entries is, I hold, December 1706, and
certainly Berkeley held the immaterialist hypothesis then.

In the first two pages of the *Commonplace Book* we see, to
adapt Reid's simile, the young Samson with his arms around
the two pillars of the house, time and space. 'Time a sensation: therefore onely in ye mind' (13). 'Extension a
sensation, therefore not without the mind' (18). The entries
read like the death-knell of a world. Yet the slight change
of rhythm—'onely in' to 'not without'—is perhaps significant. Space that is seen is more external than time that is
heard. Visible space is the stronger pillar of the two. Samson stops to think. 'In the immaterial hypothesis, the wall
is white, fire hot, &c' (19; cf. *Search*, vi. 2. 2.). There's the
rub. I see the wall and see it white. I feel the fire, and feel
it hot. This surely was the 'difficulty' of which he speaks
in the *Principles* (§ 43). In this difficulty he turns to Malebranche's rules of method. He outlines the 'immaterial
hypothesis' in its main bearings (*C.P.B.* 20–6), and then
addresses himself at once to the study of vision. In the
entries 27, 28 he sets himself in query form the main problem of the *Theory of Vision*. From that on up to the last
quarter of the first note-book topics of vision predominate,

[1] See Appendix, p. 200.

though the wider issues are never dropped. About the time he made the entries 283–7, he seems to have satisfied himself that 'seeing' is no objection to immaterialism. The 'immaterial hypothesis' thereupon or shortly after passes into the Principle. The remaining entries in that and the other note-book are about the wider issues, though an odd entry with a *Theory of Vision* marginal sign is found in the later pages (881 is the latest).

Thus the *Commonplace Book* confirms the explicit statement of the *Principles* (§ 43) about the origin of the *Theory of Vision*, 'that we should in truth *see* external space, and bodies actually existing in it, some nearer, others farther off, seems to carry with it some opposition to what hath been said of their existing nowhere without the mind. The consideration of this difficulty it was that gave birth to my *Essay towards a New Theory of Vision*, which was published not long since.' That passage makes it clear that when he began to shape the argument for immaterialism he was met at the outset by an obstacle that seemed to bar further progress— we *see* the outside world; we see the world *outside*. Therefore there is a world and it is outside. He turned aside to deal with that difficulty. His *New Theory of Vision* removed the barrier. So Berkeley's essay on vision, though presented as an independent work, and certainly possessing an independent value, is essentially and by origin an integral part of *his* new philosophy.[1] The influence of Malebranche upon this part of the Berkeleian philosophy is therefore an index to the degree of his influence upon the whole system.

Sketch of Berkeley's Theory of Vision

The developed and characteristic part of Berkeley's theory is his account of the object seen. Before discussing that part, we shall piece together his account of the subject

[1] See quotation from Collier, p. 27 above.

seeing. For Berkeley, seeing is a compound act. It is more
than the act of the eye, *qua* eye. It is shadowed by the
judgement and by incipient movements of other organs,
especially of touch. In his words, the 'turn of the eyes is
attended with a sensation' (§ 16), and he finds it acknow-
ledged, as regards remote distance, that the estimate is an
act of judgement rather than of sense (§ 3). His insistence
upon the suddenness and swiftness of the act is a recognition of this complexity, and an attempt to introduce an
apperceptive unity. As regards terms, he often uses indifferently seeing, sensing, perceiving and judging; but he
can be precise when he wishes (e.g. 'The eye, or, to speak
truly, the mind, perceiving ...' § 36). He knows well the distinction between 'the first act of vision' (§ 106) and its concomitants, between sight and perceiving by sight (§ 99).
Pure vision is simple apprehension of colour (§§ 43, 156,
158). It is the postulate of the Molyneux problem (§ 106),
and is the sole type of sensible act open to 'an intelligence
or unbodied spirit, which is supposed to see perfectly ...
but to have no sense of touch' (§ 153). Berkeley uses with
effect certain terms, which imply the complexity of the
process, but subordinate the notion of *act*. Of these the
most characteristic is 'suggestion' (§ 16 and *passim*), which
covers both the stimulus and the mind's semi-conscious
response (cf. 'unperceived transit' § 145, and the vague
terms 'attend' and 'experience', which are frequent).

He carefully characterizes one part of the subjective process. The elements that blend, be they the joint actions of
different senses, be they memory and sense, or mind and
sense, do so by virtue of custom and not of necessity. 'On
the demonstration of this point the whole theory depends'
(*T.V.*, App.). There is no necessary connexion. There is no
'natural geometry' in the act of seeing. Seeing distance or
magnitude is not like a demonstration, in which the figure

being given the properties flow by necessity. It is a mistake to confuse vision with optics. Optical angles, whether made by the axes of vision at the object or by diverging rays on the pupil, are not really there *in rerum natura*. So judgements of distance cannot, in fact, flow from them, as is generally supposed, by iron necessity. Nor can what is outside be *like* what is within the mind. 'I saw shame . . . So I see . . . distance.' This entry (240) is the only one in the *Commonplace Book* marked for insertion in all the three original parts of the essay, and to this comparison he returns repeatedly (*T.V.* §§ 9, 23, 65; cf. §§ 143–5). Thus Berkeley substitutes arbitrary connexion of unlike elements for 'natural geometry'. Colours of the countenance are not *like* passions; yet in seeing red there, by custom I learn to see shame there. Such is the proper comparison for 'how we see'.

We come now to Berkeley's treatment of the object seen. Here, too, he divides and conquers. He divides what I see from what I touch. He distinguishes what I see immediately from what I see mediately. He connects the mediate object with the object touched or tangible, and thus we have a dual object correlated with a dual activity of the subject. My eye sees the immediate object; my mind sees, i.e. I infer or perceive, the mediate object. What is presented to my eye is visible, purely and altogether visible; yet it suggests what is not visible, and what may, in most sensations, be regarded as the tangible.

That visible objects differ in kind from tangible is the key position of the new theory of vision. At this stage he is not concerned to probe the metaphysical implications of the distinction, which he says 'cannot be too often inculcated in treating of vision' (*T.V.* §91). The ideist philosophy was conveniently ambiguous, and by calling both objects 'ideas' he leaves the ground open for the ultimate argument of the *Principles*. Most of his contemporaries would admit the

propriety of calling the *datum* of sight an 'idea', and the
Lockians would admit that if it is strained to call 'what I
touch' an idea, at least there is an idea of 'what I touch'.
Locke had taught that there are ideas common to both
senses,—that, in fact, we see and touch the same thing.
Berkeley joins issue with him, asserting what I see is one
object and what I touch is another object. While both
objects may be called and are 'ideas', visible ideas are stated
by Berkeley to be in the mind, while the reader is allowed
to assume that tangible ideas are external. The design of
the essay is expressed in § 1, and the first part of the design
has caught the commentator's eye rather too exclusively. But
from §§ 119 and 127 we see that in Berkeley's opinion the
core of what is new in the *new theory* is this heterogeneity.[1]

The supposed fact that we do not see and touch the same
object had been stamped on Berkeley's imagination by the
Molyneux problem. He reproduces the problem in Locke's
words together with Locke's solution in *T.V.* § 132. The
Molyneux problem was of capital importance to Berkeley
when he was designing the essay. About fifteen entries in
the *Commonplace Book* raise questions about the blind man
made to see, and the earliest entries (27, 28, 32), dealing
with the heterogeneity of sight and touch, raise the question
in connexion with the Molyneux problem. Molyneux and
Locke both said 'no', the blind man in the problem would
not know which was the cube and which the square. Berkeley's private opinion was that the blind man would not
recognize either of them to be even bodies (*C.P.B.* 32), and
that the question would be to him 'downright bantering and
unintelligible' (*T.V.* § 135). But he makes capital for his
main thesis by saying that the solution given by Locke and

[1] So also *Theory of Vision Vindicated*, §§ 41, 42. 'This stating
of the matter placeth it on a new foot, and in a different light
from all preceding theories.'

Molyneux is wrong unless the space of sight and the space of touch are specifically distinct (*T.V.* § 133).[1]

The main and comprehensive thesis of the essay, 'so remote from, and contrary to the received notions and settled opinion of mankind', is formally laid down in the following proposition: 'the extension, figures, and motions perceived by sight are specifically distinct from the ideas of touch, called by the same names; nor is there any such thing as one idea, or kind of idea, common to both senses' (*T.V.* § 127). This proposition can be gathered from 'several places' of the essay, but in the sections immediately following Berkeley gives a 'demonstration' of its truth by three separate arguments, adding the solution of the Molyneux problem in 'farther confirmation of our tenet'.

The New Theory, then, starts from the 'heterogeneity' and works round to it again through a study of distance, magnitude, and situation. That this is the correct analysis of the essay is established by the passage above quoted, by the *Commonplace Book*, and by *The Theory of Vision Vindicated*, where he calls the heterogeneity 'this main part and pillar' of the theory.[2]

We shall now briefly review the three steps by which he leads his readers to his own starting-point.[3] The section on 'Distance' (§§ 2–51) may be summarized thus. It is physically impossible for distance itself to be seen (§ 2), as an object is seen. Distance is not perceived by means of lines and angles (§§ 13–15). Another type of medium must be

[1] Since the above was written I came across the following statement: 'His philosophy can alone be truly known, when seen germinating from the question of Molyneux' (Teape, *Berkeleian Philosophy* (1870), p. 3). For the original problem see Locke, *Fam. Letters*, p. 37.

[2] *T.V.V.* § 41; *v.* also §§ 15, 32, and *passim*.

[3] N.B. In *The Theory of Vision Vindicated* the order of these steps is reversed.

sought. Distance is suggested by the 'turn of the eye' and by confused appearance and by other contributing circumstances (§ 28). This explains the 'Barrovian case', i.e. the problem which Dr. Barrow felt so acutely that he called in question the principles of optics, and demanded a new theory of vision (§§ 29–40). From this account of distance it follows, in Berkeley's view, that not colour alone, the proper and immediate object of sight, but also extension, figure and motion, are at no distance from the mind, but as near as pain (§§ 41–4). He then introduces his readers to the principle that was his own starting-point, and explains the illusion of visual distance by our refusal to admit the heterogeneity of the objects seen and touched, called by the same name (§§ 45–51).

Berkeley's second step is to do for magnitude what the first step did for distance. The section on 'Magnitude' (§§ 52–87) follows the course of the first section. We do not perceive magnitude by means of lines and angles. Real invariable magnitude is perceived principally by three means: (1) the everchanging visible magnitude; (2) confusion or distinctness of the visible appearance; (3) its vigorousness or faintness. There are as well some secondary factors, e.g. the disposition of the eye, and the number, quality, and nature of intermediate objects. There is no necessary connexion between these features and tangible size. Great size means simply that the object contains a large number of points or minima, and minima may be either tangible or visible. There is no reason other than custom why confusion and vigorousness should suggest smaller size and fewer minima, while distinctness and faintness do the reverse. We see magnitude in no other way than 'we see shame or anger in the looks of a man' (§ 65). The apparent size of the horizontal moon is then considered and explained on these principles. The section ends with a brief discussion of the *minimum visibile* and microscopic sight. The chief new point in this section is that the connexion between the visible and tangible, while arbitrary in the sense that it might have been otherwise, is not capricious; for it conduces to the preservation of the body.

The third section (§§ 88–120) has the broad title *Situation*, but it is entirely devoted to the narrow problem of the inverted retinal image. Berkeley may have taken the title from Descartes's section on *Situs* (*Dioptrics*, c. vi., § 9). As we shall see below, Malebranche provided the model for the sections on 'Distance' and 'Magnitude', but he has nothing corresponding to this third section. The section was an afterthought with Berkeley. From the marginal signs in the *Commonplace Book* we see that the three sections originally planned were on distance, magnitude, and heterogeneity; for the corresponding entries are numbered 1, 2, 3, respectively. There are, however, 7 or 8 entries on the inverted retinal image, and these and these only are marked 3ª.[1]

This 'one mighty difficulty' (*T.V.* § 88) became to him 'the principal point in the whole optic theory' (*T.V.V.* § 52). For its solution is clear proof that the tangible object is not the proper object of sight. He first considers Molyneux's explanation, using Molyneux's own diagram. This explanation, 'allowed by all men as satisfactory', is in effect that of Descartes, and involves the absurd *geometria innata* of the blind man with crossed sticks, and the other assumptions of external visible distance. His own explanation turns on his sharp distinction between visible and tangible ideas (*T.V.* §§ 97 sqq.). By 'erect man out there' we mean a tangible man with tangible feet on the tangible earth. The rays of light from the 'erect man out there' form an inverted image on the tangible retina. Taught by experience, when we want to see distinctly the objects imaged on the *higher* or

[1] See Appendix, p. 185 and frontispiece.

lower parts of the retina, we turn the eyes *down* or *up* respectively. Hence, though we do not see 'up' and 'down', any more than we see outness, yet we *say* we see a man's head up and his heels down, because we see the head and heels distinctly by turning our eyes up and down respectively.

The remainder of the essay turns on Berkeley's doctrine of abstract ideas (§§ 122–60). This section too was an addition to the original plan.[1] He was half-way through the *Commonplace Book* before he came on the question of abstraction. There are several parallels between this section and the Introduction to the *Principles*; so we may presume that Berkeley added it in the late autumn of 1708, when, we know for certain, he was working at that Introduction. It is a highly important section, for it directly incorporates the new theory of vision in Berkeley's wider philosophy. An abstract idea of space, a mere product of fancy, is at the back of our belief that we see and touch the same object. The supposed idea common to two senses is nothing more or less than this abstraction, which gains in dignity and acquires apparent substance by being regarded as the subject-matter of geometry. Thus Berkeley brings the root-cause of men's mistakes about vision under the most inclusive of all the erroneous principles that, in his opinion, trouble knowledge.

The heterogeneity of visible and tangible ideas is the 'main part and pillar' of the New Theory. What I see is not what I touch, nor like it. This result is negative. It explains our errors, but is not positive knowledge. Berkeley is not content to leave the matter there. He discusses the question 'How visible extension and figures come to be called by the same name with tangible extension and figures if they are not of the same kind with them.' (*T.V.* § 139). His answer[2]

---

[1] Abstraction is not treated in the *Theory of Vision Vindicated*.

[2] Based, I think, on *Search*, bk. ii, pt. 2, c. 3, see below, p. 46.

leads to a positive expression of his theory. Visible words are symbols. So too are visible ideas. The series *square* is not a bit like a tangible square, yet to Englishmen that group of letters suggests a tangible square. Now a visible square, also unlike a tangible square, has parts that in some measure correspond to the parts of the other. So the visible square is a sign the world over, not conventional like the letters, not 'variable and of human institution'. Thus he reaches his highest and widest conclusion, that 'the proper objects of vision constitute the Universal Language of Nature' (*T.V.* § 147). Berkeley's reference to this passage in the *Principles* (§ 44; also §§ 66 and 108) shows that he regarded this truth as the net outcome of the essay, and in the *Principles* and in the *Alciphron* (dial. iv) he expands it into a main proof of the existence of God, and, we might almost say, into a solution of the enigma of the universe.

Praise has been given to Berkeley's theory of vision, even by those who reject the metaphysic on which it rests. It is a fine piece of constructive reasoning, involving a wide sweep of the philosophic mind, as well as exact knowledge of optical science. A young man in his twenty-fourth year wrote it. So an inquiry into the influences that moulded the work is of unusual interest. We know that Berkeley used Barrow's *Optical Lectures*, Descartes's *Dioptrics*, and Newton's *Optics*. But his two outstanding authorities in this field were Molyneux and Malebranche.

William Molyneux's Treatise of 'Dioptricks' (Dioptrica Nova)

This book was so important for Berkeley that some account of it is required. It was published apparently in 1692, with a dedication to the Royal Society.[1] It is written

---

[1] The above date seems correct, though others have given it as 1690 or 1691. The dedication is dated 1690. The T.C.D. Library copy, *ex dono Authoris*, is inscribed: 'Almae Matri

THEORIES OF VISION 39

from the standpoint of the New Learning. It claims to be the first book on the subject ever published in English. The Dedication speaks highly of Locke and of the *Recherche de la Vérité*. Berkeley relied on Molyneux's book for the technique of his subject, and actually reproduces some of the diagrams contained in it. The opening of the *Theory of Vision* is verbally indebted to pp. 113–14.[1] Molyneux treats of the physics of light and of plain vision with the naked eye. He deals with the structure and function of the eye, explaining the crystalline, retina, &c. He passes on to consider distinct, confused, clear and faint, near and distant vision. He discusses optic angles, apparent and real distance, apparent and real magnitude. He concludes with a section on glasses, concave and convex, the speculum, the microscope, and telescope. The book is only once mentioned in the *Commonplace Book* (203); but there can be no doubt that many other entries dealing with the technical side of optics are based upon it. The *Theory of Vision* (§§ 29, 40, 89) treats it as one of his primary authorities.

Now Molyneux, like Barrow and Newton, is eloquently silent at the point of contact between optics and philosophy. For instance, of the retinal image Molyneux says: 'Which representation is there perceived by the sensitive soul (whatever it be), the manner of whose actions and passions He only knows who created and preserves it' (p. 104). Or again, of the inverted retinal image Molyneux writes: 'But this quaery seems to encroach too nigh the enquiry into the manner of the Visive faculties' perception' (p. 105; cf. p. 289). He recognizes that visual perception lies outside his province, adding, '"Tis not properly the eye that sees'. Thus Molyneux's treatise points on to a metaphysic of vision.

Academiae Dubliniensi humillime offert Alumnus gratissimus Gulielmus Molyneux.'

[1] Cf. *Works*, vol. i, p. 108.

Malebranche on Vision

Malebranche's influence on Berkeley extended beyond the technique to the philosophy of the subject, and was therefore profound. It is curious that while obscure writers are named in the *Theory of Vision*, Malebranche receives neither acknowledgement nor mention. Possibly Berkeley was so conscious of the points of difference that he did not realize his debt. More probably his silence was prudence. In some quarters 'Malebranche' spelled enthusiasm, and enthusiasm was literally a sin. It was safe for Collier, settled in his Wiltshire rectory, to connect his system with that of Malebranche. It was another matter for the ambitious young Irish Protestant to do so. Only those who know the conditions can appreciate the point. Berkeley was absolutely dependent for promotion on the favour of Dublin Castle. A Roman Catholic monk who wrote bitterly of 'heretics',[1] and who called the English 'those wretched people, those children of this world', attacking the English Crown, the Church, and the State,[2] would not be the most profitable patron for Berkeley's first important venture in authorship. It seems certain that Berkeley deliberately avoided mentioning Malebranche. For instance, in connexion with the moon problem a recognition of the care that Malebranche devoted to that problem would have been easy and natural. His mention in § 75 of Gassendi, Descartes, and Hobbes is due, no doubt, to the fact that Molyneux's paper before the Royal Society, written 'to rouse philosophers up to enquire anew after this surprising Phenomenon', exposes the errors of those three thinkers. But when he goes on to review the very next paper in the *Transactions*, that by Wallis, one would have expected a mention of Malebranche among the 'others' who had anticipated Wallis's explanation. It

[1] *Search*, bk. ii, 2, c. 4.   [2] *Search*, bk. ii, 3, c. 2.

is worth noting that Gassendi's 'false principle' referred to in the Appendix to the *Theory of Vision*, namely the alteration in the pupil, is noted in the *Commonplace Book* (264) in connexion with Malebranche.

There is no doubt whatever that Berkeley studied the *Search* while he was preparing to write the *Theory of Vision*. In the *Commonplace Book* some fourteen entries name Malebranche; as many more refer to his views; two entries (264, 266) actually include the reference to bk. i, ch. 6, where Malebranche begins his study of vision.

Malebranche gives his general theory of sense perception in bk. i, chs. 10–14. His analysis of the act of perceptual judgement is close to that of the Berkeleian theory. What looks single, proves on analysis to be dual. The one world of perception turns into two worlds, the world within, and the world without (*hors de nous*). The act of natural judgement is two acts of sense, combined in 'compound sensation'. The object sensed is dual, the mediate object and the immediate. Finally existence itself is in a manner bisected, and the theory is outlined in the following words: 'There are two sorts of Beings; Beings which our soul immediately sees and others which she knows only by the mediation of the former. When, for instance, I perceive the sun arising I first perceive that which I immediately see, and because my perception of the former is only occasioned by something without me . . . I judge the former sun which is in my soul, to be without me and to exist.'[1] Vision, whether the term mean the act of seeing or the object seen, is, for Berkeley, compound sensation.[2] I suggest that Malebranche,

---

[1] *Search*, bk. i, c. 14. For the illustration cf. *C.P.B.* 898.

[2] Berkeley does not use the phrase 'compound sensation'; but his 'sudden judgement of sense' (§ 77) is close to 'judgement of the senses' which Malebranche uses as a synonym for 'compound sensation', bk. i, c. 14.

to that extent, supplied the outline of the New Theory, and that Berkeley filled in the outline by his original contributions, namely, the distinction between the *data* of sight and of touch in the complex percept, and the expression of the whole in terms of idea.

As regards motion Malebranche is close to the full Berkeleian distinction. He distinguishes (bk. i. 8) two sorts of motion, the one being visible, the other not. He argues that we do not know the true quantity of motion, adding, 'This argument is only a corollary of that which I have said of extension.' Berkeley reproduces the thought and perhaps the words of this passage, dismissing motion similarly in an offhand way. 'Now that visible motion is not of the same sort with tangible motion seems to need no further proof, it being an evident corollary from what we have shown concerning . . . extension' (*T.V.* § 137).

The Cartesian division of the primary qualities, extension, figure, and motion, without reference to solidity and the other Lockian variants, appears at most of the turning-points of Berkeley's argument. It is also the framework of Malebranche's section on vision in Book i. Chapter 6 is devoted to extension, i.e. size or magnitude. Chapter 7 considers figure. Chapters 8 and 9 treat nominally of motion, but in effect of distance. Similarly Berkeley gives a serial treatment of the primary qualities, to some extent following a line of his own, but perhaps influenced by the *Search*. Like Malebranche he gives pride of place to distance, allowing it to oust motion. To figure Malebranche concedes only a brief notice, declaring that figure is 'not a thing of an absolute kind, but its nature consists in the relation which is between the parts which terminate some space'. Similarly Berkeley twice (*T.V.* §§ 105, 124) declares that 'figure is the termination of magnitude', and he treats it along with magnitude. Berkeley's section on situation was, I have

shown above, an afterthought, due no doubt to an independent study of the retinal problem (p. 36).

The comparison of the sense-*datum* to language, the
arbitrary connexion between sign and thing signified, and
the contrast between man-made connexions and the universal connexions established by the Will of God, these
Berkeleian principles may all be found in the *Search*.
Occasionalism taught that there is no necessary connexion
between changes in the body and the accompanying changes
in the soul. Berkeley did not accept occasionalism, but this
tenet, in the form of faith in the real operation of the Will
of God, became an essential of his theory. Malebranche
points out that what we call 'heaven' the Greeks call 'oura-
nos', the Hebrews 'shamajim'. The connexion between the
word and the thing is arbitrary and man-made. But, he
notes, sensations like colour, taste, &c., have no such
variable character. No words of mine can explain to a
man what heat is or colour. If he does not know and I
want to tell him, I must speak to him in the universal
language that God has established. I must, that is, impress
his organs of sense. 'I must bring him to the fire, and
show him a piece of painting.'[1]

It would seem that in the plan of the book and in the main
lines of the argument, the *Theory of Vision* is indebted to
the *Search*. To trace the dependence further would be
tedious and unnecessary here; but I have collected in an
appendix to this chapter some of the more striking parallels.

'Dependence' seems scarcely the word in the case of so
independent a thinker. Berkeley was no copyist. His
authorities were his sources; they helped to mould but did
not make his thought. My aim is to show that the way to the
heart of Berkeleianism lies through Malebranche. If the
facts bear me out, a fair presentation of them cannot detract

[1] Bk. i. 13; see also bk. ii. 2. 3 and elsewhere.

from Berkeley's achievement. His achievement is not in question. It stands above detraction. They detract who would make his views the dreams of an egoist out of touch with his day. His Irish originality and genius stand out all the more sharply against the French background. He used Malebranche so much and so fruitfully, and yet reached conclusions so different. Malebranche's confessed aim in analysing the 'most comprehensive' of the senses is at one blow to shake man's natural faith in all his powers. His system is built upon a conscious and radical distrust of the evidence of our eyesight. It was a stroke of genius on Berkeley's part to study afresh under Malebranche's tuition, the 'most comprehensive' of the senses, and to find its evidence, misunderstood and misrepresented indeed, but in its true interpretation reliable, reassuring, and uplifting.

APPENDIX

Parallels between the 'Theory of Vision' and the 'Search'

N.B. *S.* = *Search*

Commonplace Book: the following entries refer to Malebranche on vision: 264, 266, 278, 296, and probably 60, 83, 126, 127, 441.

The term 'comprehensive' of sight is common to Malebranche, Locke, and Berkeley; cf. Descartes's *latissime patens* (*Dioptrics*, c. i).

The welfare of the body determines our visual apprehension, especially in the case of magnitude. *S.* bk. i, c. 6 and 20, *T.V.* §§ 59, 85. 'The principal thing I would have remembered' (Malebranche).

Glasses as proof of not seeing extension: *S.* i. 6, *C.P.B.* 63.

The animate atomies which indicate eternal creation: *S.* i. 6, *C.P.B.* 60; cf. letter to Percival in Rand, op. cit., pp. 83, 84.

The varying length of a six-foot rule: *S.* i. 6, *T.V.* § 61; cf. *C.P.B.* 87–9.

'If we had eyes after the manner of microscopes': *S.* i. 6; cf. 'Were our eyes turned into the nature of microscopes', *T.V.* § 86; cf. Locke, *Essay*, ii. 23, 12.

Right lines not verifiable: *S.* i. 7, *C.P.B.* 126. The cube: *S.* i. 7 and iii. 2. 2, *C.P.B.* 83.

The steeple, interjacent objects, fields, houses, &c., seen behind a wall: *S.* i. 7, *T.V.* §§ 70, 73, 76, 77.

Blind man with two sticks (optical angle): *T.V.* § 42, *S.* i. 9, and Descartes, *Dioptrics*, c. vi and diagrams.

Natural Geometry: *S.* i. 9, *T.V.* § 19 and App.

Both give great prominence to the apparent size of the horizontal moon. Malebranche refers to it under 'Figure', 'Distance' and 'Judgement'. Though Berkeley omits to mention Malebranche, there are two indications of special study of this source: (1) The moon problem leads M. to say (*S.* i. 7) that optics only instructs us 'how to put fallacies on our eyes' and he speaks of 'this cheat'. B. in the same connexion asks (*T.V.* § 74), 'What is it can put this cheat on the understanding?' (2) B. says (*T.V.* §§ 70, 74) that the visible magnitude of the moon 'remains the same or is rather lesser'. The inconsistent phrase puzzles Fraser, who asks, 'Why lesser?' The answer may be that M. says so. M., denying that atmospheric refraction is the explanation, says that the retinal image of the moon is smaller as refracted, because astronomers have proved that the moon's diameter grows greater as she climbs (*S.* i. 9).

Malebranche in *S.* i. 9 on 'Distance' distinguishes six 'mediums' of judging distance. Berkeley uses the word 'mediums' (*T.V.* § 22). B. refers to all the mediums, accepting some, rejecting others. The mediums are: (1) The optical angle, or the optical angle with the disposition of the eye; cf. *T.V.* §§ 19 and 42. (2) The disposition of the eye accompanying the angle made by the rays converging on the retina. (3) The retinal image. (4 and 5) The force of the object's action upon the eye and the distinctness and clearness, the faintness and confusion of the image. (6) Interjacent objects.

B. illustrates the relativity of sensation by the case of an Englishman meeting a foreigner who used the same words in the contrary sense (*T.V.* § 32). So Malebranche (*S.* i. 13) speaks of the foreigner, who, on a winter's day praised 'cold' water, thinking 'cold' was the word for hot.

B., contrasting geometry with algebra, speaks of the 'extra-ordinary clearness and evidence of geometry', and assigns as the reason, 'the very ideas themselves' being copied out and exposed to view upon paper (*T.V.* § 150); so also *S.* vi. 1. 3, 'By drawing lines upon paper geometricians draw, as I may say, answerable ideas upon their mind.'

'All men have the idea of a square upon sight of a square; because that connexion is natural; but it may be very well doubted whether all men have the idea of a square when they hear the word 'square' pronounced; because that connexion is altogether arbitrary' (*S.* ii. 2. 3). So B. (*T.V.* § 152; cf. § 140) says: 'There is indeed this difference betwixt the signification of tangible figures by visible figures and of ideas by words—that whereas the latter is variable and uncertain, depending altogether on the arbitrary appointment of men, the former is fixed and immutably the same in all times and places. A visible square, for instance, suggests to the mind the same tangible figure in Europe that it doth in America.'

'Outness.' Where did Berkeley find that 'barbarous but ex-pressive term?'[1] The *Oxford Dictionary* gives no instance before Berkeley. I have only met it in one other place, namely, in the famous 'Illustration' appended to the *Search* on the difficulty of proving the existence of bodies. B. refers to this 'Illustration' more than once in the *C.P.B.*, e.g. 697 and 830. The passage is: 'Is it not evident that there are outnesses (des dehors) and remotenesses . . . in the intelligible world which is the im-mediate object of our mind?' N.B. There are many other indications, amounting to proof that Berkeley read Male-branche in Taylor's translation, e.g. *C.P.B.* 812: 'Malbranch in his Illustration'. Taylor invariably gives 'Illustration' for the technical term 'Éclaircissement'.

[1] Thomas Brown, *Philosophy of the Human Mind*, 1820, vol. i, p. 491.

III

THE BACKGROUND OF IMMATERIALISM

PROFESSOR DAWES HICKS and Professor Aaron have stated
that immaterialism was 'in the air' when Berkeley wrote.
That statement is correct, if it means that immaterialism
is strongly suggested to us by Cartesian ideism, but not, I
think, if it be taken to mean that there were Berkeleians
before Berkeley. The reception accorded to Berkeley's
Principles[1] shows that immaterialism was not in the air of
London. Collier too had no hearing. Thinkers were not
waiting for immaterialism, nor ready for it. As we study the
books Berkeley read, we shall see that his contemporaries
differed about the nature of matter, but were ready to turn
and rend any one who denied its existence. Materialism
was much 'in the air' that Berkeley breathed.

Religion was the driving-force of his immaterialism—
'Matter once allowed, I defy any man to prove that God is
not matter' (*C.P.B.* 634; cf. 308). But Berkeley did not
isolate his religion. Philosophy, mathematics, and science
combined with religion to thrust upon his notice the problem of matter. Mathematicians needed matter, for they
demonstrated its infinite divisibility, the postulate of the
new theory of infinitesimals. Physics assumed matter, for
'attraction', the 'great mechanical principle now in vogue'
(*Prin.* § 103), required something to attract. The microscope
was exploring the microcosm of matter, and had confirmed
the doctrine of the infinite divisibility. A world lies hid in
a mite. In a seed there lies a tree itself seeding yet another
tree (*Search*, i. 6). The telescope had advanced the frontiers
of knowledge and of matter. Lastly, under the influence of
Spinoza's 'infinite attribute', theologians were beginning to

[1] *V.* Percival to B. August 26, 1710 (Rand, op. cit., p. 80).

regard extension or real space as an attribute of Deity, and Clarke had based on matter a demonstration of the essential attributes.

Matter had only recently become a problem. Norris[1] writes: 'Suarez proves that first matter is not *so a pura potentia* but that it has some entative actuality belonging to it, that is, that tho' it be in *pura potentia receptiva* as to any formal act, yet it is not in *pura potentia objectiva* as to reality of being, but is a real something (however incomplete) and actually *extra nihil.*' This elusive ghost, Pura Potentia extra Nihil, could never be a danger to religion, nor to anything except clear thinking. Indeed, the ghost was much in demand to support certain dogmas of the medieval church. Transubstantiation had shielded matter down the centuries, as matter was the ground of transubstantiation.[2]

The scholastic tradition died hard. Sir Kenelme Digby, writing about the middle of the seventeenth century, devotes 400 pages of his *Two Treatises* to the physics of bodies, in preparation for his lofty address to his soul. The type of his physics can be gathered from his definition of colour, 'the term of the diaphanous body', the definition being 'confirmed by Aristotle's authority, reason, and experience' (c. 29). Though clearly he believed in matter, he scarcely mentions it. It was of no interest to him. He says in effect (p. 426), 'It is unnecessary to study matter after bodies'.

Half a century of the method of doubt changed all that. Cartesian metaphysic raised the status of matter and focused attention upon its nature. The speculative examined the evidence for its existence. Physicists studied its content and when, with the discrediting of Descartes' vortices, the

---

[1] *Theory of the Ideal World*, 1701-4, pt. i, p. 78.

[2] A. Collier, *Clavis Univ.*, pt ii, c. 9, assembles several definitions and descriptions of matter, and in his Conclusion connects matter and transubstantiation.

force of cohesion was transferred from the thing to the ether, the *solidity* of matter vanished, leaving behind it the clear and distinct idea of extension. In England Hobbes's materialism had taken deep root, and Locke's material substance was solid extension, divisible and mobile, which might even think. Subtle French matter and solid English matter, both were fair targets for the young Irishman.

A brief account of Raphson will illustrate the mathematician's attitude to matter. Joseph Raphson, F.R.S., in 1697[1] published his vigorous essay *De Spatio Reali seu Ente Infinito*, annexed to a mathematical treatise. Berkeley's first mention of it is in his essay *Of Infinites* (1706–7). He criticizes Raphson for speaking of the infinitesimal as 'quasi extensa'. In the *Commonplace Book* Berkeley twice names Raphson (308, 839; cf. *Prin.* § 117). In both these entries Berkeley has a serious charge to make. Raphson, although a critic of Spinoza, followed him in so interpreting the divine immensity as, in effect, to make God extended, demonstrating (ch. v) that space is, *inter alia*, 'actus purus, incorporeum, immutabile, aeternum, omni-continens, omni-penetrans, attributum (viz. immensitas) primae causae'. Each of these phrases constitutes an infringement of the divine prerogative. Raphson opposes Inextensionism, which is the doctrine of those who hold that there is no extension in addition to matter. He maintains that space is real and is distinct from matter, claiming antiquity and the authority of Henry More for this view. Berkeley long remembered Raphson. Writing to the Reverend S. Johnson on March 24, 1730, he speaks of mathematicians who have attributed extension to God, 'one of whom in a treatise *De Spatio Reali* pretends to find out fifteen of the incommunicable attributes of God in space'.[2]

We pass on to a tougher type of 'materialism'—that of Dr.

[1] Fraser, vol. ii, p. 19 n., gives 1706   [2] *v. c. v* especially.

Cheyne. He also was a Fellow of the Royal Society. In 1705 he published his *Philosophical Principles of Natural Religion*. Like Raphson, Keill, Barrow, and almost all the 'mathematicians', he held the infinite divisibility of matter, and gives a full geometrical demonstration of it (c. iv. §7). His words on infinitesimals are quoted and criticized by Berkeley in his *Of Infinites*. Three entries in the *Commonplace Book* name Cheyne (388 duplicates 931, 458). His book must have impressed Berkeley. Its style is clear and vigorous. It is theistic. It strongly maintains Providence and the Divine Conservation. Cheyne expounds the mechanics of bodies, celestial and terrestrial, the anatomy of the human body, the philosophy of the organism, of sensation and colour. He disagrees with Raphson as to extension, saying, 'Time and Space are no real things, nor complete substances' (c. iv. § 8). His is a robust doctrine of matter. He writes that gravitation is 'a principle annex'd to matter by the Creator' (c. i, § 27), and again: 'The existence of matter is a plain demonstration of the existence of a Deity. I believe nobody doubts that there now exists a quantity of solid mass, out of which the celestial and terrestrial bodies were form'd; and tho' perhaps in our most solid bodies there be more Pores than Parts, or more vacuity than solidity, yet there is still sufficient not to permit us to doubt of the existence of matter' (c. iii, § 3).

The Newtonian principles are too well known to need notice here. Berkeley refers to them repeatedly in the *Commonplace Book*, and one of his early queries is 'How to reconcile Newton's 2 sorts of motion with my doctrine?' (30). He discusses the *Principia* with special reference to absolute motion, in the *Principles* (§§ 110–15). In his letter to Johnson (*Works*, vol. ii, p. 19), he says: 'Sir Isaac Newton supposeth an absolute Space, different from relative, and consequent thereto; absolute Motion different from relative motion; and with all other mathematicians he supposeth the infinite divisibility of the finite parts of this absolute Space; he also supposeth material bodies to drift therein.'

Since Berkeley's immaterialism is as much an assertion of a spiritual God as of an ideal world, it is of importance to glance at the view of matter held by the theologians whose works he read. King's *De Origine Mali*[1] (1702) opens with a statement about sense-perception and sensible qualities in Lockian terms. He then contrasts the variable qualities and 'that which continues under all these changes'. When greater changes happen to a piece of wax, its essence and appellation change. Still, under all mutations it is always extended, capable of motion and rest, and has always some parts separable and mutually exclusive. The substance which carries along with it these qualities is called matter. When a portion of matter is removed another succeeds into its place. Place or space is distinct from matter because the same space receives successively different bodies (cf. *C.P.B.* 137). King is a tough 'materialist', but he decides definitely against extensionism. No doubt with Spinoza and Raphson in view, he denies the necessary existence of space. He says that we attribute necessary existence to space as the vulgar attribute existence to secondary qualities. Again, he says, 'Whether there be any such thing as space or no, whether its extension be distinguished from the extension of body or not: be it nothing at all, be it mere privation of contact, as some are pleased to term it: be it mere possibility or capacity of existing . . . yet still it is an indolent thing, it neither acts nor is in the least acted upon. . . . It cannot therefore be the cause of matter, or impress motion on it. There must then necessarily be another Cause of matter and motion'.[2] This passage well illustrates the theologians' interest in matter and the points at issue as regards space.

---

[1] The references to this work in the *C.P.B.* 143–6, 158–62 have hitherto escaped notice. See App. p. 187.

[2] King, *De Orig. Mal. c.* 1, § ii. 18, trans. 1731.

Clarke's *Demonstration of the Being and Attributes of God*[1] defines the contemporary English attitude to the Cartesian doctrine of matter. He says that the known properties of matter are dependence, finitude, divisibility, passivity, and unintelligence. It has therefore no active powers. He says that the Cartesians are reduced to the absurdity of making matter a necessarily existing being; and he maintains that Spinoza holds that the material world is the only self-existing, or necessarily existing being. Matter is not a necessary being. Answering the objection, derived from Hobbes and tenderly treated by Locke, that perception might arise out of matter, as colours and sounds do from figures and motion, he says that there is nothing in the bodies that is like the secondary qualities, but that the secondary qualities are thoughts or modifications of the mind. He charges Hobbes and his followers with holding an 'ambiguous and confused use of the word matter', and says that thinking and willing cannot possibly be qualities or affections of matter, unless we will confound the ideas of things and mean by matter not what the word commonly is used to signify, a solid substance capable of division, figure, and motion, but substance in general or the unknown substance, capable of powers or properties entirely different from these. Clarke thus is definitely opposed to both the Cartesian and the Hobbesian conceptions of matter. In effect he says 'matter need not have been, but it is there, and is extremely important to us for purposes of life and thought'. He holds that matter is not required for demonstrating the being of God, but is required for demonstrating the attributes of God. He says for instance (3rd ed., p. 55), that the intelligence of the self-existent being 'cannot be demonstrated *a priori*; but *a posteriori* almost everything in the world demonstrates to us this great truth'.

[1] Boyle Lectures preached 1704-5, published 1705-6.

From this review of typical contemporary thought, it is clear that the view that Berkeley's immaterialism expressed 'what was in the air at the time' is paradoxical. Any one can throw a stone at matter to-day. It was not so then. Matter, as well as being, as it always is, an object of the popular imagination, was then a mathematical object, a scientific object, a metaphysical object, and a theological necessity. Berkeley approached the subject of matter from all these angles, and had read most of the relevant contemporary literature.[1] Against this popular, perplexed, but, in his view, idle entity he brought to bear all the engines of his resourceful mind.

A review of the background of Berkeley's immaterialism would be incomplete without a reference to the Cartesians. Malebranche is dealt with fully in the next chapter. Here something must be said of Bayle. I suspect that Bayle exerted considerable influence upon Berkeley, but I cannot prove it. A copy of the *Dictionary* was sold at the auction of the Berkeleys' library. A duplicated entry in the *Commonplace Book* (373, 420) couples Bayle with Malebranche. The remaining evidence is subjective. In his early published works Berkeley never mentions the *Dictionary*,[2] and there are obvious reasons for his silence. Yet he could hardly have left that famous work unconsulted, and the following articles seem to me to have left their mark upon the *Principles*: 'Anaxagoras', 'Epicurus', 'Leucippus', 'Rodon', 'Rorarius', 'Zabarella', and, more especially, 'Pyrrho' and 'Zeno'. The main topics concerned are the infinite divisibility, the nature of extension, and the sensible qualities.

---

[1] Barrow's lectures on geometry, mechanics, and optics, and Keill's *Introductio ad veram Physicam*, 1702, are referred to repeatedly in the *Commonplace Book*. Their point of view is that of the mathematicians above reviewed.

[2] Bayle is mentioned in *Theory of Vision Vindicated*, § 6.

Who, if not Bayle, taught Berkeley to reject so uncompromisingly and with such repeated emphasis the infinite divisibility[1]? Keill, Cheyne, Barrow, Raphson, Newton, and Malebranche—all the great names supported it. Locke, following Descartes, speaks of the difficulties whether 'we grant or deny it' (*Essay*, ii. 23. 31; cf. ii. 17. 12). Berkeley in his early paper *Of Infinites* cites Locke's distinction between *infinity* and *infinite* as decisive. But Locke's criticism of 'the idea of a body infinitely little' is very guarded, and in great contrast to the conviction expressed by Berkeley and Bayle. Bayle, speaking of Anaxagoras and the Homoeomeriae, says: 'He cannot get out of this difficulty but by the divisibility of matter *in infinitum*, which is to imitate a man, who, to avoid the thrust of a sword throws himself headlong into a precipice.'

Bayle seems to have reserved the full vigour of his amazing pen for his article on 'Zeno'. Here we have an extraordinarily clear analysis of deep and abstract subjects. Point after point in it would have come home to Berkeley. Bayle's problem here is the relation between the infinite divisibility and extension. The entry in the *Commonplace Book* (26) which rounds off the opening sketch of the immaterial hypothesis, relates the infinite divisibility and external extension exactly in Bayle's logical way. Bayle says: 'The divisibility *in infinitum* is an hypothesis embraced by Aristotle and almost all the professors of philosophy.... You ought to lay aside your disjunctive syllogism and make use of this hypothetical one. If extension existed, it would be composed of mathematical points or physical points or of parts divisible *in infinitum*. But it is not composed of mathematical points or physical points or of parts divisible *in infinitum*. Therefore it does not exist.'

[1] Some fifteen entries in the *C.P.B.* name it. Scores refer to it. See also *Prin.* §§ 123–32.

Then after two formal disproofs of the divisibility, he connects the issue with sensible qualities, bridging the gulf between primary and secondary in Berkeley's manner (v. also sub art. 'Pyrrho'): 'all the ways of *suspension* which destroy the reality of corporeal qualities overthrow the reality of extension. The modern philosophers . . . have so well apprehended the foundation of the *epoche* with relation to sounds, odours, heat, cold . . . colours, &c. that they teach that all these qualities are perceptions of our mind and do not exist in the objects of our senses. Why should we not say the same of extension? If a being void of colour, yet appears to us under a colour determined as to its species, figure, and situation, why cannot a being without any extension be visible to us under an appearance of determinate extension?' Bayle then refers to those geometrical problems, which students of the *Commonplace Book* know to have been much in Berkeley's mind. These are the sides of a square equal to the diagonal, and the equality of concentric circles. Bayle says that these do not prove that matter is divisible *in infinitum*, but only make it appear 'that extension doth not exist any where but in our minds'. He quotes from Malebranche's 'Illustration on Bodies', and adds: 'I was obliged to prove that there are stronger objections than those of Malebranche.' Bayle concludes the 'Zeno' article with a severe criticism of the principles of mathematics, and of the doctrine of infinitesimals. Sir William Hamilton[1] pointed out that Bayle anticipated Berkeley as regards the assimilation of primary and secondary qualities. Ought not *we* who have the *Commonplace Book*, and can watch Berkeley's thought in the making, to go farther than Hamilton, and see in Bayle one of Berkeley's important sources, perhaps ranking next in importance to Malebranche and Locke?

[1] Reid, *Inquiry*, c. vi, § 6. n.

IV

PROBLEMATICAL IDEALISM AND *ESSE PERCIPI*

IF Berkeley's immaterialism had a source other than his own genius, there is, I think, no clear evidence as to what that source was. There is, however, abundant evidence that for the argument supporting immaterialism, expounding it, developing it, Berkeley was greatly indebted to the Cartesian idealism, and more especially to Malebranche's *Search*.[1]

Immaterialism, as expounded in the *Principles*, was a new thing. It was Berkeley's invention. He was 'the founder of a sect called the Immaterialists'.[2] No study of sources is likely to upset his claim to that title.

It is very extraordinary, we think, that a young man should have invented a philosophy that still grips European and American thought. But youth has these great thoughts. Berkeley had remarkable natural endowments. He could look within and without, up and down with equal facility and interest. He received a broad-based liberal education that encouraged expression and that did not condemn him prematurely to middle-aged caution. His words on the education of the ancients apply to his own education. Like theirs, his mind 'seems to have been more exercised and less burdened, than in later ages' (*Siris*, § 298). Further, Berkeley believed in God with heart and mind. In his meta-

---

[1] Berkeley seems to have confined his reading of Malebranche to the *Search*. Possibly there are echoes in his writings of the *Méditations Chrétiennes*, e.g. 'Tu pénètres les Cieux, tu perces les abîmes'; cf. Intr. *Prin.*, § 24. But the same thought occurs in the Preface of the *Search*. So also *Nature and Grace* gives most of the accidental evils mentioned in *Prin.* §151, but no doubt they were stock subjects.

[2] Swift to Lord Carteret, September 3, 1724. *L.L.* p. 102.

physic he took God seriously. For God's sake he wanted to prove immaterialism, and perhaps that wish was father to the thought. He speaks once as if immaterialism had been an intuition, disclosed to him, long debated, and finally made public. Stung by the charge of insincerity, he writes to Percival on September 6, 1710, about his three-months-old book: 'God is my witness that I was and do still remain entirely persuaded of the non-existence of matter and the other tenets published along with it. . . . Nothing less than a full conviction not only of the truth of my notions but also of their usefulness . . . could have engaged me to make them public. I may add that the opinion of matter I have entertained some years; if therefore a motive of vanity could have induced me to obtrude falsehoods on the world, I had long since done it when the conceit was warm in my imagination and not have staid to examine and revise it both with my own judgment and that of my ingenious friends.'

He was aged 25 when he wrote the words, so that the 'long since' is relative to the train of his thronging ideas; but the 'some years' is more precise. We may be certain then that the immaterialist conceit warmed in his imagination not later than 1706–7, perhaps earlier. Berkeley graduated in 1704. Then he stayed on in college, waiting no doubt for a fellowship to fall vacant, and reading the course for the fellowship examination.[1] Some time during that three years' post-graduate reading, the great thought came to him. Certainly by the end of 1706 he knew well Malebranche's *Search*. If he drew his inspiration thence, and if, as seems probable, he began the *Commonplace Book* soon after winning a fellowship in June 1707, we understand how he was able to begin it with a full-fledged statement (*C.P.B.* 1–26) of the 'immaterial hypothesis' in all its main bearings.

[1] Cf. 'aliis studiis occupato', *De Ludo Alg.*, and *v.* Appendix, p. 189.

The *Commonplace Book* is certainly part of the 'revising it with my own judgment', of which he wrote to Percival. When he had filled 30 or 40 of its pages, the hypothesis became proof, and the negation, immaterialism, took positive shape as the New Principle. Malebranche figures in these pages,[1] and it will therefore be in place here to give an account of his doctrine of matter.

Malebranche's Doctrine of Matter

As a headline for his discussion of the secondary qualities, Malebranche writes (i. 10): 'We often see things that have no existence, nor ever had, and it ought not to be concluded that a thing is actually without us, from our seeing it without us.' Things have 'a real existence . . . though it be a very hard thing to prove it'. He speaks to the same effect in bk. vi. 2. 6. As an elucidation of these two passages he appends his well-known 'Illustration' (*éclaircissement*, i.e. excursus), entitled 'that 'tis very difficult to prove the Existence of Bodies; what we ought to esteem of the proofs which are brought of their existence'. We are on firm ground in making this Illustration our starting-point. For the *Commonplace Book* refers to it several times (697, 698, 812, 813, 830, and perhaps 274). Malebranche does not distinguish here between body and matter. He passes from the one to the other as if they were synonyms. He is discussing matter as embodied and body as material. The discussion is carried on in full view of the distinctions already established by him between immediate and mediate object, between *voir* and *regarder*. Malebranche does not doubt, in fact he here affirms, the *in*-existence of what we *see* (*voir*)—the visual *datum*. He does doubt, is not far from denying the *out*-existence of what we behold (*regarder*).

[1] Especially in those represented by entries 260–300, where Berkeley's sense of discovery is at its height.

The Illustration opens with a résumé of Malebranche's general teaching about the double union. Knowledge arising from the soul's union with the body is not comparable to knowledge arising from her union with the Word of God. Circumambient bodies have not in them to inform us of their existence. As has been already proved by him, 'The testimony of the senses is never exactly true, but commonly every way false.' Here the senses do not report 'for' or 'against'. 'What reason is there from the reports of our . . . senses to conclude there are actually bodies without us and that they are like those we *see*, I mean, those which are the immediate object of our soul?' It is then idle, he thinks, to say 'We *see* external bodies', for in point of fact we do not. External bodies, if such there be, are not and cannot be the immediate object of our minds. The same argument holds of *the* body. The body, which is united to the soul, 'cannot give light to reason'. Therefore Malebranche appeals to another court. Since things cannot speak, and the senses do not speak (nor would be decisive if they spoke), only God can prove to us the existence of matter. Has He done so?[1] His answer is 'Yes' and 'No', inclining to 'No'. Malebranche is trying to reconcile conflicting interests. He has in view different types of knowledge, and different sources of knowledge. So the issue becomes perplexed and his answer indeterminate. To such an extent is the issue perplexed that Malebranche here advances from the pros and cons of the materialist hypothesis to the pros and cons of the immaterialist hypothesis. The Illustration which begins with the difficulty of proving the existence of matter

---

[1] Malebranche's theory of the union of man's intellect with the Word of God enables him to pass easily from theological terms to rationalist. So the same question appears in the alternative form: Only reason can prove to us the existence of matter. Does reason prove it?

ends with the possibility of proving the non-existence of matter.

Descartes, he says, has gone as far as bare reason can go towards proving the existence of bodies. But he has not proved their existence. God speaks by evidence and by faith. Faith assures us of the existence of matter. But this may mean no more than that material bodies exist for faith, are, in fact, part of the setting of the Christian Faith. It does not prove that they would exist if not believed in. There can be no cogency, for faith, in a proposition about a world of unfaith. Revelation assures us that 'prophets, apostles, sacred writ, and miracles' exist; but, he holds, the appearance of these things would have the same effect as the reality.

Malebranche passes then from faith to evidence. Here reason is inconclusive. 'We are not invincibly carried to believe there is anything existing besides God and our own mind.' We know in general that God is no deceiver. But has He in this particular told us *by reason* that matter exists? In effect Malebranche answers in the negative. He grants to Descartes that God has given us a 'strong inclination' or 'natural propension' to believe in matter. But, he holds, God does not compel us to believe it. If we believe it, *we* believe it, not God in us. Besides, the 'natural propension' works by the sensible impression, and the fallibility of the senses has been proved up to the hilt. If they are wrong in the one deliverance, they may be wrong in the other.

In his final summing up, Malebranche's hesitation is very marked. He puts revelation on one side, and proceeds to reason thus. We have naturally a strong inclination to believe there are external bodies. Therefore we have more reason to hold the existence of matter than its non-existence. This argument is clearly based on a consideration of prob-abilities, and falls far short of demonstration. If it were not for scripture, the question would be unresolved. Malebranche the monk gives a decision; Malebranche the thinker leaves it undecided. He says, 'We cannot deny the existence of bodies, through a principle of religion'. The reference is probably to transubstantiation; it supports Hamilton's contention that only fidelity to the Catholic doctrine stood between Malebranche and Berkeley's views on matter.[1]

Berkeley writes (*C.P.B.* 697): 'Scripture and possibility are the onely proofs with Malbranch. Add to these what he calls a great propension to think so.' Malebranche himself had exposed the 'propension'. Berkeley searches Scripture and finds no matter there, and he had only ridicule for the poor 'bare possibility' (*Principles*, § 75). Malebranche was a 'patron of matter'; he could not therefore teach immaterialism. But there can be little doubt that he set forward on his way thither the travelling man. 'From Malbranch, Locke, & my first arguings it can't be prov'd that extension is not in matter' (*C.P.B.* 274). He had tried Malebranche and Locke. He had under their guidance analysed the sensible qualities. He had steeped himself in the relativity arguments. He failed to find there a basis for immaterialism. So he sought and found another foundation. But before dealing with his intuitive approach to immaterialism, we must discuss the argument from the sensible qualities in which Malebranche was his chief guide.

Primary and Secondary Qualities

Berkeley wanted no half-measures. He was not content to deny the matter of metaphysicians. He did so, but he went farther and denied the matter of the 'man in the street'. He came down to empirical facts, and challenged the qualities of things. We suppose, rightly or wrongly,

[1] Sir W. Hamilton, Note P, on Malebranche's theory, appended to Reid's *Works*.

that there is in the things about us something that enables them to stand on their own feet. This is their material quality. It guarantees, we think, material reality apart from mind. Of material qualities we make material things. Of material things we build the material world. Material quality is therefore the foundation of the whole structure of reality external to the mind. So in attacking such qualities, Berkeley was striking a blow at the heart of materialism.

That an examination of the sensible qualities gave direction to his immaterialism, we see from the marginal signs of the *Commonplace Book* . In Berkeley's own index we find the two abbreviations 'P' for 'primary and secondary qualities' and 'M' for 'matter'. There are some 36 'P' entries. Of these 8 mention Malebranche or the Cartesians, and another 10 or 12 contain references to the *Search*. Three 'P' entries mention Locke and possibly 4 others refer to him. Several 'M' entries also refer to the *Search*. About half of the 'P' entries are also marked 'M'. So probably his first intention was to treat the qualities by themselves; but afterwards he decided to treat matter and its qualities together.

Locke taught that qualities in bodies fall under three heads (*Essay*, ii, c. 8): (1) Primary qualities, viz. bulk, figure, number, situation, and motion or rest of their solid parts. These are inseparable and original. (2) Secondary qualities immediately perceivable, viz. colour, taste, &c. These are powers to produce different ideas in us, and are usually called *sensible* qualities. (3) Secondary qualities mediately perceivable, e.g. the sun's power to make wax white. These operate on other bodies and make them able to produce varied ideas in us. They are usually called 'powers'.[1]

---

[1] King had given great vogue to the doctrine in Dublin, not only in his *De Origine Mali*, but also in his famous sermon on 'Predestination' (May 15, 1709). He says: 'Light and colours are

Malebranche does not use the terms primary and secondary, but he recognizes corresponding categories. The former category, dealt with in Book i, cc. 6–9, comprises extension, figure, and motion. These are real qualities, though our judgements concerning them are mostly false. They are extrinsical, without us, and 'wholly independent on our mind.' (i, c. 10). Save for solidity, the list agrees with Locke's primary qualities. The other class consists of the sensible qualities proper. They correspond roughly to Locke's secondary qualities. As studied *seriatim* in Book i, cc. 10–13, they are pleasure, pain, heat, cold, light, colour, sound, touch, &c.[1] The order is of importance in Malebranche's argument. These qualities are not external to us, but are modifications of the soul.

Malebranche tries to keep these two categories of qualities distinct. The former qualities as apprehended are ideas, the latter are 'sentiments'. Malebranche is, by his own admission, loose in his use of the term *idea* (see Illust. on bk. i, 3). But whenever he is speaking precisely he draws a sharp line between the idea which represents that which is outside us and the sensations which represent to us what we find within us, and are therefore called technically 'modifications of the soul'. The distinction is essential to his system. In order that our calm clear ideas may be in God, and be seen there, they must be cut clean away from the disturbing obscure modes of mind which arise from union with the body, and which cannot without impiety be attributed to God. The secondary qualities then, for Malebranche, are modifications of the human soul caused by the general Will of God on the occasion of motions of the animal spirits, sense-fibres, and brain.

nothing but effects . . . no such things at all in nature but only in our minds.'

[1] For other lists slightly varying see bk. iii. 1. 1. and bk. iii. 2. 5.

Bayle pointed out that 'sauce for the goose is sauce for the gander'. The argument that internalizes the secondary internalizes the primary.[1] Locke,[2] apparently blind to the same difficulty in his own system, shows that on Malebranche's principles the colour of the marigold and the number and figure of its leaves must be on the same footing in respect of mind, divine and human. Berkeley, whether he read it in Bayle or Locke or thought it out for himself, made the assimilation of primary and secondary qualities the spear-head of his attack. In the opening statement of the immaterial hypothesis (*C.P.B.* 20) he writes: 'Primary ideas prov'd not to exist in matter after the same manner yt secondary ones are prov'd not to exist therein.' His resolve to equalize the status remains unaltered throughout the *Commonplace Book*.[3] He must have noticed the difference of opinion as to which qualities were primary and which were not, as well as the arbitrary character of the distinction. But his main argument is simply that in point of fact colour is always extended.

In the *Principles* we find this argument at the outset. In §§ 9–13 he develops the thesis that primary and secondary qualities are in point of fact inseparable. That is his own line of proof. In § 14 he glances at an auxiliary line of proof. Primary qualities can be shown not to be in matter 'after the same manner as modern philosophers prove certain sensible qualities to have no existence in matter'. His two illustrations of this 'manner' show that he has Locke (ii. 8. 21) and Malebranche (i. 13) in view. Berkeley goes on to show his dissatisfaction with this mode of arguing. In effect he says that arguments based on the variability of primary qualities, and on the relativity of sensation, carry you only part of the

---

[1] So Hamilton, Reid, *Inquiry*, c. vi. n.   [2] *Exam. Maleb.*, §§ 40–1.
[3] *v.* 123, 330, 380, 452, 813, 894, 938 for extension and colour; cf. 231, 704, 844, for the generalized thesis.

way. At best they form arguments *ad hominem*, and they represent little advance upon Descartes's problematic idealism. They prove that we do not know the absolute magnitude and distance of objects; they do not prove that there is no absolute magnitude nor distance. With these unsatisfactory lines of argument he contrasts 'the arguments fore-going', i.e. those of §§ 9–13 which are his own, and are based upon intuitive perception of the meaning of the existence (§ 3) of sensible things.

The assimilation of primary and secondary qualities might well support scepticism, as with Bayle, or indeed materialism. That it became a leading argument for immaterialism should be traced probably to its conjunction with the doctrine of modifications of the soul. Primary qualities are where secondary qualities are. But where is that? Malebranche might have supplied the answer. Secondary qualities are *in* the soul, because they are *modifications of* the soul.

The term 'modification' involved a break with scholasticism, as Bayle shows (*sub* 'Spinoza'). It cut across the old doctrine of substance and accidents. While Locke left the secondary qualities dependent on the mind, Malebranche, calling them 'modifications', takes them into the mind and makes them part of it. Light and colours then are not only relative to mind, but mental, as are love, joy, and hatred. They are so near us, he holds, that we cannot cause them nor comprehend them. In the attempt to grasp them, we extrude and externalize them. Yet our clear and distinct idea of extension excludes them. They must be, he argues, in the mind, because there is nowhere else for them to be. The most serious consequence of this doctrine, patent to the true Cartesians and to Berkeley, was its reaction upon our conception of the mind. Descartes's 'first knowledge' disappears. The idea of the soul must go (*Search*, i. 12, 13).

We simply do not know *what* we are. We have no knowledge of the fabric of the mind, and cannot know what modifications it can endure. Our partial self-knowledge is no more than *conscience* or *sentiment intérieur*. Cartesians resented this perversion of the master's doctrine, and ridiculed Malebranche's 'rain-bow soul'. It may be noted that Clarke, who in general opposed Cartesianism, accepted the view that the secondary qualities are 'thoughts or modifications of the mind' (*Dem.*, 3rd ed., p. 59).

Did Berkeley accept it? He was profoundly influenced by it. It was the background for his assimilation of the primary and secondary qualities. Both are alike in being 'not without the mind'. Further, the method of the first *Hylas* dialogue follows the lines of the *Search* (i. 12). Both arguments take the qualities *seriatim* and internalize them all. Malebranche treats pain and pleasure first. They are 'strong and lively sensations'. They modify the soul so sensibly that, for instance, we never locate the pain in the needle (cf. *C.P.B.* 441). Heat and cold also are vigorous and readily become pain. Unfelt they would be nothing; yet, with an effort, at times we locate them in the object. But light and colours, *qua* sensations, are faint. So we divest our own soul, where they properly belong, 'to cloathe and beautify the objects that are without us'.

Berkeley takes the qualities in the same order; he uses the same terms, strong, lively, vigorous, faint, of ideas of sense (§§ 30, 33), and he adopts in part (§ 27) Malebranche's argument that having no idea of the soul we do not know what modifications she is capable of. Once at least, (*T.V.* § 94) he uses the technical phrase 'modifications of the soul', coupling it vaguely with 'thoughts, desires, and passions'; and he approaches Malebranche's doctrine in the *Theory of Vision* § 41, where, summing up his account of distance, he states that the objects of sight are 'thoughts or sensations each whereof is as near to him as the perceptions of pain or pleasure or the most inward passions of his soul'.

Influence is one thing, doctrine another. On the whole it would not be correct to say that Berkeley accepted Malebranche's doctrine of modifications. This is an important point for interpreters of Berkeleianism, involving the issue closely and acutely argued by Dr. Dawes Hicks[1] as to the way of *mode* versus way of *idea*. I quite agree with Dr. Dawes Hicks that Berkeley 'in his more guarded moments' held firmly the 'duality of subject and object', but I am not convinced that instances of less guarded moments are many or serious. There were definite obstacles in the way of his acceptance of Malebranche's 'modifications'. The chief obstacle was his distinction between active spirit and passive idea. Light and colours, tastes and sounds cannot, for Berkeley, be modifications of mind, part of the fabric of the mind; for they are passive and not active. They are idea-things, not spirit-things. They are objects that are not subjects though necessarily related to a subject.

Although he did not accept the implications of the 'modification' doctrine, yet from it Berkeley would get the support he needed for his assimilation of the primary and secondary qualities, thereby laying a strong foundation for his argument for immaterialism. If a ray of light, composed of globules, almost a mathematical line, is in the truth of things an intimate part of the mind, then there can be no absurdity in stating that the very elements of the world we see are not without the mind. Where lines of light are, there colour must be. Therefore length and breadth and depth along with light and colour are not without the mind.

The term 'conversion' has been used to describe the beginnings of Berkeley's immaterialism. The term is not

[1] *Berkeley*, pp. 110 sqq. Note the explicit 'not generated from within by the mind itself' (*Prin.* § 90).

inappropriate, provided we remember that here, as in most conversions, the sudden and the gradual were blended. In Berkeley's conversion we may distinguish three crises. First came the initial intuition or inspiration. All we know of it is what he says in his letter to Percival quoted above (p. 57). We may presume that the 'conceit' came to him in 1705–6, tracing it to the religious motive at work in his mind, critical from childhood and now aghast at the rising tide of materialism. He turned it over in his mind and discussed it with his friends. Then came the second crisis, probably in the summer of 1707. The 'conceit' now takes written form as 'the immaterial hypothesis'. The young Lockian is thinking of turning Malebranchian. In accordance with Malebranche's rules of method, he compiles the *Commonplace Book*, testing the hypothesis by the facts. After pondering the mathematical problems involved, and making a careful study of vision mainly under Malebranche's tuition, and scrutinizing the material qualities in close connexion with Malebranche's doctrine of modifications of the soul, he met the third wave, perhaps early in 1708. At the third crisis the 'convert' found full salvation. The hypothesis that matter is nothing is verified, and takes positive shape in the affirmation of the New Principle. At this point Berkeley consciously transcended his sources, went beyond Locke, beyond Malebranche, beyond his own 'first arguings', and launched out into the uncharted sea of *esse percipi*. The *Commonplace Book* supplies the evidence. Towards the end of the first note-book we find entries touched with ·the discoverer's joy. We see (274) the young thinker at the end of his tether, and his first method bankrupt. Locke, Malebranche, and his own 'first arguings' have brought him far, but have failed him. So he turns to a new method, and in the entry 287 he records his *Heureka*. From this on, he subordinates the argument from sense relativity, and substitutes that from the clear and distinct idea of perception or existence. The terms become interchangeable. The hypothesis of matter is not needed, for spiritual substance explains all the facts. His parallel study of vision reached a head about the same time (277, 283, 286). The inverted retinal image points to the same conclusion. For if the retinal image were a photograph of something outside the mind, erect vision by inverted image would be impossible. At the same time too (272-3) he seems to have satisfied himself as to one of the most urgent of the mathematical problems in the case, the incommensurability of the diagonal and side. 'The diagonal is commensurable with the side', and accordingly a proof of the infinite divisibility of matter falls to the ground. So on all the main counts Berkeley concludes that there can be no 'Outside the mind'. 'Me percipit... horror' exclaimed Lucretius,[1] when he saw the secrets of existence. Just so, his great antithesis, Berkeley, is staggered by the very simplicity of his intuitive solution. He writes: 'I wonder not at my sagacity in discovering the obvious tho' amazing truth. I rather wonder at my stupid inadvertency in not finding it out before. 'tis no witchcraft to see we know nothing but our thoughts or what these think' (287, *prima manu*).[2]

[1] *De Rerum Natura*, iii. 28-9: 'His ibi me rebus quaedam divina voluptas percipit adque horror . . .'

[2] Berkeley's denial of matter is not to be limited in scope, nor his belief in real things impugned. The unflinching letter of Sept. 6, 1710 (Rand, p. 81) shows that he had not a particle of doubt of the existence of sensible things created by God, yet had not a shred of belief in any sort of matter. It is instructive to compare his 'entirely persuaded of the non-existence of matter' with his more guarded, 'non-existence of what philosophers call material substance' (Aug. 7, 1713, Rand, p. 123). Yet the two phrases differ only in prudence, not in meaning. For the second *Hylas* dialogue (1713) lists seven types of exploded matter, and concludes that matter is proved impossible 'in every particular sense that either you or any one else understands it in'. *Works*, vol. 1, pp. 437-40.

V

SEEING ALL THINGS IN GOD

BERKELEY's denial of matter is not to be divorced from his affirmation of ideas. The denial catches attention; but the affirmation holds it. The present-day and permanent attraction of Berkeleianism lies not so much in its challenging negation as in its bold assertion as to the nature of the object perceived and known. This assertion is implicit in Berkeley's use of the term *idea*. So it is important to watch the usage in the making, to see the new coin struck, and to take note of the mint from which it issued.

Berkeley thought out his doctrine of idea gradually during the years 1707–8. A marked change in his style of writing the word 'idea' occurred in that period.[1] The change is so pronounced that it is probably significant. The introduction of the capital letter seems to show that Berkeley meant to give the word a new meaning. In any case the term *Idea* at the end of the *Commonplace Book* had richer connotation than the term *idea* at the beginning. In the interval Berkeley had learned to idealize the thing and to spiritualize the idea.

These two lessons could be learned from the *Search*, but not from Locke's *Essay*. From Locke Berkeley would learn to think and speak and try to know in terms of idea. But Locke could not teach any deeper lesson about ideas, for he nowhere gives a critical study of the nature of idea. He keeps clear of material ideas and of such views of ideation as Hook had laid before the Royal Society.[2] But as to the stuff of which they are made, their *habitat*, and the relation between

---

[1] See Appendix, p. 194.

[2] 'The ideas of sight, he thinks, are formed of a kind of matter resembling the Bononian stone or some kind of phosphorus.' Reid, *Intell. Powers*, Essay II, c. 9.

my ideas and yours Locke is virtually silent. In the opening of his *Examination of Malebranche's Opinion* he speaks of his 'unaffected ignorance' as to the nature and manner of ideas in our understanding. In the *Essay* he takes ideas for granted, as elements in thought recognized by all. There is no knowledge without them, there is real knowledge by their means. Each man finds the simple ideas in his mind and manipulates them, framing, compounding, abstracting, and comparing them. Locke in fact gives a psychology of idea and a metaphysic by means thereof, but he attempts no metaphysic of the idea itself.[1]

Clearly a young Lockian would have much to learn about ideas and much to unlearn. A study of the nature of idea was an essential part of Berkeley's struggle for consistent expression. The famous Malebranche-Arnauld controversy, a brilliant discussion of the status of idea, must have been known to him.[2] He would have found a clear outline of the points there at issue in Leclerc's little manuals of the new Logic which we know he used (*C.P.B.* 361). But in the *Search* itself he would have found all he needed. For Book iii, Part 2, the section in which the theory of seeing all things in God is expounded, has the title 'Of the Nature of Ideas', and justifies its title. Chapters 1–6 coupled with the 'Illustrations' constitute a searching and instructive analysis of idea which could not fail to further in Berkeley's alert mind the twofold process of idealizing the object and spiritualizing the idea.

The *Commonplace Book* throws considerable light upon this process. In the first note-book the word 'idea' occurs

---

[1] In the *Essay*, bk. ii, c. 1, §§ 1–5 he glances at their source and nature, assuming their origin in things and their representative function. See also J. Sergeant, *Solid Philosophy*, p. 22.

[2] Leclerc, *Pneum.*, Sect. I, c. v, *De Idearum Natura*, 'ut uter vicerit haud facile constet.'

often in the Lockian sense, but only one or two entries (e.g. 392) towards the end disclose any reflection upon the nature of the idea. It is otherwise in the second note-book. Here ideism is a recurrent theme. The relations of idea to idea, of idea to word, of idea to thing, and of idea to soul are discussed over and over again, and looked at from many angles.[1] During the months[2] occupied in the filling of that note-book Berkeley consciously discarded several Lockian doctrines. He gave up the distinction between adequate and inadequate ideas. He considered abstract ideas and abstract particular ideas and abstract general ideas. He reached his revolutionary doctrine of abstraction. Nearly as momentous, yet commonly ignored, was his tacit abandonment of the Lockian doctrine of simple and complex ideas. This distinction, fundamental for Locke, is prominent at the opening of the *Commonplace Book*,[3] but towards the end, and in the published works it has practically disappeared from sight.

There are certain entries, viz. 492, 576, 591, 615, 665, which seem to me to decide the interpretation of *Principles*, § 1, an important and recently disputed paragraph. Dr. Dawes Hicks (op. cit., p. 109) writes: 'At the beginning of the *Principles*, he starts by accepting, somewhat precipitately, Locke's threefold division, according to which there are simple ideas of sense, simple ideas of reflection, and complex ideas', and he adds in a footnote to 'precipitately': 'Because later he is all the while contending that of the mind and its operations there are no "ideas". I do not think that Dr. G. A. Johnston's interpretation of this

[1] *v.* 424, 471, 479–80, 486, 492, 510, 527–8, 575–6, 591, 615, 653, 665, 670, 696, 770, 788, 819, 855, 884.

[2] No doubt, the spring and summer of 1708.

[3] The entries are marked +, which I take to be the obelus; *v.* Appendix, p. 186.

passage is tenable.' Here I side with Dr. Johnston. The missing word must be 'objects' not 'ideas'. In his formal opening 'survey' of the objects of human knowledge Berkeley could not, so it seems to me, have accepted Locke's ideas of reflection; nor, in view of the entries[1] cited above, could it be said that haste had betrayed him into accepting them. Berkeley had deliberated upon this opening sentence. It shows every sign of careful wording. Possibly, so as not to estrange readers at the outset, he meant it to suggest the well-known Lockian distinction. He may be insinuating his point of view; he may be so stating the Lockian divisions that in the stating they are quietly transformed. That may be so. Yet no tactics of his could alter the fact that he had irretrievably made up his mind that the perception of white is not different from white.[2]

What, then, does Berkeley in the first sentence of the *Principles* mean by 'or else such as are perceived by attending to the passions and operations of the mind'? He is surveying 'the objects of human knowledge' in their tripartite division. So grammar requires, as Dr. Johnston points out, that *such* should qualify 'objects', and not 'ideas'. What objects he has in view seems to me quite clear. But Dr. Johnston,[3] I venture to think, has missed giving an adequate exegesis of the passage, because he looks almost entirely to Locke for the origins of Berkeley's thought. The clue to the passage is,

[1] e.g. 'not to call the operations of the mind ideas' (492). 'Mem. To begin the 1st Book not with mention of sensation and reflection' (576). N.B. The word printed 'sensation' in the second half of 576, i.e. 'instead of sensation', is almost illegible. It cannot, in my opinion, be 'sensation'; it might be 'reflection', but is probably 'those'.

[2] *v. C.P.B.* 591, correct reading, 'Wherein I pray you does the perception of white differ from white.' N.B. Berkeley does not equate the act of perceiving and the perception.

[3] *Development*, pp. 143–6.

I think, Malebranche's statement 'there are things we know without ideas'. These 'things' for both Malebranche and Berkeley are God, the self, and other spirits. It would be impossible, surely, for Berkeley to exclude these from his opening 'survey of the objects of human knowledge'. To pass them over would have been virtual scepticism. This class of objects is set aside during the first half of the *Principles*, but it is resumed in § 86, and comes in for detailed treatment from § 135 on, when he has 'dispatched what we intended to say concerning the knowledge of ideas'.

The opening sentence of the *Theory of Vision* states the design of the book. Just so the opening sentence of the *Principles*, rightly understood, outlines *its* scope and contents. The principles of knowledge are concerned with objects of knowledge, and those objects are, for Berkeley, ideas of sense, imagination, and memory, on the one hand; on the other, the objects which are not ideas but spirits, namely, the self, other finite spirits, and Deity. If this be the correct interpretation, the question must be faced: does the phrase 'such as are perceived by attending to the passions and operations of the mind' adequately describe that hemisphere of knowledge, called 'knowledge of spirits'? I think it does. It is not a full description, but it is not positively incorrect, and therefore it is sufficient for Berkeley's immediate purpose. The self is thus known. Knowledge of God is based in § 29 on attention to the contrast between 'passions' and 'operations'. Knowledge of other minds is mediated by the other modes of knowing. So considering that Berkeley's argument is new, and that knowledge of ideas was his main concern in Part I, the description is adequate for the purposes of his opening survey of the field.[1]

[1] Fraser misquotes the passage in his footnote '*ideas* perceived by attending etc.', *Works*, vol. i, p. 272. Browne, *Procedure*,

Malebranche's Doctrine of Ideas

Berkeley would meet Malebranche's doctrine of ideas in two forms: in the *Search* itself and in Locke's *Examination of P. Malebranche's Opinion*. This latter work, posthumously published, appeared in 1706. Berkeley speaks highly of the little volume that contains it, in his *De Ludo Algebraico*. But it is far from likely that Berkeley owed to it his knowledge of the famous theory. It is certain that he went to the fountain-head and studied the nature of ideas in the *Search* itself. It must be remembered that for Locke all our ideas, if not man-made, at least arise in the process of man's knowing. For Berkeley the major part of our ideas are not human in origin or in nature. Idea is the characteristic word of Locke's *Essay*. Idea is the characteristic word of Berkeley's *Principles*. But in the interval the word has been transformed. In Locke's *Essay* 'idea' speaks of sober English common sense, of sunlight, and the highway of life. In the *Principles* 'idea' suggests Celtic twilight and Gallic enthusiasm. It is haloed with mystery and awe.

Book iii, Part 2, of the *Search* opens with a clear statement of representationism, viz. 'I suppose that every one will grant, that we perceive not the objects that are without us immediately and of themselves. . . . The immediate object of the mind when it beholds the sun . . . is not the sun, but something intimately united to the soul, and that same thing is what I call our Idea.' For Malebranche, then, ideas are not 'nothings', they are not merely functional parts of the process of thinking. Ideas differ from one another. This idea is not that idea. An idea can be compared with another idea. Again the idea differs from the thing it represents, and, as we see from dreams, it may exist *in vacuo*. Ideas have a 'most real existence'. They are 'beings and

i. 2, ii. 3, who probably taught Berkeley in college, vigorously opposes Locke's ideas of reflection.

beings spiritual'. He almost calls them substances.[1] We sometimes think them 'small and despicable'. 'Merely an idea', we say. We think of ideas as brief and flimsy, called into being and annihilated by transient turns of attention. But it is self-flattery, says Malebranche in effect, that makes us depreciate the status of ideas. We mistake occasions for causes, and like to fancy ourselves as sharing the Creator's powers, as producing and destroying ideas at will.

This stress on the actual distinct being of the idea is required by Malebranche's quasi-physical view of presence to the mind. Representationism requires the absence of the thing; therefore it demands the presence of an idea of the thing. The mediate object being physically absent, the immediate object must be actually comprescent with the mind. For Malebranche, as for many moderns, the seeing eye and the thinking mind apprehend X, if they try to apprehend Y. From the crude form of representative perception Berkeley turned away. But he may have learned from this passage to take the idea as a real being, and to distinguish sharply between 'within the mind' and 'without'. The quasi-physical 'without the mind' toned down later to 'without my will' (*C.P.B.* 379–80). But the early entry (906) 'all ideas come from without or from within' may well be an echo of Malebranche's statement (iii, 2. 1), 'Whatever things the soul perceives are only of two sorts; and are either within or without the soul.'

If from Book i of the *Search* Berkeley learned the internality of 'what we see', from Book iii he would learn the internality of 'what we know'. For as Malebranche developes his view of the contents of the mind, the internality of the object receives increasing emphasis. If the bright sun out there and up there, the most impressive instance of externality, has to surrender its light and heat, parts

[1] *v.* Locke, *Exam. Mal.* § 17.

apparently of its very being, and to make them over to the observer's mind, as really parts of mind's very being, and if, further, the geometrical properties of the apparent sun, the circle of the orb and the line of light, prove to be 'pure idea' in the mind, what then is left of the real external object? Berkeley in *Hylas* says that his purpose is to turn ideas into things. It is a daring attempt. It compels him to say among the learned that 'we eat and drink ideas, and are clothed with ideas' (*Prin.* § 38). It takes courage to say 'idea', where other folk say 'thing'. He did not rush blindly upon that usage.[1] He knew he was taking liberties with language, and the decision to do so was deliberately taken after debate. It is probable that he had some philosophical guidance and leading in his revolutionary usage. Locke supplied none here. The New Principle rent the old bottles of Lockian ideism. But Malebranche's tough substantial 'ideas', were the proper model for Berkeley's idea-things.

The ideas under discussion in the *Search*, as in the *Principles*, are the ideas of, or for Berkeley the ideas which constitute, the material world. The theory 'that we see all things in God', when expressed precisely becomes, as its author admits, 'that we see all *material* things in God'.[2] The other objects of knowledge, God, the self, other selves, and 'Intelligences' will be under discussion in the next chapter. Confining here our attention to unthinking things, we shall outline Malebranche's classic conclusions. So far we have seen that the idea is there, and there for study. It is no mere trace, nor motion. It is to be taken seriously. It is a real being, distinct from the thinker, distinct from the thing

---

[1] The *C.P.B.* is full on the point. It was to have been a theme of the Introduction; *v.* 492, 510, 527, 653, 696, 770, 819, 884; cf. *Prin.* § 39.

[2] Cf. *Prin.* § 91: 'The Eternal Mind wherein they suppose only Ideas of the corporeal substances . . .'

thought about. Each idea is a spiritual entity. It serves a definite purpose in knowledge, enabling me to know what you know without losing my identity in yours. Malebranche carries the study into deeper waters. He examines the *whence*, *the why*, *the where*. He tries to state the cause and provenance of ideas, and to rise thence to an understanding of the mystery of being and knowing.

Malebranche follows the method of exclusion. There are five possibilities he says, and only five (cc. 2–6).

(i) Ideas arise from *Species Impressae*, emitted by material objects and resembling them. This is the Aristotelian and Scholastic view. Malebranche rejects it for various reasons, amongst others the impenetrability of bodies.

(ii) Ideas are produced by the soul on the impulse of impressions made by objects upon the body. This is the common view. It is, for Malebranche, incompatible with what we know of the nature of man and the status of idea. It overrates human powers and flatters human vanity. It implies that man can create and annihilate—powers reserved to the Creator. It depreciates the idea, taking it to be a being 'slender and contemptible', brought to nothing as soon as out of mind. Further, if man made ideas, he must first have had an idea of what he was going to make. Finally, the view mistakes occasion for true cause.

(iii) All ideas are created with us—the 'magazine theory' (perhaps in view in *C.P.B.* 658: 'There are innate ideas, i.e. ideas created with us'). The theory errs in over-estimating the capacity of the mind of man and his powers of selection. Man's finite mind cannot contain an infinite 'magazine'; nor if it could, would it be equal to the task of taking from the 'magazine' the idea appropriate to each occasion.

(iv) Ideas are modifications of the soul, the soul being regarded as a sort of Intelligible World, containing in herself the ideas of external things and seeing them by considering her own perfections. This theory is a counterpart, or parody, of Malebranche's 'Divine in-Vision' on a lower and human level. He sees various objections to it. It implies that each soul is a light to herself. It requires the soul to see in herself what she does not contain. It degrades pure luminous ideas to the level of the obscure *modifications de l'âme*.

(v) There is, then, only one possibility left, viz. ideas representative of material things are in the infinite mind of God, and by our union with the Word we see them there.[1] Malebranche's starting-point, adopted by Norris,[2] is the necessity that God should have in Himself the ideas of all the beings He has created; for otherwise He could not have produced them. God sees created things 'by considering the perfections He includes whereunto they are related'. By strict union with God the mind of man can see 'what there is in God which represents created beings'. God's ideas are therefore the essences of things, and the incomprehensible simplicity of the Divine Essence includes the ideas. Malebranche warns us not to conclude that our minds see the Essence of God. 'What they see is most imperfect, whereas God is most perfect.' The union is in the Presence of God, not in His Essence. This important distinction is sometimes overlooked. In the *locus classicus*[3] Berkeley virtually admits his close resemblance to, and even partial agreement with, Malebranche, denying what Malebranche did not affirm, that we see things in the Essence of God. Finite spirits therefore do not merge in the infinite, any more than bodies do in space.

Reflecting then on his theory, Malebranche adds five

[1] For the infinite comprehension *v. C.P.B.* 181, 361, and especially 686, 'God may comprehend all ideas', and *Rand*, p. 84.

[2] *Theory of the Ideal World*, pt. i, c. 2, especially § 19.

[3] *Hylas*, p. 427, 1st ed., and less clearly in *Prin.* § 148.

considerations in support of it. (*a*) The only plausible alternative is the 'magazine' theory, and this is contrary to the principle of Divine Economy or Parsimony. (*b*) His theory has the merit of 'instating created minds in an absolute dependence upon God'. (*c*) It corresponds to psychological fact. In order to think of 'this' we must first think of All. 'We first cast about our view upon all beings in general and afterwards apply ourselves to the consideration of the object we desire to think on.'[1] (*d*) The theory, and it alone, accounts for our 'seeing' universals. (*e*) God's purposes are self-contained. He has no other end of action but Himself. 'If God had made a mind and given it the sun for its idea . . . God, we should think, had made that mind . . . for the sun and not for Himself.'

In this theory it is essential to distinguish idea from sensation. Malebranche, of course, denies that we have sensation in God. The sensation is a modification of the soul which God causes without having. The idea is 'joined' to the sensation, and is in God, and we see it there because He is pleased to show it us. The chapter (vi) concludes with an impressive passage: 'God is the intelligible world, or the place of spirits . . . From His power they receive all their modifications; in His wisdom they discover all their ideas; by His love they are influenced with all their regulated motions; and because His power and His love are nothing but Himself, let us believe with St. Paul, that He is not far from every one of us, and that in Him we live and move and have our being.'

The six chapters in which Malebranche exhibits his theory of ideas and the vision of all things in God form an imposing façade of argumentation whose inconsistencies Locke easily exposes without doing much harm to the intuition behind the argument. Berkeley knew the *Search*

---

[1] Cf. *C.P.B.* 605, and note the same phrase 'cast about'.

when he was writing the *De Ludo Algebraico* and the *Commonplace Book*. He was familiar with it when he was writing the *Theory of Vision*. Its main argument was in full view when he was writing the *Principles*. To know the argument was to be moved by it.[1] I would urge that the *Search* left a profound and indelible impression upon Berkeley in his plastic period, an impression that conferred character, an impression that is the key to the interpretation of Berkeley's system.

Berkeley nowhere formally denies the debt. He had good prudential reasons[2] for not parading it. Several passages virtually admit it. All his main works, *Principles*, *Hylas*, *Alciphron* lead up to the Vision of all things in God. The *Hylas* dialogues contain a dramatization of his own philosophical experience, and perhaps what Hylas in the finale says of himself was true of Berkeley, namely, that he did not thoroughly comprehend the course that brought him to his position; but certainly what Hylas there says of Philonous was autobiography, 'You set out upon the same principles that Academics, Cartesians, and the like sects usually do.' Berkeley advanced to 'opposite conclusions' as regards the senses and matter, but what Malebranche taught him about God remained with him, and passed into his published philosophy. Berkeley's disclaimers have been misunderstood. They are partial, not total. They concern final position, not origins. The extreme occasionalism, the doctrine of 'intelligible matter', the union of the 'pure intellect' with God, certain Spinozistic developments of Malebranche's theory, as that we literally see and are united to the Essence of God—these things Berkeley disclaimed

---

[1] Even Locke was affected by the 'many very fine thoughts, judicious reasonings, and uncommon reflections contained' in the treatise he criticized. *Exam. Mal.* § 1.

[2] See above p. 40.

and disowned. Even his protest that he does not understand the theory should not be taken too seriously. He protests too much. Besides, the unintelligibility of the theory was the fashionable criticism in England.[1] It was a safe criticism because Malebranche admits somewhere that he does not understand parts of his own theory, accepting them on faith of reason. Anyhow, Berkeley's contemporaries connected his teaching with that of Malebranche, and he seems to have gone as near the doctrine of seeing all things in God, as one who was not an occasionalist could go.

Characteristic of Berkeleianism is the theocentric solution of the problems of being and knowing. It is no reflection on Locke's deep piety to say that this mark is absent from his system. God is in the background of Locke's *Essay*, in the foreground of Berkeley's *Principles*. The two thinkers conceived Deity differently. Locke's deity is transcendent, Berkeley's deity is immense.[2] With the text of immanence (more correctly, immensity), 'In Him we live and move and have our being', Malebranche clinches the argument, as we saw above, for the Divine in-Vision. There are several striking occurrences of that text in Berkeley's writings, most of them being apropos Malebranche (*Prin.* § 149; *Hylas, Works*, vol. i, pp. 427, 453; *Alciphron*, iv, 14; cf. *C.P.B.* 839, *Essays in Guardian, Works*, vol. iv, p. 181, and title-page *Theory of Vision Vindicated*). The former of the *Hylas* passages is particularly striking in the first edition, though an inartistic[3] addition in the third edition (1734) has obscured the point.

---

[1] v. Keill, *Examination of Dr. Burnet's Theory*, pp. 7–9, and Locke, *Fam. Letters*, p. 45.

[2] This term, once technical, remains in the Articles of Religion (1562–3), 'immensae potentiae, sapientiae, ac bonitatis' (*Art* i). It occurs frequently in the *Search*.

[3] 'Inartistic' because Philonous shows full knowledge of the system though he has just asked for information about it.

Hyl. But what say you? Are not you too of opinion that we see all things in God? If I mistake not, what you advance comes near it.

Phil. I entirely agree with what 'the holy Scripture saith, 'That in God we live and move and have our being.'

The reply goes as near as possible to saying 'I agree with that part of Malebranche's philosophy'.

An immense, immanent Deity, substance of real ideas, thinker of the unthinking, will of the inactive, makes possible the *esse percipi*. For Locke, the way of ideas was a human path. In the *Search* ideas are always thought of in connexion with Deity.[1] Malebranche did more than weaken the evidence for matter. He showed Berkeley, if I mistake not, how to construct a system dispensing with matter. He substituted the God of ideas for the world of ideas. He showed Berkeley how our ideas can be also God's ideas, thereby laying a foundation for inter-subjective thinking. We may with confidence take § 6 of the *Principles* as expressing Berkeley's primary and controlling conception of unthinking reality. For that intuition possessed for him 'all the light and evidence of an axiom' (ib., 1st. ed.), and the elevated diction suggests a mystico-religious experience as its source. The seer sees 'all the choir of heaven and furniture of the earth' laid out in the mind and will of some Eternal Spirit, like a great cathedral church in the mind and will of a creative architect, being there because thought there. 'All those bodies which compose the mighty frame of the world' may be called things or ideas (that point matters comparatively little), provided that the primary truth is kept, namely that they, one and all, lie there in the mind of God, being because thought on by Him, always

[1] In the 'Conclusion of the three first books' Malebranche shows in detail that all modifications and ideas are received from God.

thought on by Him, sometimes thought on by me, by you, by us, because always thought on by Him. Instead of starting inquiry, as we do, with an oblong florin or some other little bit of a sense *datum*, Berkeley began from a vision of the total *datum*, of heaven and earth lying there passive in the vaster mind of God. Berkeley is not seeing this or that in the mind of man. He is actually 'seeing all things in God'.

Real things, then, for Berkeley, are in God and are ideas. I have real ideas; therefore some of my ideas are also God's ideas. This twofold status of the idea comes out repeatedly in the *Principles*, and as we have seen, it is one of the major results of Malebranche's study of the nature of ideas.[1] Ideas of sense are 'our ideas' (*Prin.* § 25 &c.), because we perceive them; yet clearly they are not creatures of my will (*Prin.* § 29). They are produced by the will of God and excited in my mind. So that also they are God's ideas, just as our world is also God's world. When Berkeley is pressed on the score of sameness (e.g. *Hylas*, *Works*, vol. i, p. 466) he bids the reader choose between the abstract idea of identity, which no one can grasp, and the familiar use of words. I have an idea, I write it in a book and publish it. The idea that was private becomes public without ceasing to be, for all practical purposes, the *same* idea. My idea does not cease to be mine because it becomes yours too. Sharing it makes it more richly mine, if it is true. Malebranche spoke of God 'discovering' his ideas to us. That 'discovery' is a simple corollary of the fact that 'in Him we live'.[2] Berkeley had the same view-point here as Malebranche, I think. Both thinkers agree in the prin-

[1] So Locke, *Exam. Mal.* § 24: 'God hath the same ideas we have.'

[2] 'Whose Will it is they should be exhibited to me.' *Hylas*, p. 428.

ciple 'in tuo lumine lumen videbimus'. If God is left out of account or brought in *ex machina* to the system, then, no doubt, Berkeleianism is unsatisfactory on the score of sameness. But seeing all things in God and holding that God maintains intercourse between spirits, Berkeley could no more dispute as to whether two spirits see the same thing, than he could dispute as to whether they see it by the same light.

The same Substance is, for Berkeley, the solution of the problem of permanence. There is nothing so impermanent as man's ideas *qua* fancies; but if his ideas are also God's ideas, they last, though 'out of mind'. If Deity be immense, unbounded by time and space, limitless in thought and act, it seems reasonable to conceive Him as minding the *aurum irrepertum* of the *Commonplace Book*, *cum terra celat* (say, from 1753 to 1870), and as not ceasing to mind it when a man's intelligent activity, drawn from the same abyss, 'finds' the book and makes it current coin in the republic of letters.

As regards archetypes, in Dublin in 1710, as in America twenty years later, Berkeley was very guarded. He would affirm them or deny them according to the sense in which the word was used. The word is used in the *Commonplace Book* (701, 835) and in the *Principles* (§§ 45, 87) much as Locke uses it, for material originals. Two other passages in the *Principles*, §§ 71 and 99, call for mention. The latter passage speaks vaguely of archetypes existing 'in some other mind'; the former so rejects 'intelligible matter' in the mind of God, as to leave open the possibility of Ideas in the mind of God. Berkeley believed, of course, in ideas in the mind of God.[1] But, θνητὰ φρονῶν, he took little interest in God's ideas when they are not also our ideas, and did not pretend to any knowledge of the topography

[1] *v.* his letter to Johnson, March 24, 1730. *Works*, vol. ii, p. 19.

of the 'intelligible world'. In the third of the *Hylas* dialogues he goes rather further, and pressed for a philosophy of Creation he admits archetypes 'external to your own mind' and a 'two-fold state of things—the one ectypal or natural, the other archetypal and eternal'. But he is always afraid of matter creeping back in disguise, as a Third Nature, or Divine attribute, or *Spatium Reale*, or Intelligible Matter, and his guarded admission of the archetypal state is always to be qualified by the governing principle, 'No idea or archetype of an idea can exist otherwise than in a mind' (*Hylas*, *Works*, vol. i, p. 425).

Ideas of the Imagination—Occasionalism

Leaving real ideas, we come to the important group of objects of knowledge called 'ideas of the imagination'. This group gives a definite and distinctive character to Berkeley's system. Here he may be indebted to Malebranche, though the difference in doctrine is very marked. Berkeley could hardly have framed this part of his theory without reference to the *Search*, for Malebranche devotes Book ii *in toto* to the imagination and considers the imagination again in Book iii in connexion with the Divine in Vision. Malebranche isolated the imagination and thereby perhaps drew Berkeley's attention to the metaphysical importance of the faculty.[1] Berkeley here would find no guidance in Locke. The peculiar character of imaginative perception is scarcely mentioned in the *Essay*. Locke speaks of 'Invention or voluntary putting together of several simple ideas' (ii. 22. 9), and he opposes fantastical ideas to real ideas, but he gives no systematic treatment of the imaginative faculty. It is simply lost among the various modes of thinking. Descartes touches on the imagination in the second

[1] This, however, was a commonplace. As regards the imagination, I merely state, without pressing, the evidence for dependence.

Meditation, and discusses it at greater length in the sixth. But Descartes could hardly give more than hints.[1] The *Search,* however, devotes a whole book of three parts to the imaginative faculty, and treats it as one of the primary parts of the human understanding co-ordinate with sense and intellect.

The opening of the second *Hylas* dialogue affords some evidence of dependence. The account there given of the brain and animal spirits may be a summary of Malebranche's account of the physiological concomitants of the imagination (bk. ii, 1. 4, 5, perhaps referred to in the petulant *C. P. B.* 432). Perhaps we may trace an even earlier connexion. For in his essay on the *Cave of Dunmore* (1705–6) Berkeley has a paragraph on the imagination reminiscent of the *Search.*[2] In the *Commonplace Book* the imagination receives considerable attention and is constantly isolated, in Malebranche's manner, as one of the three primary modes of apprehending ideas, e.g. 'the existence of our ideas consists in being perceiv'd, imagin'd, thought on' (471). Imaginable and sensible ideas are contrasted in 581, 588, 667. From 804, 830, and 835, we see that sense and imagination are the only two of the three faculties left for the time being; for in the meantime Berkeley has developed his doctrine of abstraction, and 'pure intellect', *qua* faculty of abstract ideas, is eclipsed (822). In 788 he defines idea, and it is interesting to see that he first wrote 'by idea I mean any sensible or

---

[1] Berkeley knew Molyneux's translation (1680) of the *Meditations* with Hobbes's objections. *v. C.P.B.,* 807–10.

[2] 'Men of a strong imagination . . . fancy the petrified water stamped with the impressions of their own brain' and 'the clouds so far comply with the fancy of a child, as to represent to him trees, horses, men, or whatever else he's pleased to think on.' Cf. 'The brains of men of strong imaginations receiving deep impressions of the subject' (*Search,* ii. 3. 1) and 'chariots, men, lions, and other animals in the clouds' (*Search,* ii. 2. 2).

imaginable or intelligible thing', subsequently erasing the last three words (cf. 790). So we can see that his doctrine of ideas of sense and imagination was well thought out, and its main lines may have been reached by the impact of his doctrine of abstraction upon the tripartite division of the understanding, viz. sense, imagination, and pure intellect, which occupy respectively Books i, ii, and iii of the *Search*.

Malebranche found the fact of the imagination a grave difficulty. His problem was this: how can ideas, obviously the result of human fancy, obviously inconsistent with truth and reality, be in God and be seen in Him? Accordingly he goes very carefully into the nature of the image, in order to solve this problem and save his theory. He divides the imagination into two faculties, active and passive. The passive imagination is what we should call the part played by the nervous system. A good deal of the physiology of Malebranche's account is on modern lines. He lays down that memory consists in the traces left by the animal spirits in the brain (cf. 'you make certain traces in the brain to be the causes or occasions of our ideas.' *Works*, vol. i, p. 421, where Hylas expounds 'the modern way'). The active imagination receives no separate treatment (*v.* bk. ii, 1. 1). It is the element due to the imagination's dependence upon the soul. It consists in 'the action and the command of the will', to which the animal spirits that delineate the images, and the brain fibres that take the images, pay obedience. In bk. iii, 2. 3, he considers the imagination in connexion with the intellect. One great source of error, Malebranche thinks, is the confusion between two representative entities —the image engraved on the brain and the idea which accompanies it. The idea 'regulates the image'. The idea tests the agreement of the image with reality. In respect of both entities appearances deceive us. We find the idea present to our mind when we will to have it. We ought to conclude that our will is a *sine qua non*, but not that our will is the *vera causa*; our will does not show the idea to the mind, much less create it *de nihilo*. Similarly, we appear to produce the brain image, but we do not do so, for we do not know how to do so, nor how it is done. We are not then the cause of the image on the brain, and we may not call ourselves *cause* of ideas of the imagination. Our active part is to make the mind more attentive to the ideas of 'pure intellect'. When, for instance, we imagine a square, an auditory image of the sound of the word provokes a visual image of a shape. These images come to us. Our part is to go to meet them, and direct the mind towards the pure ideas of extension that lie behind the image of the square.

Malebranche's argument is a product of his occasion-alism. God is 'the one true cause'. Man is always trying to evade this truth. Man thinks, in defiance of reason, that a bowl in motion (cf. *C. P. B.* 36) communicates motion to the bowl it meets; but it does not; for *non dat quod non habet*. The bowl is in motion, not the motion in the bowl (*Search*, iii, 2. 3). Malebranche's more famous instance is that a man thinks he moves his arm, but does not. Moving the arm is a very complicated business, and a man cannot do it, because he does not know how. The arm is moved on the occasion of his willing to move it. Just so men take the act of applicative will which accompanies and occasions the production and preservation of ideas to be a *vera causa*, and overlook the true cause, the Will of God.

Now here we have a main point at issue between Berke-ley and Malebranche. One wonders if this was a topic dis-cussed at their alleged meeting[1] in the Paris monastery, when Malebranche raised his voice and lost his temper, and according to the *bon mot*, Berkeley became unwittingly 'the occasional cause of his death'. Here at any rate was

[1] See Appendix ii, p. 208.

inflammable matter, a point of acute difference. Perhaps Berkeley was familiar with Malebranche's doctrine of the image, and perhaps he was indebted to it. If so, he departed widely from it. Fortunately we are in no doubt as to the reason of the divergence. We have Berkeley's own statement of the case. Poking sly fun at the 'arm' argument, he writes in his note-book (*C. P. B.* 553): 'We move our legs ourselves. 'Tis we that will their movement. Herein I differ from Malbranch.' It is a summary description. There are other differences, three of which Berkeley specifies in the second *Hylas* dialogue.[1] But leaving matter out of account, which Malebranche the monk retained but Malebranche the thinker discounted, there is little else to separate the two systems, as philosophies of ideas. This difference is no slight one. It is grave and far-reaching. Berkeley, loyal as ever to empirical fact, recognizes the reality of finite activity. He comes to terms with it, makes it indeed one of the poles on which his system turns. For if we move our legs ourselves, we make ideas ourselves. We make and unmake ideas (*Prin.* § 28), as really as we stretch and relax muscles.

Berkeley steers as it were a middle course between Malebranche and Locke. He granted to Malebranche that some (the majority) of our ideas are also God's ideas. He granted to Locke that some ideas are made by man. The connexion between idea and will comes in for repeated notice in the later portion of the *Commonplace Book* (801–45). 'Every idea has a cause, i.e. is produced by a Will' (843). This is not, as in ordinary Christian apologetic, a deduction from Divine attributes, but is a matter of observed fact from which the being of God is correctly inferred. 'When in broad daylight I open my eyes, it is not in my power to choose whether I shall see or no' (*Prin.*§ 29). Ideas of sense 'are not creatures

[1] 1734 ed.; *v. Works*, i., p. 427.

of my will. There is therefore some other will or spirit that produces them'. So the real ideas that are the real world are God's ideas discovered to us and becoming *pro tanto* our ideas. But there is also, for Berkeley, the plain matter of fact which any one can verify in his experience, that we command, control, make, and unmake some of our ideas. 'This making and unmaking of ideas doth very properly denominate the mind active. Thus much is certain and grounded on experience.' Thus the imagination with its ideas takes a defined place in the Berkeleian system. Sensation proper is, for Berkeley, a sphere of God's manifest operation. Imagination proper he views, I think, as a sphere of man's free activity, into which God wills not to enter. The two spheres are in theory distinct, but it is not likely that Berkeley regarded them as actually separate. The distinctions of theory are blurred in living fact. Berkeley contrasts ideas of sense and ideas of imagination on the score of regularity, vividness, and constancy; he contrasts them with regard to their source, and their metaphysical implications. He could scarcely have made a clean cut between them. In actual fact image blends with percept, and percept with image. So, on Berkeley's principles, there is no need to regard our fancies as entirely godless, nor our imaginings as lying outside God's general Will.[1]

[1] With regard to this and to similar questions which arise out of Berkeley's doctrine of ideas, it would be rash to infer that Berkeley did not see the difficulty and had no answer ready. The *C.P.B.* contains several indications that psychological questions were reserved for the second Part of the *Principles*, which Berkeley lost in Italy after making 'considerable progress in it'. On divine and human agency *v. Hylas*, p. 454.

VI

THE PRINCIPLES OF KNOWLEDGE

BERKELEY'S denial of matter with its complement, the assertion of ideas, is his characteristic performance. Upon it he concentrated his attention in Part I of his *Principles*. But it is not the whole of his philosophy. There are for him other realities besides ideas, other objects of knowledge, and therefore other principles of human knowledge. In connexion with these other objects he outlines his views on the Knowing of Knowing.

Berkeleianism is popularly supposed to reduce everything to mere idea. Nothing could be further from fact. It is usually classified as idealism, and regarded indeed as the head and front of idealism. That classification is open to serious criticism. Fraser often speaks of Berkeley as a realist. It is arguable that his principles have more in common with our realism than with our idealism. But an adequate discussion of the use of those labels would be a long matter, and perhaps not profitable or conclusive. Suffice it here to say that when Berkeley denied matter and refuted materialism, he did not assert mentalism, nor put the human mind in matter's place.

It is not even correct to say that Berkeley lays all the stress upon ideas. He preserves his sense of balance.[1] Ideas form, for him, simply one hemisphere of things, and, even so, not the more important. His ideas are in their nature passive and inert. They do nothing, cause nothing, cannot even resemble an active being (*Prin.* § 25). There is something else in the universe (*Prin.* § 2). There is something entirely distinct from idea. There is what perceives ideas, wills, imagines,

[1] Cf. *De Motu*, § 21: 'Duo sunt summa rerum genera, corpus et anima'.

remembers them. There is what I call 'mind, spirit, soul, or myself'. This rather ego-centric account passes soon (*Prin.* § 27) into the account of spirit as 'one simple undivided active being' whose two main operations are understanding and willing. Spirit, by denotation, divides into the infinite Spirit and finite spirits, and in the later sections, more precisely, into God, myself, and other spirits.

Thus the component parts of Berkeley's experience are familiar elements. His world is the world of common sense. So the interest for us in what he says about spirits is not so much his assertion of their existence as his meaning in calling them 'known'. Are spirits 'known' in the same sense as idea-things are 'known'? The *Principles* is a treatise designed to express the principles of human knowledge. The first half of the book expounds immaterialism and defends it against objections. The second half fulfils the promise of the title by offering a co-ordinated statement of the wider principles of knowledge, dealing *seriatim* with knowledge of ideas, of the self, of other spirits, and of God. It may be noted that Berkeley in his Preface makes a point of inviting his readers to suspend judgement till they have read the whole through. The last section, that on the knowledge of God, is the keystone of the fabric, and his doctrine of idea-things, if sundered from that section, is certainly one of the 'passages . . . liable to gross misinterpretation, and to be charged with most absurd consequences'. Before dealing in order with the four sections, which treat of the four objects of knowledge, we shall glance at the genesis of Berkeley's epistemology.

'Certainly we do not know it. This will be plain if we examine what we mean by the word knowledge' (*C.P.B.* 582). Berkeley conducted this examination. He studied the nature of knowing, and tried to co-ordinate the varieties of knowledge that arise under his system of reality, making critical use of the epistemological teaching of both Locke and Malebranche.

The fourth book of Locke's *Essay* is an elaborate treatise upon the nature, modes, extent, and certainty of knowledge. It opens with the statement, 'since the mind, in all its thoughts and reasonings, hath no other immediate object but its own ideas... it is evident that our knowledge is only conversant about them. Knowledge then seems to me to be nothing but the perception of the connexion and agreement or disagreement and repugnancy of any of our ideas.' Locke goes on to consider agreement of ideas under four heads: (1) Identity or diversity, (2) Relation, (3) Co-existence, (4) Real existence. Locke's controlling principle is clearly expressed in the words 'we can have knowledge no farther than we have ideas' (bk. iv. 3. 1). The field of our knowledge can be no wider than the field of our ideas. Where there is no idea there is no knowledge. Upon this principle depends his account of the various modes and degrees of knowledge.

Locke's view of knowledge is reflected in the first half of the *Commonplace Book*. When the second note-book is well advanced a break-away begins. In the formal demonstration of the new principle *more geometrico*, with which Berkeley experiments at the end of the first note-book (903–24), the second on the list of axiomatic principles is, 'all knowledge about our ideas'. There the Lockian principle is endorsed. But by the time we reach the important series 740–52 a revolution in outlook has occurred. Berkeley now writes 'we may have certainty and knowledge without ideas'. In the entry 752 he takes up Locke's four heads of agreement of ideas, tears three of them to pieces, establishes the fourth, pointing out, however, that Locke had misjudged its extent.

Berkeley's acceptance of 'knowledge without ideas' was a turning-point. This meant a positive break with repre-

sentationism, and at least a partial assertion of direct
awareness. Further, it released the term 'idea'. The term
being no longer required for the *tertium quid* of indirect
knowledge, can be used now for the supposed direct object
of knowledge, usually called material thing. Now was
Berkeley self-taught in this matter? In asserting that we
have knowledge without ideas, and in making that position the corner-stone of the second half of the *Principles*,
he was abandoning Locke's first epistemological principle.
In this grave departure had he any support and guidance
besides his own 'arguings'? It seems probable that here
again he is indebted to Malebranche. Berkeley must have
read chapter vii in the second part of the third book of the
Search. It immediately follows the exposition of our seeing
all things in God. It is indeed a necessary supplement to the
main theory. For the very notion of man-knowing-in-God
obliges Malebranche to draw the line between material
things which we know in God by representative idea, and
other objects known, but not known in that way. Accordingly
Malebranche marks off 'four manners or ways of knowing
things', corresponding to the four objects, God, bodies, the
self, other spirits. God, and God alone, is known 'by
himself' with 'an immediate and direct view, without the
Deputation or interposition of any creature'. Bodies and
their properties are seen in God and by their ideas, and
therefore 'the knowledge we have of them is most perfect'.
The soul we know not by idea, nor in God. 'We know her
only by conscience, and for that reason the knowledge we
have of her is imperfect.' Other spirits, human or super-
human, we know only by 'conjecture'.

Malebranche's quadrilateral of knowledge rests on the
principle 'We see only those things in Him whereof we
have ideas, and there are things we see without ideas'
(*Search*, iii. 2. 7). That passage may have been Berkeley's

authority for his 'knowledge without ideas'. Allowance made for his peculiar use of the term *idea*, the head-line of the second half of the *Principles* (§ 86) 'Human knowledge may naturally be reduced to two heads, that of ideas and that of spirits' seems to be an echo of Malebranche's words 'All things in the world whereof we have any knowledge are either bodies or spirits.' His immaterialism compelled Berkeley to modify the details of Malebranche's epistemology, but the *Search*, I think, suggested the general plan.

Knowledge of Ideas (*Principles*, §§ 86–134)

The second half of the *Principles* was, it would seem, conceived separately. It was drafted in a separate note-book.[1] It assumes the results of the former half, but it can stand as an independent study of the fourfold object of knowledge.

The first division (§§ 86–134) examines knowledge of ideas. Sections 86–91 repeat previous arguments. They form a strong assertion of the reality of knowledge, and an exposure of the sceptical alternative. Both Malebranche and Locke are included among those who have given a sceptical turn to the theory of knowledge. In § 87 he has Malebranche in view. Using Malebranche's phrase[2] he speaks of the sensible qualities as 'perfectly known', assigning in effect the same reason—'there being nothing in them which is not perceived'. He then outlines the arguments of problematic idealism as expounded in the *Search*, bk. i. In § 88 he passes to Locke's 'assurance that deserves the name of knowledge'. In the draft copy § 88 Berkeley first wrote '*intuitive* or demonstrative knowledge of the existence of sensible things'. This fixes the reference of the passage to Locke's 'sensitive knowledge' (*Essay*, iv, 2.14). Against such problematical knowledge Berkeley asserts that we know one

---

[1] British Museum Add. MS. 39304.

[2] i.e. for the intelligible ideas of bodies.

hemisphere of reality in apprehending (§ 89) 'inert, fleeting, perishable passions, or dependent beings; which subsist not by themselves, but are supported by, or exist in, minds or spiritual substances'.

After some recapitulation and a brief discussion of time Berkeley passes from knowledge to science, that is, from unsystematic knowings to the two 'great branches of speculative knowledge', and he outlines an epistemology of physics and mathematics. He maintains (§§ 101–17) that physics as knowledge does not differ in kind from sense-perception. Science has no claim to an exclusive knowledge of reality. If she makes the claim, scepticism ensues. Science has not even an exacter knowledge of efficient causes. The excellence of science resides in the scientist's largeness of comprehension, from which springs the 'endeavour towards Omniscience' (§ 105), with its attendant dangers. In §§ 118–34 he considers pure mathematics, discussing the genesis of both arithmetic and geometry. Their subject-matter too is grounded in sense-perception. Intelligible number and pure intelligible space are empty notions arising from the false doctrine of abstraction.

This whole passage (§§ 85–134) is tantalizing. Berkeley says in it startling things about ideas and yet leaves much unsaid. We feel that he ought to have attempted a more systematic answer here to the big epistemological questions which arise out of his statements about ideas. Very possibly he shows a calculated restraint in this matter, and perhaps he had a good reason for not disclosing at this stage his full doctrine of knowledge.

Knowledge of ideas is, for Berkeley, first and last, sense-perception. It differs from sense-perception, as ordinarily understood, in omitting the external or, more precisely, the material object.[1] The psychology of the imagination and

[1] 'Externality' with regard to origin is granted in *Prin.* § 90

memory is not discussed in the *Principles*, but from the *Commonplace Book* it is quite clear that Berkeley held that the image arose from the percept.[1] Even the two great provinces of speculative science, natural philosophy and mathematics, are 'conversant about ideas received from sense and their relations' (§ 101). The idea, then, for Berkeley is the foundation of the whole fabric of human knowledge, and we look to him to tell us the nature of the idea, and how it is related to the percipient.[2] The idea, as the name implies, has no independent nature. Relation to spirit makes ideas what they are. That relation is percipience or knowing, which is an ultimate, unanalysable fact, vouched for by every man's experience. Ideas from their birth to the moment of their annihilation are known. Not occupancy of space-time, but occupancy of mind is their *esse*. Yet ideas are not spirit, nor are spirits ideas. Spirit and idea have it in common to be immaterial, if you like, but that is saying little or nothing, if matter *non est*. My ideas, *qua* mine, are made by me, and held in brief existence by me; but they are not the *me*, nor part of it. Ideas are neither modes of spirit, nor states of mind. 'In' mind, they are not 'of' mind. They are essentially unlike spirit. Spirit can act, ideas cannot. The Berkeleian idea is object which is not subject, and which, being made and conserved by spirit, has no independent nature.

of things perceived by sense, i.e. of all ideas except those of the imagination and memory.

[1] The following entries are explicit: 536, 588, 667, 804, 830, 835.

[2] If he has not told us systematically, he has put us in the way of finding out. Twenty years later in a letter to Johnson he admits 'defects' in his early publications. He still thinks their teaching true, but does not pretend that his 'books can teach truth. All I hope for is, that they may be an occasion to inquisitive men of discovering truth, by consulting their own minds, and looking into their own thoughts' (*Works*, vol. ii, p. 18).

Further, the idea imprinted on the sense is real, and a criterion of reality. The idea of the 'great square tower' on the bend of the River Nore, Berkeley's reputed birth-place, seen from the Thomastown road, is small, round, and can be covered with a pencil. But it is a *datum*. In some sense it is *there*. The visual idea is the visual *datum*. It is what we see. As seen it is perfectly apprehended. There is nothing in it not seen. The idea has no inside and outside, no back and front. We can walk away or round, and see adjacent *data*. But once we select an object for vision, what we see is all there is to see. Malebranche says that we should like fuller knowledge of ourselves and of other spirits; but that we cannot desire knowledge, fuller than we have, of the representative idea of body. Being in God, it is perfect in its kind. Now Berkeley's idea is presentative. It is not, like Malebranche's idea, 'different from' the thing (*Search*, iii. 2. 7). But when he calls it 'perfectly known'[1] he means by the phrase just what Malebranche meant.

There is no occult universality in the idea, any more than there is occult materiality. The idea is just what it pretends to be, a particular.[2] This idea is not that idea. The visual idea that I just cover with my pencil is not the visual idea that I just cover with my book. The idea imprinted on the senses is a real thing that really exists. So it is a particular. Since, however, one particular idea can stand for another particular idea, the idea is a proper and adequate basis for general knowledge. The mind is liable to be in too great a hurry to form general theorems; but if we check this 'endeavour towards omniscience', we may attain 'the greater largeness of comprehension whereby analogies, harmonies, and agreements are discovered in the works of nature and the particular effects explained, that is, reduced to general rules'

---

[1] *v. Prin.* §§ 87, 101, and elsewhere.
[2] Cf. *Intr. Prin.* § 15 and *Hylas*, *Works*, p. 403.

(*Prin.* § 105). This symbolic universality is due to the will of the author of nature; things are so made by him that we read general rules in particular phenomena, as surely as we read meaning in letters of a book (*Prin.* § 108).

Ideas then are the unthinking things that compose the world. Excited by man (§ 36), excited by God (§ 57), they are never excited by 'matter'. The conception of unthinking things that are always thought is undoubtedly difficult, but it is neither arbitrary, absurd, nor alien. It is no harder than rival conceptions, e.g. a subject that makes itself its object, or the too familiar notion of an external thing 'acting on' our minds or brains.

Berkeley is his own best expositor. But perhaps this amount of exegesis may be permitted as a background to a brief reference to certain 'defects' in his treatment of ideas. The four difficulties commonly felt about his ideology are that the ideas are incoherent, private, impotent, and flimsy. The opposite features in matter attract us. This is the source of the dreamlike character usually attributed to the Berke-leian world. As regards the incoherence of the ideas, Berkeley just says that they are 'combined, blended, or concreted together' (§ 99) to form objects of sense; but he gives no adequate treatment of the nature of body. His silence is marked, because we know from the *Commonplace Book* (290, 302–3, &c.) that he had considered the question. The difficulty of the idea's privacy is scarcely even approached in the *Principles*. Yet if my idea is only mine, how can two people see the same thing? The third *Hylas* dia-·logue (*Works*, vol. i, pp. 466 sqq.) to some extent repairs the omission. As regards the impotence of the idea, the fact is stressed often, and made the basis of an argument for the existence of God; but no adequate explanation is advanced of the appearance of causality between things (*v.* §§ 51–60). Locke had said, 'pure matter is only passive' (ii. 23. 28), but to all intents and purposes he treats matter as able to act, e.g. ii. 8. 10. Berkeley, one might almost say, tacitly transfers this part of the occasionalist teaching, viz. the impotence of matter, into his own system, *mutatis mutandis*. However, the permanence of ideas is the fundamental and primary issue, for permanence involves substance. The other characters of the Berkeleian idea are dependent. Berkeley leaves us in no doubt that God is the substance and ground of the permanence of ideas, but he develops the notion hardly at all. All the other characters of the Berkeleian idea turn on his conception of the nature of deity. Because God is, ideas form bodies round which socialized human knowledge and joint action can revolve. Because God wills, ideas are changed by the divine operation. Now had Berkeley at this stage attempted the explanation of these problems he would have been speaking of deity in a language incomprehensible to most of his readers, and one likely to prejudice the acceptance of the immaterialist argument, which, for Berkeley, is the 'principle or main point, from which, and from what I had laid down about abstract ideas, much may be deduced' (letter to Johnson, *Works*, vol. ii, p. 20). In fact Berkeley could not fully explain the knowledge of ideas until his view of the other three types of knowledge was familiar and accepted.

Knowledge of the Self

Berkeley had trouble with this question. Its intrinsic difficulty, disclosed in the conflicting views of Locke and Malebranche, was heightened for him by his peculiar doctrine of ideas. Berkeley states his views on self-knowledge in the *Principles*, §§ 135–44.[1] From the concluding words

---

[1] Fraser's text mixes the editions and is confusing. As we are studying origins, the first edition, 1710, will be our main topic.

of that section, and from the large number of neglected 'S' entries in the *Commonplace Book*, we may be sure that he intended to carry the discussion further in the lost Part II. The dominant theme of this section is the bifurcation of knowledge. 'Our souls are not to be known in the same manner as senseless inactive objects, or by way of idea' (§ 142). A man sees and touches parts of his body. Those objects being, for Berkeley, ideas, and the 'material' body being non-existent, his question shapes itself as follows, 'Can I, who know the inactive idea, also and in the same sense of the word, *know* the active spirit?' His answer is an unwavering affirmative, coupled with the proviso that the fact that both are knowable does not mean that they are in any way alike. Berkeley here is not trying to apprehend a higher faculty resident in a material body, but a self-conscious centre of real finite activity.

The novelty to many of his English readers would be Berkeley's refusal to recognize the term *idea* in connexion with our knowledge of the soul. In this refusal we may trace the influence of Malebranche. For Locke, our knowledge of the soul is intuitive and of the highest degree of certainty, but, like all Lockian knowledge, it is knowledge by idea. Our idea of the soul is, for Locke, a complex idea of an immaterial spirit. The substance of spirit baffles us, he holds, but the primary ideas of spirit, thinking, willing, and motivity are as clear as our ideas of body (*Essay*, ii. 23. 15–26).

Malebranche's doctrine is more subtle. Like Locke, he admits that there is an idea of the soul; otherwise God would not have known what He was about to do when He created the soul. Unlike Locke, he denies that we know the soul by its idea. He says that God has not given us an idea of our own soul, so as not to weaken the union of our soul with our body. We know the soul; otherwise we could not prove its immateriality, immortality, and liberty; but this knowledge, in fullness and clarity, falls far short of Descartes's 'first knowledge'. In point of fact, Malebranche thinks, we do not know the soul as well as we know body. We can define and know all the properties of extension;[1] but we do not know all the modifications of the soul nor what she is and is not capable of. From this comparative ignorance arises our difficulty in admitting colour and light to be modifications of the soul. If we knew the soul by idea, we should see it in God and should be as gods—which may not be. He gives various names such as *sensation*, *sentiment intérieur*, and *conscience*, to the rush-light self-knowledge that we have (*Search*, iii. 2. 7: "tis possible that what we know of her is the least part of what she is').

There is a good deal here that Berkeley accepted or agreed with and a good deal that he rejected. Agreeing with Malebranche against Locke that we do not know the soul by idea, he went a stage further and said that there is no idea of the soul to know. In the *Commonplace Book* (900) he refers to Malebranche's distinction between knowing the mind by idea and 'sensation conscientia'. He calls it 'vain'. But the entry is cryptic, and the reading doubtful. Berkeley does not characterize self-knowledge with a technical name in the *Principles*; but as with Malebranche, it rests upon immediate feeling. In the *Hylas* dialogue (*Works*, vol. i, p. 447) he says: 'I know what I mean by the terms *I* and *myself*; and I know this immediately or intuitively.' Again (ib.) 'my own mind and my own ideas I have an immediate knowledge of', and in the same context self-knowledge is described as 'reflex act'. In the *De Motu* (1721), § 21, Berkeley says explicitly 'rem sentientem, percipientem, intelligentem, conscientia quadam interna cognovimus'. In the addition, made in 1734, to the *Principles*, § 89, the term

[1] Cf. *Prin.* § 142 'know a spirit as we do a triangle'.

'inward feeling' is found. So it is clear that Berkeley regarded our self-knowledge, as Malebranche did, as partial and imperfect but immediate and quite real. Berkeley is tactically in a difficult position. He is fighting on two fronts. His first concern is to prevent self-knowledge from being a support for materialism. He is answering the argument latent in Locke's words, 'the substance of spirit is unknown to us; and so is the substance of body equally unknown to us' (*Essay*, ii. 23. 30). The obscure in self-knowledge imperils his consistency.[1] He has to meet the objection that there may be matter, though we are only dimly aware of it; for there is a soul, though we have no idea of it. In order to repulse the threat from materialism, Berkeley has to establish the radical difference between spirit and idea. In so doing he exposes his flank to the attack of scepticism, and repels it by maintaining that the soul is really known, though it is not known after the manner of ideas.[2]

Commentators usually make a great deal of the alterations in the later editions and of the stress there laid on the term 'notion'. It is doubtful whether the alterations represent any change of view. Berkeley had long held that self-knowledge and knowledge of ideas differ in kind, and it seems improbable that he could ever have come to regard notional knowledge as a third kind. The word 'notion' had been used in the schools, and Berkeley would meet it in Malebranche, Locke, Sargent, and many other writers, and he uses it in a simple innocent sense[3] in the first editions of the *Principles* and the *Hylas*. A notion was not, I believe,

---

[1] 'To act consistently you must either admit matter or reject spirit.' *Hylas, Works*, vol. i, p. 449, added 1734.

[2] Reid, rather superficially (*Inquiry*, c. vii), urges the objection which Berkeley had anticipated.

[3] As e.g. Locke, *Essay*, ii, 23. 35, 'the idea or notion we have of God'.

for Berkeley, an epistemological *tertium quid*. In the third
Hylas dialogue (all editions, *Works*, vol. i, p. 448) it is
explained that 'having a notion' of God means knowing Him
by 'reflexion and reasoning'. In all the editions of all his
books[1] Berkeley's doctrine of 'notions' is capable of being
interpreted within the scheme of knowledge laid down by
him in 1710, and we should not give to it a turn inconsistent with 'The Principles of Human Knowledge'.

The term 'notion' is not a new departure, but an addi-
tional safeguard against sceptical misinterpretations of
Berkeley's doctrine of knowledge of spiritual objects. The
critic could, and, no doubt, did say 'the bishop denies that
we have an idea of God and the soul'. Berkeley supplies the
retort, 'True, but he affirms that we have a *notion* of God
and the soul'. He knew from personal experience the need
of such a term. From the *Commonplace Book* we see that
if he had not plumbed in person the depths of doubt, at
least he had been to the brink of the precipice, and had
looked over. In the early entries (25, 44) self-knowledge
is more or less certain and complete. He seems to accept
(552 corrected reading) by implication Locke's doctrine of
intuitive self-knowledge. The soul is a complex idea, known
and defined (156). However, the series 581 to 588 contains
an important revelation of a change of view. He asserts that
it is mere prejudice to deny that we have an idea of the soul;
but, as he immediately (583–7) gives a tentative account of
the soul, indistinguishable from Hume's, it would appear
that for the time being he had given up the fact while
retaining the name 'soul'. Later on, he revised that page,
adding 582 on the verso and marking with the marginal sign
÷ (? the obelus) the entries 583, 585, 586, 587. In 751 he
expresses the view that the *Cogito ergo sum* is a tautology,

[1] Even, I think, the 'such are *notions*' of *Siris*, § 308. *v. infra*,
p. 176.

and in the next entry he records the devastation in the Lockian theory of knowledge caused by the New Principle. His earlier uncertainty is thus in marked contrast with the certainty eventually reached.[1] His fear of scepticism is not feigned. So he concedes, as Malebranche had conceded, that 'in a large sense we may be said to have an idea of spirit'.[2] Subsequently he formally expresses this concession by using the term 'notion'.

Malebranche had insisted that, however imperfect our knowledge of the soul, it is yet sufficient to demonstrate her immortality, spirituality, and liberty. The same three items are dealt with by Berkeley. In § 141 he declares that the soul is indivisible, incorporeal, unextended, and therefore incorruptible and naturally immortal. In § 144 he hints at a projected treatment of liberty, which he intended to give in *Principles*, Part II (*v. C.P.B.* 511). Berkeley's firm faith in God and life would not permit any permanent scepticism about self-knowledge. In his view the soul must be real and really known, because God, who encompasseth us, made and knows it.

Knowledge of other Finite Spirits

Knowledge of other finite spirits is recognized by Malebranche, Locke, and Berkeley as a special branch of epistemology. No one of the three, however, treats it with fullness, though Malebranche and Berkeley are far from neglecting it. Berkeley has been severely criticized on this score. Reid wrote (*Int. Powers*, Essay II, c. x): 'I can find no principle in Berkeley's system which affords me even probable ground to conclude that there are other intelligent beings like

[1] As e.g. in *Hylas*, *Works*, vol. i, p. 446, 'I might as well doubt of my own being'.

[2] *Prin.* § 140. Cf. *Search*, Illustration on bk. i, c. 3: 'I have sometimes said we had an Idea of the Soul, and sometimes denied it.'

myself', and he says, unjustly I think, that Berkeley 'seems not to have attended to' this difficulty. Dr. Dawes Hicks (*Berkeley*, pp. 147–50) appears to find Berkeley's treatment of the question highly unsatisfactory. The charge he makes seems to be one of inconsistency rather than, as with Reid, of neglect. I have not been able to see the full force of either charge, while admitting that the form in which Berkeley has stated his doctrine leaves a good deal to be desired.

Berkeley was no solipsist. Few philosophers have had wider and more fruitful contacts with their fellow men than he had. It is hardly likely that his thought could belie his action. Might it not be the case that an interpretation of Berkeleianism that tends towards solipsism is neglecting the Malebranchian strain in his teaching? Just before the sentence quoted above, Reid says, 'What I call a father, a brother, or a friend, is only a parcel of ideas in my own mind'. That is a parody of Berkeley's teaching, owing all its point to the Lockian interpretation of 'idea' which Reid habitually places on the Berkeleian 'idea'. To reach a coherent and sensible account of Berkeley's teaching about the 'Thou', we must piece together several passages, and to appreciate it we must read it in connexion with his account of our knowledge of God.

We shall first glance at Malebranche's teaching (*Search*, iii. 2. 7). Other spirits are known, says Malebranche, by 'conjecture'. After a visit to an exhibition of wax-works we are inclined to agree with him. Certainly we do not ordinarily feel the existence of other spirits, in the same manner and with the same directness as we feel our own existence. Yet the term 'conjecture' does less than justice to Malebranche's view. He was no sceptic. His attitude towards 'other spirits' is like his attitude to matter. He is certain of the existence, but he doubts the evidence. Conjecture to us means little more than 'not knowing'; to Malebranche the term meant analogy. He says we know by conjecture when we think some things (different from ourselves, from those we know in themselves, and from those we know by ideas) 'are like some others that we already know'. He grants that conjecture is unreliable where the physical factor is prominent; but he thinks that we reach virtual certainty in the spheres of law and righteousness. The truths that twice two make four, that it is better to be just than rich, that God acts equally on all spirits, are social principles, postulating a society of men. What 'thou' art thinking and feeling on any given occasion must be conjectural, being based for me on the precarious ground of analogy; but God is 'the place of spirits', and so the existence of other spirits is, for Malebranche, a postulate of piety and a dictate of the moral sense. (Locke's few remarks on this topic are contained in *Essay*, bk. iv, c. 3. 17, and c. 11. 9–12.)

Knowledge of other spirits is one of the very few topics of the *Principles* not discussed in the *Commonplace Book*. From the entry (406) 'God knows how far our knowledge of Intellectual beings may be enlarg'd from the Principle', we may gather that a speculative development of the topic had crossed Berkeley's mind, but there are, I think, no entries dealing with the problem nearer home. We cannot then study his view 'in the making'. As we find it in the *Principles*, his account of our knowledge of other spirits, that is, of the spiritual or mental character of the men we meet, is like that of Malebranche. Both thinkers mark it off carefully from knowledge of ideas and from knowledge of God and the self. Both regard it as a complex process, and take similitude as its objective basis. Berkeley intended § 145 to be his formal statement. But that curt, compressed section should be taken along with the relevant passages from the flanking sections on self-knowledge and knowledge of God. God, the self, and other selves have it in common to be spirits. So Berkeley cannot neatly isolate and treat separately these connected types of knowing. The relevant passages in the *Principles* are §§ 140, 145, 147, 148, and with them should be read *Hylas*, *Works*, vol. i, pp. 448–9, and *Alciphron*, iv. 5.

Knowledge of other spirits is distinguished by Berkeley both from knowledge of ideas and from knowledge of the self. Ideas are known immediately. The self is known immediately. Other selves are known mediately. This mediate knowledge is none the less knowledge; for it is the product of two immediacies. Self and my ideas are both known immediately, and both these elements enter into our mediate knowledge of the 'Thou'. 'We know other spirits by means of our own soul . . . it having a like respect to other spirits that blueness or heat by me perceived has to those ideas perceived by another' (§ 140). Again (§ 148) certain ideas 'serve to mark out unto us the existence of finite and created spirits like ourselves.' In *Hylas* (p. 449) the process is referred to as 'mediate apprehension by similitude of the one or the other' (i.e. idea or self). In the second edition of *Prin*. § 89, Berkeley introduces the term 'reason'. The new term is not a new departure. It simply means that we must take steps to know the existence of other minds. The objective basis of the transition constituting the act of 'reason' is, to use Malebranche's term, 'likeness'. The blueness I see is to the blueness thou seest as *I* to *Thou*. Hearing thy voice is like, but not the same as, hearing my own voice. Resemblance and difference combine to make me refer the idea 'thy voice' to an agent like myself; in fact to thee.

The manuscript draft of the *Principles* breaks off in the middle of § 145, as if perhaps Berkeley stopped to devote special care to the section. Fraser notes that 'this is one of the notable sections in the *Principles*, as it suggests the *rationale* of Berkeley's rejection of Panegoism or Solipsism'. Berkeley's world is peopled with plural spiritual existences. He never shows the slightest doubt of the existence of other minds. His assured certainty on this point is not only consistent with his immaterialism but explanatory of it, and perhaps even expository of it. Repeatedly (e.g. § 34) he insists that the New Principle sacrifices no item of reality, sensible or conceptual. To make this evident, Berkeley has to pass on from knowledge of ideas to knowledge of finite spirits, and thence to knowledge of God. There must be choristers in the choir of heaven; real men are part of the furniture of the earth. But the idea-things composing heaven and earth are not private sensa, any more than they are only atoms or merely electrons. The idea-things are mental, only if 'mental' means inter-subjective and inter-spiritual. My thinking 'makes it so' to a minute extent and for a moment of time; but *our* thinking (thine and mine) finds, not makes, a vast, stable system of idea-things, that could not be unwilled, unwanted, unknown by God.

Hence it is that the knowledge of other spirits (§ 145) leads straight on to the knowledge of God (§ 146). Berkeley here restates, almost in terms, the well-known argument of § 29 for the existence of God, with the significant changes of *I* to the first person plural, and of 'my will' to 'the wills of men'. Then he passes at once to the language and the thought and, in a measure, to the system of Malebranche. Malebranche had said 'everything proves God'. Berkeley here says (§ 147) in effect, 'everything that proves man proves God'. Malebranche calls God 'the place of spirits'. Berkeley says (§ 147), 'He alone it is who "upholding all things by the word of his power" maintains that intercourse between spirits whereby they are able to perceive the existence of each other.' There is the key of Berkeley's solution of the problem of the *Thou*. The world of ideas or unthinking things would drop to pieces if its substance were removed. Just so, in Berkeley's system the social and spiritual order would be shattered, if God were not.

Knowledge of God

How God is known and what He is known to be are, no doubt, distinct questions; but Berkeley does not keep them altogether separate, though the epistemology of the subject is, in the main, reserved for the concluding sections of the *Principles*.

The *Principles* contains over twenty divine titles. Of the 156 sections about 70 mention God or consider the point at issue in relation to God. The cause of this stress on deity is not only the piety of the man, but the character of the system. Berkeley's philosophy apart from Berkeley's God falls. God in Berkeley's system is no *deus ex machina*, introduced as an afterthought or conventionally connected with the new way of ideas. He is its source and mainspring and secret strength. Each of the other three types of knowing, as we have just seen, involves a reference to the highest object of human knowledge. To study Berkeley's conception of deity is to go to the heart of the system.

Early training and education would dispose Berkeley to take the Lockian view. Locke's doctrine of deity, for all its deistic tendencies, is in itself orthodox, endorsing as it does the traditional and rational attributes. Yet the *Commonplace Book* shows us Berkeley profoundly dissatisfied with Locke's doctrine. 'God Space', followed by two references to Locke's *Essay*, is one of the very early entries. The danger of 'making God extended' is referred to in 299, 321, and 936 (*v.* also 634). In 308 Locke, More, and Raphson are named as seeming to make God extended. In 707 he mentions amongst Locke's dangerous opinions 'the infinity and eternity of space and the possibility of matter's thinking'.

We know that Berkeley studied King's *De Origine Mali* (*v. C. P. B.* 161–8) and King's characteristic title for Deity 'Active Principle' occurs in the *Principles* (§ 66). Berkeley must have known Clarke's writings, and the statement (*Prin.* § 63) that God prefers to convince our reason of his attributes by the works of nature rather than by miracle is reminiscent of Clarke's Boyle Lectures on the Attributes.

Traditional theism and transcendence are reflected in such titles as the Governing Spirit, the Supreme Agent, the Author of Nature—titles that abound in Berkeley's writings. But those titles are not sufficient for the needs of the New Principle. Immaterialism placed new stress upon another aspect. A Governing Spirit might conjure up ideas, and impose them upon men as realities. But Berkeley's *ideas* are no fancies. The permanent ideas whose *esse* is *percipi* are grounded in Deity, but could scarcely be related in any satisfactory way to the Deity as conceived by Locke and by contemporary British theology. It seems that French philosophy supplied the decisive conception.

We referred above, pp. 68–9, to the *Commonplace Book* entry, 'I wonder not at my sagacity in discovering the obvious tho' amazing truth . . . ' (287). One feels the half-suppressed exultation of the entry. It was a moment of enlightenment. The scales fell from his eyes. But what was his discovery precisely? What was 'the obvious tho' amazing truth'? It could hardly have been the denial of matter. That principle with its corollary, the ideality of sensibles, he had entertained for some years as an hypothesis. Surely his discovery was a sudden perception of the main condition that made immaterialism possible, that verified the hypothesis? If he saw in a flash the *Esse Percipi* against the background of the Immensity of God, his 'stupid inadvertency' would be his previous blindness to that aspect of

Deity which is the sole possible basis of the New Principle. Now it is worth noting that the pages of the note-book preceding this declaration show marked traces of the influence of Malebranche. The entry in question is 287. The entries 239, 264, 266, 274, 278, and 296 name Malebranche and, probably, other entries in these pages refer to his writings.

Locke (*Essay*, iv, 10. 1) had called the proof of God's existence 'most obvious', but his laboured demonstration makes it seem anything but *obvious*. We meet the phrase 'obvious truth' used of Deity both in the prologue and at the climax of the *Principles* (§ 149). An examination of these two passages, the alpha and the omega, makes it probable that the Immensity of God was Berkeley's master-light, and that he thought of it in connexion with Malebranche. In § 6, Berkeley declares, in lofty language, that God is the substance of all the choir of heaven and of the furniture of the earth, and that this truth is 'near and obvious to the mind'. That passage states with restraint and in untechnical terms Berkeley's primary vision of all things in God. In the second *Hylas* dialogue (*Works*, pp. 422–4) the same vision is painted on a larger canvas. Berkeley gives the rein to his fancy there, and describes the high arch of heaven, the abyss of space with all its 'glittering furniture', and 'the vast bodies that compose this mighty frame', and strikes the formal inference 'there must be some other mind wherein they exist'. The difference between this doctrine and the usual method of proof is explained, and at once (p. 426) Hylas asks the question: 'But do you not think it looks very like a notion entertained by some eminent moderns of "seeing all things in God"?'

At the close of the *Principles* (§ 149) Berkeley rises to his climax, and there we find the same sense of discovery, similar language, and the same 'great truth which lies so near and obvious to the mind' and yet is 'attained to by the reason of so very few'.[1] That truth is, 'God . . . is intimately present to our minds, producing in them all that variety of ideas or sensations which continually affect us, on whom we have an absolute and entire dependence, in short "in whom we live, and move, and have our being"'. Here Locke is left far behind, and the setting of the passage and several of its phrases are taken, apparently, from the *Search*. God as the home of 'our' ideas, God as intimately present to our minds, God as the Being upon whom we have an absolute and entire dependence, God in whom we live and move and have our being—in this divine quadrilateral the theory of seeing all things in God is framed.

For Malebranche, the knowledge of God differs intrinsically from the other types of knowing. It is knowledge of 'things by themselves'. It is immediate knowledge, knowledge without ideas. As far as we know, God is the only object so known. An object must be of a most intelligible nature if it is to penetrate the mind and discover itself to the mind. None but God penetrates the mind, and discovers Himself to it. ''Tis God alone that we see with an immediate and direct view.' What makes this possible is the union that our intellects have with Him. He is the 'Master who presides over our minds without the deputation or interposition of any creature'. A representative idea of God then, for Malebranche, would be impossible and unnecessary, impossible because an idea is a created being and cannot represent the universal Being, unnecessary because 'God is intelligible by Himself'. This is Malebranche's true opinion, strictly expressed.[2] In Book iv, c. 11, however, he seems to express an inconsistent view, asserting that the idea of God is no fiction. He is here using,

[1] With the 'sad instance of the stupidity and inattention of men', cf. 'my stupid inadvertency' *C.P.B.* 287.
[2] *Search*, iii. 2. 7.

as he says, a 'personal not a universal argument'. In one sense we must have an idea of God; otherwise we could not answer the question 'Is God round or square?' The argument is *ad hominem*. Malebranche is defending the ontological argument in its Cartesian form, rather than expressing his own proof of the existence of God.

Locke's account of Deity is of a different strain. Malebranche starts from God and works down to human knowing. Malebranche's God discovers himself to us. Locke discovers God (*Essay*, iv, c. 10. 1, 12) by working upwards from man's ideas. First (bk. ii, 23, 33–5) there is the idea of God that we make. That idea is complex, though God Himself be simple and uncompounded. Then (bk. iv, c. 10) we come to the real existence of that idea. This is known by demonstration. It is the 'most obvious truth that reason discovers'. We have no innate idea of God; yet we have a clear proof of Him, as long as we 'carry ourselves about with us'. The evidence amounts to mathematical certainty. Man knows that he himself is. Since nothing cannot produce a being, there must have been Something from eternity. I have power and I know. Therefore that Something must be powerful and knowing. We have a more certain knowledge of God than we have of anything not immediately discovered by the senses. Of the ontological argument Locke says that it is not the only argument, and that it is a mistake to concentrate attention upon it to the exclusion of those proofs 'which our own existence and the sensible parts of the universe offer so clearly and cogently to our thoughts'.

Now Berkeley's theology goes its own way. While he learned from both authorities, he agreed fully with neither. His affinities of spirit on the whole were with Malebranche. Locke's cold recognition of the province of faith would scarcely attract one who was warmly attached to Christian mysteries. In passing we may note that Malebranche habitually speaks of revealed religion and the mysteries of faith, as things apart, requiring the submission of the intellect, just as Berkeley does.[1] In spite of differences of creed the conservative Protestant and the liberal Catholic shared many beliefs of heart and head.

The *unio mystica* between man's 'pure intellect' and the Word of God is a hinge of Malebranche's system. Berkeley does not recognize the *unio* as such. He had not Malebranche's conception of the soul and body relation, and he was critical of the 'pure intellect'. 'Pure intellect I understand not', he wrote in his note-book (822). He never admits 'pure intellect' as a faculty of abstraction, but, I think, he never denied 'pure intellect' as a faculty of the supersensible. In the first *Hylas* dialogue (*Works*, p. 404) he recognizes 'pure intellect and its spiritual objects, as virtue, reason, God'. Berkeley is careful not to merge the finite spirit in the infinite, but there is nothing in his outlook formally inconsistent with the *unio*. Indeed the *unio* may be said to appear in Berkeleianism in the form of God's intimate presence. The 'Intimate Presence' is predicated in the *Principles* not alone of Nature (§ 151), but of our minds (§ 149), and, of these, not one-sidedly, for (§ 155) 'He is present and conscious to our innermost thoughts'.

The formation of Berkeley's natural theology can be, to some extent, traced in the *Commonplace Book*. A considerable group of entries has the marginal sign 'G' (= God). Quite early (41) he intends a 'brief demonstration of an active powerful being'. The characteristic proof of the *Principles* makes its appearance in 111, 724 and 850. In 180 he is pondering the difficulties in the Lockian 'complex and

compounded idea of God'. In 795 he gives up the idea
of God completely, thereby breaking with Descartes and
Locke and rejecting the ontological argument. In 825 he
states that he is certain there is a God, though he does not
perceive Him. This statement is supplemented in 850 and
there branches out into the typical argument of the *Principles*, incorporating a notion that appears in Clarke (*Dem.*
3rd ed., p. 55) and more forcibly in the *Search* (iv, c. 2):
'Every of His works is a proof of it. All the actions of men
and beasts prove it. Whatever we think, whatever we see,
whatever we feel, demonstrates it. In a word, there is
nothing in the world but proves that there is a God, or at
least may prove it.'

In the *Theory of Vision* there is scarcely a reference to
Deity, except for the hint of the Divine Visual Language
dropped in § 147. The *Essay* at its appearance seems to
have been criticized on that score.[1] In the *Principles* the existence of God is in the foreground throughout. In §§ 26–9
we have the brief proof, based on the contrast between our
voluntary and involuntary ideas, of God as the active substance and cause of the regular succession in our ideas.
There is a marked resemblance between § 29 and Locke's
Essay iv. 11. 5, in respect of language and the example.
One would think that Berkeley designed the echo. Locke
says: 'If I turn my eyes at noon towards the sun, I cannot
avoid the ideas which the light or sun then produces in me.'
Hence Locke infers 'the brisk acting of some objects without me'. From the same instance Berkeley brings out his
rapier thrust, 'There is therefore some other Will or Spirit
that produces them' (§ 29). In §§ 30–2 Berkeley considers
the nature of the connexion between ideas and their relation to human good, and thence he establishes the goodness
and wisdom of the Governing Spirit. In §§ 53, 61–6 he

[1] Rand, op. cit., pp. 72–3.

turns to the power and operation of God. Apparently he has Malebranche in view when he speaks of 'modern philosophers who though they allow matter to exist, yet will have God alone to be the immediate efficient cause of all things'. Without here defining his attitude to occasionalism, he puts his finger on a weak point in Malebranche's system. If the material bodies are impotent, and if God works all without their help, is not their very existence, if possible, at least 'a very unaccountable and extravagant supposition'. This is the argument against matter from Parsimony, to which Berkeley returns in § 61, demanding 'To what end God should take those roundabout methods of effecting things'. It is worth noting that Berkeley here may be turning against Malebranche the latter's own argument against the 'magazine' theory, viz. 'God never effects by most roundabout and difficult ways what can be done in ways most simple and easy' (*Search*, iii. 2, c. 4, 6).

Berkeley did not accept the full occasionalist doctrine of the divine operation; for he always recognized the finite spirit as a centre of real activity, but he agreed with part of the occasionalist creed. He accepted the passivity and impotence of the idea, and the absence of the second or material cause. For corporeal causality Berkeley substitutes the categories of sign and things signified, regarding ideas as the language of the Author of Nature (§ 66). In § 150 he expands this notion of the divine operation, and there his debt to Malebranche becomes marked. Nature, he says, if regarded as something distinct from God, 'is a vain chimera, introduced by those heathens who had not just notions of the omnipresence and infinite perfection of God. . . . Fain would we suppose Him at a great distance off, and substitute some blind unthinking deputy in his stead'. Malebranche writes to the same effect and in similar language, 'Of the most dangerous errour in the philosophy of the ancients' (vi. 2. 3)—a passage which culminates in the daring statement, 'There is then but one true Cause, as there is one true God. Neither must we imagine that what precedes an effect does really produce it. God Himself cannot communicate his Power to creatures, according to the light of reason. He cannot make them true causes and change them into Gods. . . . Bodies, spirits, pure intelligences, all can do nothing . . . tis the author of our being that performs our desires. Semel jussit: semper paret. He moves even our arms when we use them against his orders. . . . All those little divinities of the heathens, all those particular causes of philosophers are chimeras.'

No wonder that Berkeley when he reached Paris wanted to go and see the man who could write like this. For Berkeley's theism is inseparable from his ideism, as concave from convex. He expounds it simply and unsystematically throughout the *Principles pari passu* with his doctrine of ideas. Apart from the Active Principle 'in whom we live and move and have our being', his world of idea-things is scarcely intelligible. But it is a mistake to approach Berkeleianism with preconceptions of deity. The system is difficult, if we come to it, thinking we know already what God is. Berkeley in effect teaches what God is rather than what ideas are. Deity, as seen by Berkeley, has to be always everywhere, always supporting the idea-things, controlling their changes, discovering them to finite spirits, and that not in the manner of a scene-shifter or conjurer, but like an Immense Power, silent and pervasive as attraction, conscious as the human will, intelligent as reason, wise as law, strong as love, good as Christ. Was there a Deity in the philosophies known to Berkeley, outside the pages of Malebranche, conceived on that grand scale?

There follows the inevitable question—*How* can such a Being be known by brief man? Berkeley does not shirk that question. He describes in outline in § 146 *how* God is known. In §§ 147–9 he classifies the knowing of God and compares it with other knowledges. From § 150 onwards he explains the difficulties men have in accepting it. The ease, the subtlety and the fire of this exposition are remarkable. This is the climax to the epistemological section of the *Principles*, begun in §86. Of the four types of knowing, correspondent to the four objects of knowledge, he takes the knowing of God *last*, not as most obscure but as most comprehensive. We saw above that knowledge of other spirits is a synthesis of knowledge of ideas and self-knowledge. The same seems to be true on a wider scale of man's knowledge of God. Ideas and self and finite spirits enter into it. We advance from knowing idea-things to self-knowledge, thence to knowledge of other selves, thence 'after the same manner' (§ 148) we reach the knowledge of the Boundless Spirit.

The concluding paragraphs of the *Principles* do not always receive from readers adequate attention. Berkeley attached great weight to them and devoted care to their composition. Perhaps their piety and homiletic undertone make them seem alien to metaphysics. Yet they enshrine the purpose of the book. Berkeleianism is a philosophy of God, not of mind alone. Berkeleianism is a religious philosophy, as Berkeley's was a philosopher's religion. His published writings, his correspondence, his private note-books, his public and private life all prove his absolute genuineness and unswerving conviction. From his early days in Trinity College to his closing days at Oxford his opinion never varied as to 'what deserves the first place in our studies . . which to promote . . was the main drift and design' of his labours (§ 156).

Any one trying to describe how God is known and to relate that knowing to other knowings is faced with a great difficulty. He is trying to express that which, in our

thoughts, is most luminous and most obscure. He is trying
to combine the deep of inherited feelings with the surface
of individual experience. Consequently the reasons he
gives are not adequate to the reasons he feels. Our knowledge of God is a clear dictate of reason shadowed by a complex of obscure feelings. We may detect in it the feeling
of the part for the whole, of the branch for the stem, of the
marching soldier for his battalion, of the man for his
country, of the son for his father. Those intermittent, blind,
inarticulate feelings blend with the rational Attributes, and
the resulting apprehension may become at times as clear as
daylight, as cogent as a *Barbara* syllogism.

Berkeley faces the inherent difficulty of his task. For
him, our knowledge of God is like sense-perception in its
cogency, like self-knowledge in its intimacy, like knowledge of other minds in the conscious reasoning involved.
As portrayed in § 146, the knowledge of God partakes of
three elements. First, there is the intelligent study of idea-
things, 'which are called the Works of Nature', with the
unavoidable inference to some Spirit other than man.
Second, there is the attentive consideration of certain qualities of value in the things, viz. order, greatness, beauty,
purpose, laws of pain and pleasure, and animal instinct.
Third, there is attention to the meaning and import of the
Attributes, as they appear in rational theology.

Having thus recognized in it reason and feeling, intelligence and instinct, Berkeley passes on to characterize this
type of knowledge. At the outset we find a difficulty which
is perhaps also an inconsistency. The opening sentence of
§ 147 appears to state that God is known certainly and immediately, but the statement is qualified almost to the point
of withdrawal by the addition of the words, 'as any other
mind or spirit distinct from ourselves'. Berkeley has just
said (§ 145) that our knowledge of other spirits is not

immediate. Having compared our knowledge of God to mediate knowledge, he virtually states that it is immediate. Berkeley has not blundered or changed his mind; for the same difficulty meets us in the *Hylas* and the *Alciphron* dialogues. 'We have at least as clear, full, and immediate certainty [of God] . . . as of any one human soul whatsoever besides our own' (*Alc.* iv. 5). In the second *Hylas* dialogue (*Works*, p. 424) Philonous 'immediately and necessarily' concludes the being of a God; in the third *Hylas* dialogue (*Works*, p. 448) Philonous 'has a notion of Him, or knows Him by reflexion and reasoning'—a process which lower down is explained as 'collect it by reasoning from that which you know immediately'. Perhaps to some extent Berkeley is being swayed by the opposing influences of his primary authorities. For Locke, knowledge of God is a much mediated demonstrative knowledge. For Malebranche it is the clearest type of immediate knowledge. More probably Berkeley is simply putting common sense before technical accuracy. The technical distinction between immediate and mediate is a good servant but a bad master. When dealing with a process like knowing, especially the knowing of an Immense Object, where no clean cut between knowledge of His existence and knowledge of His nature is practicable, a man of Berkeley's stamp, hating jargon, loving fact, will not oppose too strictly mediacy and immediacy. Our knowledge of God, in fact, is immediate, in that we are in God and that immediate facts not representative ideas are the ground of our assurance. Our knowledge of God, in fact, is mediate, because we are not God but men; reflexion on our part is required and we must 'open the eye of the mind' (§ 154). All said and done, it is possible for us to neglect or to refuse to know God. So our awareness of Him cannot be altogether direct.[1]

[1] Professor Jessop suggests to me that the vacillation between

God is immense and omnipresent and all encompassing,[1] for Berkeley, and therefore in one sense we must have immediate contact with Him. The resemblance of this part of Berkeley's theology to that of Malebranche is too close to be accidental. In each of Berkeley's major works, as soon as he has outlined his own conception of Deity his thoughts pass to that of Malebranche (*Prin.* §§ 147–8; *Hyl.*, *Works*, pp. 424–6; *Alc.* iv. 14). Nor is the debt other than emphasized by the pains Berkeley takes to underline the points of disagreement. Berkeley is, perhaps, not unwilling that the disagreement should seem greater than it really is. From § 148 we can see that there are three things in Malebranche's theology to which Berkeley takes exception: (1) It leaves the door open to a materialist interpretation of the term 'seeing'. Even philosophers were saying 'Jupiter est quodcumque *vides*'. (2) The representative ideas supposed to be seen by us. (3) A literal union of man's mind with the substance or essence of God. When he has shown his disagreement on these points, he proceeds to show his agreement on others. Having denied what Malebranche affirmed, that 'we see God by a direct and immediate view', he goes on at once to admit, with reservations, that we see a man, and to conclude that 'after the same manner we see God'. In the next section (149) Berkeley, for all his disclaimers,[2] throws himself almost into the arms of Malebranche, using two of the other's characteristic phrases, 'intimately present', 'absolute and entire dependence', and quoting the text with which Malebranche

mediacy and immediacy represents the passage from unreflective knowledge to demonstrative justification of that knowledge.

[1] Also omniscient; but never omnisentient. The term 'omnipercipient' might be allowed, subject to the proviso, 'God . . . perceives nothing by sense'. *Hylas*, p. 459.

[2] *v.* Rand, op. cit., p. 89.

closes his famous chapter (iii. 2. 6) and which Berkeley quotes elsewhere in connexion with Malebranche's doctrine (*Hylas*, *Works*, p. 427; *Alciphron*, iv. 14)—'In Him we live and move and have our being'.

The *esse percipi* is unintelligible apart from 'the intimate presence of an All-wise Spirit who fashions, regulates and sustains the whole system of Being' (§ 151). The *esse percipere* is an idle boast, if divorced from the truth 'that He is present and conscious to our innermost thoughts; and that we have a most absolute and immediate dependence on Him' (§155). For Berkeley, then, in knowing God, we know Something not ourselves, a conscious encompassing Spirit all good and wise. From the nature of the case, every sort of representative entity, except signs, is excluded; therefore that knowing is, to all intents and purposes, immediate. Thus Berkeley's world is seen in God. His idea-things are stable by God's law, regulated by God's ordering Will, luminous in His light. As a twentieth-century thinker can only with difficulty prevent himself from seeing all things in evolution, so Berkeley when he had read Malebranche could scarcely help seeing all things in God.

The Vision of all things in God is the alpha and omega of the *Principles*. Berkeley never attempts to interpret material things by our powers of perception. Not *our* thinking makes them so. Neither does he rise by inference or analogy from our thoughts to God's thoughts. Rather he puts himself into the scheme of things and finds God there. Nor does he lose himself in so doing. He never forgets that he is a free though finite centre of real activity. He takes the facts of life as they come, reading in the facts what many people in thoughtful moments read there but cannot express, namely the Mind and Will of the Creator who 'can indifferently produce everything by a mere *fiat* or act of His Will', not less because He 'produces in our mind all that variety of ideas or sensations which continually affect us'.

Berkeley's ideism is theological realism. Its basis is not strictly mind but deity, and though he often speaks of God as Mind, in the last resort he considers God and the human mind as distinct as are the One Infinite Spirit and the many finite spirits. The New Principle of seeing all things in God without matter or representative idea derives in the main from Malebranche's *Search*. That was the derivation assigned to it by the leaders of English thought in his day, Clarke and Whiston, who read the *Principles* in 1710 a few months after it appeared.[1] Fifteen years later (July 24, 1725) Bolingbroke writing to Swift speaks of that derivation casually, as if it were admitted matter of fact, lamenting that he will lose the opportunity of meeting Berkeley, 'a man who can espouse in good earnest the system of Father Malebranche'.[2]

[1] Rand, op. cit., pp. 87, 89.
[2] A considered judgement. Bolingbroke knew both systems well, and brackets them in his *Philosophical Works*, ed. 1754, vol. i. p. 16 and vol. ii. p. 141.

VII

ABSTRACT IDEAS

BERKELEY'S doctrine of abstraction, through Hume's appreciation of it, made his philosophy famous at a time when his immaterialism was ignored. To-day the estimation is reversed. His immaterialism is admired, if at a distance; on all hands his doctrine of abstract ideas is cried down. Accordingly a somewhat full treatment of its origin and objective seems called for. The doctrine is primarily a weapon of destruction, an answer to objections; so its use is of more importance than its origin, and I shall not stress the influence of Malebranche. But for the sake of completeness I have stated the evidence for the connexion (below, pp. 143–7). Berkeley was a pioneer on this point. Hume at any rate took him to be such. It seems unlikely that he would strike out on a new line without suggestion and support. Berkeley was intrepid and original. Percival records of him that he said, 'I know not what it is to fear'.[1] But even so he might think twice before pitting himself against Locke on a subject of supreme consequence to both. Berkeley of course *had* to attack abstract ideas. It is no good telling folk that matter does not exist, unless at the same time you make it clear to them why they are inveterately disposed to think matter does exist. Collier taught immaterialism about the same time, but he did not attack abstraction. So he died and Berkeley lived.

The entire Introduction to the *Principles* is devoted to the theme. The Introduction as originally planned was more ambitious[2] but could hardly have been more effective.

[1] In the *Egmont Papers*, vol. ci, I found the note, indexed under *Dean Berkeley*, 'I know not what it is to fear, said Mr. Berkeley, but I have a delicate sense of danger': see *Hermathena*, vol. xxiii, p. 28. [2] *v. C.P.B.* 220; cf. 516, 592, 696, &c.

'To say no more, it is an abstract idea' (§ 13). There is his all-inclusive answer to objections. Matter is the abstract idea in chief; but there are others. Extension, time, motion, unity, happiness, power, will, identity, all these *qua* abstractions fall before Berkeley's razor. Berkeley may not at first have realized the full positive consequences of his denial of abstract ideas, but he knew that he was attacking roundabout methods of thinking, which issue in scepticism, and was defending direct awareness and true contact with reality.

What doctrine of abstraction was Berkeley attacking? The question has been raised. Berkeley leaves us in no doubt. He is attacking every doctrine of abstraction, except that which contents itself with stating that we can and do consider separately *separable* parts. He summarizes his views in § 10 of the Introduction to the *Principles*, and there specifies as the 'Two proper acceptations of abstraction' (i.e. of the false abstraction which he denies): (1) conceiving separately *inseparable* parts or qualities, (2) framing a general notion by abstracting from particulars in the manner aforesaid. It is interesting to note that this summary from 'To be plain' was added in the table of *Errata*, 1st edition.[1] This fact does not mean that the addition was substantially an afterthought, which was clearly not the case, but it may indicate a certain degree of haste in the composition. I do not think that this expression of his views is as well considered as the succinct description of the 'twofold abstraction' in *Principles*, § 99. In this latter

---

[1] It fully covers, I think, the ground of the addition to § 16, 1734 ed., which Professor Laird calls 'a dubiously consistent addition', and regards as 'throwing up the sponge' (*Hume's Philosophy*, pp. 56–8). If Berkeley was inconsistent on the point, he was inconsistent in 1710 and time brought no change of front. *v. infra*, p. 156.

passage we find, in place of two propositions separately
denied, one denial of a twofold abstraction. This distinction, though a fine one, considerably eases a difficulty in
Berkeley's doctrine. As regards the false abstraction in the
second acceptation (No. 2 above), there is neither ambiguity nor inconsistency. Berkeley always explicitly denied
a general notion framed by abstraction. The difficulty concerns the other acceptation (No. 1 above). It is extremely
difficult in certain cases to draw the line between the 'conceiving separately *inseparable* parts' which Berkeley denies,
and the 'considering separately *separable* parts' which he
affirms. I can concentrate my attention on an inseparable
part nearly as easily as I can on a separable part. To take
Berkeley's instances, it is easy to consider head and body
separately; but what are we to say of his stock instance
of inseparables, motion and the body moving? Since the
body may come to rest, it seems a hard saying that we
cannot conceive separately it and its motion. True, I cannot conceive that while it is moving it is not moving. But
that is another matter. Surely a particular motion may be
singled[1] from a particular extension, and vice versa. Consequently, with diffidence I suggest that the addition to the
table of *errata* in § 10 of the Introduction should be interpreted in the light of other passages, as e.g. § 99 of the
Principles. When Berkeley denies that we can conceive
separately and denies that we can frame, these are not perhaps two distinct denials. He may be denying that we can
conceive separately inseparable parts *in the supposed process*
of framing an abstract idea. That at any rate is the real
substance of his double denial. For the admission that it
is psychologically possible to conceive separately a moving
body and its motion, or an extension and its colour, would
not, I think, carry with it any admission of the framed

[1] i.e. be the focus of attention. Berkeley is fond of the term.

abstract idea of motion in general, or of the 'entity of extension' (*Prin.* § 99).

What historical system of abstraction was Berkeley attacking? He was, in the main, attacking the Lockian system. But this was no personal attack; for in the Introduction (§§ 17, 21) he throws a glance over the history of the subject, in so far as he knew it, and briefly considers the 'ablest patrons' of abstract ideas, from Aristotle to Locke. In the draft introduction he calls Aristotle 'a great admirer and promoter of the doctrine of abstraction', and to prove it, he quotes in Greek from the *Metaphysics* (*Works*, vol. iii, p. 368). He excuses himself from the task of tracing the doctrine through 'the Schoolmen, those great masters of abstraction', concluding that of all false principles 'none hath a more wide influence over the thoughts of speculative men' (*Int.*, § 17).

So the attack on Locke is an attack on Locke in a representative capacity. 'A faulty and unskilful abstraction', Bacon taught,[1] is one of the idols of the market-place, and Locke's doctrine therefore, Berkeley came to think, was more than a blemish in his system; it was a relapse into 'idolatry', an original sin of human thought. Berkeley concentrated his fire upon Locke as the latest exponent of an old error. His formal statement of the doctrine (*Int.*, § 7), prefaced by 'we are told', is based upon the two passages in the *Essay* where Locke states the doctrine '*ex professo*'.[2] These passages are bk. ii. 11. 9 and bk. iii. 3. 6. The abstract idea of colour is Locke's illustration in the former passage, and that of man and animal in the latter. Berkeley uses both illustrations, repeating Locke's words 'body, life, sense, and spontaneous motion'. Berkeley quotes several

[1] Berkeley knew the passage, *v*. *C.P.B.* 569, reading *Bacon* for *Barrow*, and *Nov. Org.*, bk. i, Aph. 59–60.

[2] Locke's own term, *v*. Note A, bk. ii. 23.

long passages on the subject from the *Essay* in his Introduction, and makes several references thereto in the
Commonplace Book.

But did Berkeley mistake his target? Did Locke actually
hold the view that Berkeley attacked as his? Berkeley in
his lifetime was charged with misrepresenting Locke's
doctrine of abstract ideas, and the charge has been recently
repeated.[1]

Locke's doctrine of abstraction is undoubtedly complex,
developing as he wrote. But that consideration, though it
lends colour to the charge against Berkeley, is really beside
the point. For certain parts of Locke's doctrine of abstraction, as e.g. the singling of separable parts, Berkeley
accepted and made his own. The issue really is: Does the
doctrine of the fourth book, in particular the passage about
the abstract general triangle (c. 7), the exposure of which
Berkeley styled his 'killing blow' (*C.P.B.* 699), represent

---

[1] In *Geometry no friend to Infidelity*, 1734, by Philalethes
(Jurin), pp. 71 sqq. and by Professor Aaron, *Locke's Theory of
Universals*, Arist. Soc., 1933. In addition to using the argument
answered above, Dr. Aaron, like Philalethes, argues that Berkeley
puts a misconstruction upon Locke's words 'some parts of several
different and inconsistent ideas are put together'. I doubt if
Dr. Aaron's two arguments are on all fours. For he wants to
defend Locke's statement, at the same time pleading that it is
not typical of Locke's teaching. His point here is that Locke
means 'consistent parts of inconsistent ideas', whereas Berkeley
makes him mean 'inconsistent parts of inconsistent ideas', and
thereby depicts the triangle as 'made up of manifest staring
contradictions' (*T.V.* § 125). I do not think that Dr. Aaron's case,
though ably pleaded, is made out. Locke seems to have meant
by the words what Berkeley said he meant. For if the abstract
triangle were made up of judiciously selected consistent parts,
what is the point of the passage? Locke's whole point here is
that the abstract idea is a mass of inconsistencies, and is therefore
difficult to frame, imperfect and non-existent. If in saying so, he
gives his case away, it is Berkeley's right and duty to point it out.

Locke's considered views? The reader will be able to judge
for himself, after reading the sketch of the doctrines of
Locke and Berkeley which I give below. Here I will only
say that there is no indication that any part of Locke's complex doctrine escaped Berkeley's notice. Berkeley was a
fighting Irishman, and when he saw a head to hit he hit it.
The triangle argument was his 'killing blow', but he had
given plenty of other shrewd blows before administering
that *coup de grâce*. It is sheer paradox to say that Locke did
not hold the doctrine. Berkeley takes it from the *Essay* in
Locke's own words. Locke did say that the 'absurd triangle'
must be 'all and none of these at once', and he meant it. So
far from the 'triangle' passage being an aside, it appears to
represent the culmination of Locke's thought on the subject.
For in the fourth book he has reached the conception of
mathematics as the true type of knowledge, and the contemplation of abstract ideas as the main method of advancing
knowledge. He would naturally therefore look for an illustration of his doctrine in the field of pure quantity. Surely
then, a mode of extension such as the abstract general triangle,
would be for Locke, the abstract general idea *par excellence*.[1]

The *Analyst* controversy called forth from Berkeley in
1735 an admirably lucid commentary upon his own attack
on abstraction and his relation to Locke.[2] At times he
speaks with some heat. It was natural that he should do so,
for Philalethes was, in effect, attempting to 'save Locke's
face' at the expense of Berkeley's judgement and candour.
Philalethes had said in effect, 'this account of a general
triangle was a trap which Mr. Locke set to catch fools'.
Berkeley in reply gives a patient exposition of Locke's
teaching, and then sums up in the words, 'This doctrine
of abstract general ideas seemed to me a capital error,

[1] *v.* e.g. *Essay*, iv. 12. 12–15.
[2] *Defence of Free-thinking in Mathematics*, §§ 45–8.

productive of numberless difficulties and disputes, that runs not only throughout Mr. Locke's book, but through most parts of learning. Consequently, my animadversions thereupon were not an effect of being inclined to carp or cavil at a single passage, as you would wrongfully insinuate, but proceeded from a love of truth. . . .'[1]

Locke on Abstract Ideas

The chief passages are Book ii. 11. 9 and Book iii. 3. 6–9 and Book iv. 6 and 7, and 12. 7–15. The above passages in Books ii and iii are stated by Locke to be his official or *ex professo* expositions. They are mainly psychological accounts of the process of abstracting, while the fourth book carries the doctrine out to its epistemological consequences. There are many incidental references to and sidelights upon the doctrine in these books, and, remembering that Book i (cc. 2. 14 and 4. 24) on 'Innate Ideas' finds the solution of its main problem in the faculty of abstraction, we see that Berkeley's statement that the doctrine runs through the whole *Essay* is correct.

Locke's abstract idea vacillates between subjective and objective, between function and product. At its first occurrence (i. 2. 15) the term is 'abstracting', the process, one of the steps by which the mind attains truth. In the note on ii. 2, when Stillingfleet advances 'substance' as a rational concept not derived from sense or reflection, Locke counters with 'the abstraction of the mind', which from ideas of sense and reflection derives the obscure vague idea of substance. In the first of the two official accounts, abstracting is simply one of the given functions or operations of the mind, like comparing, compounding, and naming. It arises in fact out of naming. There are not enough names

---

[1] Browne (*Procedure* p. 187) and Bolingbroke (op. cit. vol. i. p. 114) treat Locke's triangle as a typical passage.

to go round, and so the mind makes particular ideas to become general. The process of generalizing is called 'abstraction'. There is no substantial difference between the two official accounts. The first is the fuller as to the psychological process; the second shows in greater detail the function of the abstraction in making sorts and species. The term 'appearance' for idea occurs in the first and is dropped in the second. The second introduces the doubtful term 'framing'. In both accounts the essence of abstraction is the notion of separating. The abstract idea is a separated mental appearance; it is separated from the *here* and the *now*, and from other ideas that in actuality are connected with it. These 'precise, naked appearances' are thus fitted for generality. They are named, and laid up in the mind 'as the standards to rank real existences into sorts'. 'Thus universals, whether ideas or terms are made.' Thus far the abstract idea represents a return to the pure *datum*, and the agency of the mind is conceived as entirely selective. In the course of the *Essay* this simple and fairly innocent notion of abstraction takes on far-reaching developments. As the work proceeds, the abstract idea becomes more and more concrete. Even in Book ii (c. 32, 7–8) the abstract idea is 'something in the mind, between the thing that exists, and the name that is given to it'. It must have a 'double conformity', to thing and to name; otherwise there will be neither valid thought nor intelligible speech. In Book iii the subsistence of the abstract idea becomes more marked. In the second *ex professo* passage the term 'framing' is used, but Locke is careful to point out that the framing results in 'nothing new'. If abstract ideas are *framed*, they are framed as a postage stamp by perforation, or as a field by a sunken fence. This is framing by diminution, and Locke repeatedly uses the term 'partial' as equivalent to abstract, and against Stillingfleet (Note A on bk. ii,

c. 23) he insists that 'abstracting and enlarging' differs from 'complication of ideas'. However, a framing is a making. Locke has to relate the abstract idea to the word in Book iii, and to assign its place in Knowledge in Book iv. So naturally the idea takes shape and substance, and the mind's contribution becomes more positive as the *Essay* advances. In one passage, indeed, Locke speaks as if he were conscious of the development. He writes (bk. iii. 5. 16) of 'an argument that appears to me new, and a little out of the way (I am sure it is one I thought not of when I began to write)'. The reference is not quite certain. But since the term 'nominal Essence' comes into use in Book iii for abstract idea, and he speaks here of 'the pudder made about essences', it seems probable that he had grown convinced as he worked at the problem of abstraction, that the abstract idea was an entity, an essence actually made by the mind, mistaken by scholasticism for real essence, and restored to its true status by his slow-motion picture of the mental process.

Locke, no doubt, began to realize that abstraction raises in an acute form the problems of universality and of the one and the many. Abstracting then, for him, is no longer one among several activities of the mind, but takes a place apart. It has a distinctive value; for brutes abstract not, and the faculty puts a perfect difference between them and us. The abstract idea becomes the goal of clear reasoning and the *sine qua non* of intelligible discourse. The original notion of separating what is already there becomes that of framing or constructing what was not there. Abstract ideas are 'fictions and contrivances'; they are 'put together', and with great difficulty. If the abstract idea were simply the sense *datum* isolated, abstraction would be easy for children and possible for animals; for they attend to the sheer *datum* and owe little or nothing to memory, imagination, and suggestion. The stress laid upon the *difficulty* in Book iv, c. 7 is a symptom of the development of the 'precise naked appearances' into 'fictions and contrivances of the mind'.

The study of words as signs in Book iii gives Locke occasion for his closest examination of the abstract idea, and the term there is usually followed by 'to which the name is attached' or similar phrase. The name would be of little use, Locke thinks, without the abstract idea. It would be a sign signifying nothing. When Adam said 'niouph', Eve might think 'kinneah', and both be wide of the mark as regards Lamech's trouble (bk. iii. 6. 44). The sign is arbitrary in that there is no resemblance between it and its meaning, but it may not be capricious; for caprice in the use of significant words is the death of knowledge. By receiving a name the abstract idea attains its full status and becomes the nominal essence (bk. iii, c. 6) which in substances is distinct from the real essence, and yet is of tremendous significance for human knowledge. Thus in Locke's system an *appearance* has flowered into an *essence*. Ultimately the paradox springs from the attempt to combine the fact of generality in a representationist system with the traditional principle that all existents are particulars, a principle which is set as a headline in both of Locke's *ex professo* accounts of abstraction.

The theory of universals now (bk. iii) passes into a theory of species. It had generally been held that species and genera were made by nature, and that 'general natures', otherwise called 'substantial forms', constituted the kind after which things were created; and that in apprehending the 'general nature' the mind finds its satisfaction. Locke is not concerned to deny that there is a general nature in the sense of *real* essence; only he suspects that it is not the mysterious entity written up by the scholastics. We cannot know it in the case of substances, but it probably consists in the arrangement of minute material parts. For us the nominal essence is all-important. This is what makes the sorts. This is what we *know* when we have general knowledge. By its aid we 'shorten our way to knowledge' (bk. ii. 32. 6), and learn to think correctly and talk intelligibly. The denomination *per se* will not make the unlike like. Locke expressly recognizes objective similitude (*passim*, especially bk. iii. 3. 13). Natural things are made alike. Organisms are the most obvious instances. It is, however, also evident in the cases of artificial things like watches, and of mixed modes like covetousness that the making and naming of the sort is the workmanship of the mind. Nature, Locke holds, did not make the abstract idea of man, and in the cases of monsters and changelings, &c., *real* essence fails us. The real essence of rain, snow, and water may be the same, but the nominal essence or abstract idea of each is different, and Locke draws the corollary that there is a distinct sort for every named abstract idea. The abstract idea is what the sortal name stands for, the hypostatization of the standard notion, the boundary of the man-made species.

The controversy with Stillingfleet brought out some other points (Note on bk. iii, c. 3). Stillingfleet said that the abstract idea was the work of the mind, but not the creature of the mind, and that though there be only one individual in the sort, e.g. the sun, yet there is a real essence, which if there were more suns would still constitute them. Locke replies that abstract general essences have no being outside the understanding, that we know not the real essence of the sun, and that the only essence of the sun he talks about is the nominal. Stillingfleet sees that the nature of knowing is involved, as well as its objects, and maintains that 'the general idea is not made from the simple ideas by the mere act of the mind, but from reason and consideration of the nature of things'. Locke's reply is that reason and consideration are acts of the mind, mere acts of the mind. Conceding that there is an 'internal constitution of things on which their properties depend', he argues that if we wait till we know it, we shall have to wait a long time without species and sorts. Our thinking cannot alter the nature of things, but it can and does alter the meaning of their names, i.e. make or remake the boundaries of the species. God makes the real essence, man the nominal. To Stillingfleet's contention that real essences are immutable, Locke rejoins that that holds solely of the essence of God Himself. His creatures are in essence mutable. What is grass to-day may be sheep to-morrow and man the day after, the nominal essence of grass remaining unchanged.

An important distinction is then made between substances on the one hand and simple ideas and modes on the other (bk. iii. 3. 18. and 5. 14). In the case of substances real and nominal essences always differ. In the case of simple ideas and modes they are identical. The distinction has consequences for his theory of knowledge. I know or can come to know what men call a gold ring; but I can never know the real nature of this gold ring. On the other hand, the definition of a triangle is the essential being from which all its properties flow. It is both nominal and real essence. It is the abstract idea of the triangle. So the general knowledge of substances attainable was for Locke very limited; whereas mathematics seemed to offer the true type of method and the sure prospect of certain knowledge. This teaching, in physics, put conventional rules in place of scientific law. Indeed what Locke says about antimony, sulphur, and vitriol shows the deplorable state of chemistry at that time. That two sorts of sulphur may show qualities very different is accepted by him as simple fact, not as an urgent problem. The true method of advancing knowledge is, Locke holds, to consider our abstract ideas, and 'by what steps we are to proceed is to be learned in the schools of the mathematicians' (bk. iv. 12. 7). He goes so far as to state that all general knowledge 'consists barely in the contemplation of our own abstract ideas'. For instance, our working knowledge of man is based upon an idea of a shaped body with powers of sense, voluntary movement, and reason. This is the abstract idea of man and the essence of our species. All universal knowledge of man is the perception of the agreement or disagreement of another abstract idea with this. But we do not know the real essence of man, and so cannot affirm, for instance, that all men sleep by intervals, but simply that these men do so. Opinions and judgements we may have through 'hints well laid together'. But 'this is but guessing still'. We must glean by particular experiments and may thus gather a little knowledge of quinine, the compass, &c.; but it is idle to attempt to know 'general natures' and to 'grasp at knowledge by sheaves and bundles'. We never can know the minute changes in material substances, nor how they affect our senses and produce secondary sensations. Natural philosophy then cannot *know* for certain; and so Locke comes back to mathematics with its clear abstract ideas of triangles, angles, &c., and its art of finding out intermediate ideas as the true type of epistemological method. Locke's sceptical tendencies and his doctrine of abstraction were closely knit, and in attacking his doctrine of abstract ideas Berkeley was raising a fundamental issue.

The Commonplace Book and Abstract Ideas

Berkeley was trained[1] in the Lockian system. In his early college days he took the faculty of abstracting as a matter of course, was rather proud of it, and regarded the

---

[1] Not uncritically. Provost (afterwards Bishop) Browne took an independent line as regards the *Essay*, see above, p. 74 *n*.

abstract idea as the fine flower of intellect. This was one
of the few principles firmly held at the start of the *Commonplace Book* and discarded before the end. In fact the rejection of the abstract idea is one of the chief results of Berkeley's 'wonder year' (1707–8).

In his earlier writings he had spoken contemptuously of
'specierum supellectilem' (*Arithm.*, pt. 2, c. 5), and of
'lapidific virtue' (*Dunmore Cave* Essay), but all adherents
of the New Learning had, since Bacon wrote, broken with
that type of jargon. Half of the *Commonplace Book* is
written before Berkeley comes fairly in sight of the problem
created or reshaped by Locke's *Essay*. The first entry on
the subject is '*Qu.* Is it not impossible there shou'd be
General ideas?' (329, corrected reading). The implied
answer is 'Yes', and the next entry gives the reason, namely,
that all ideas are particular. The line between General
ideas and Abstract ideas is fine, but here, I think, we must
draw it. For in the first note-book abstraction is scarcely
mentioned and was not originally discussed, and the for-
mulation of the Principle at its close (904–24) gives no
hint of the doctrine. The editions might give the contrary impression, but the references to abstraction in 53,
113, and 385 occur on the verso, and are therefore late;
while 'abstractible' ideas in 55 (we owe the reading to
Professor Aaron) is a later insertion (N.B. 'or both'). In
141 'abstracting' merely equals 'singling'. 'No idea of
circle, &c., in abstract' (247) may be an anticipation of his
later doctrine; but I doubt if there is much conscious
thought about abstraction behind it. The entry concerns
the problem of the infinite divisibility. The fact is that
during the first part of the work Berkeley's interest in ideas
was confined to simple and complex ideas. Not till that
problem sank (it is scarcely mentioned in the publications,
and the *C.P.B.* entries are almost all marked with the

obelus, *v*. Appendix, pp. 186–8), did the problem of abstraction rise.

Berkeley wrote in the draft Introduction that there was a time when he did not doubt in the least that he had the faculty of abstracting.[1] To that period we may assign the first note-book. His doubts seem to have come gradually and to have begun with the problem of General ideas, which with a sweep are denied in the second entry of the second note-book (397). In his publications he rejects abstract ideas and accepts general ideas. It was the other way about during the transition period. Setting aside the reconsidered or correcting statements on the verso, the first clear statement about abstraction is 437. Here his horizon is limited to extension, but as far as that instance goes, his doctrine is complete; for he not only denies the abstract idea, but in the words 'as any one may try' he expresses his ultimate court of appeal in the finished argument. He then in the next twenty pages concerns himself successively with abstract ideas of colours, tastes, sounds, substances, and existence. Here he uses the term 'abstract' quite neutrally, as we may suppose Locke did at first. Abstract means 'separated'. He speaks of abstract simple ideas (498). He asserts that all abstract ideas are particular, and distinguishes abstraction of an idea from another of a different kind, and abstraction of an idea from all particulars of the same kind (499). At the same time he follows up the denial of general ideas. He seems to have reached this conclusion first in the case of figure. In 247 he had denied the circle in abstract, and now in 485 he denies general figure and in 515 general body. About this time the breach with Locke widens. In 496 he raises an important new question, prefacing it with *Qu.*, 'how can all words be said to stand for ideas?' A short time before (371 = 418) it had been to him

[1] *Works*, vol. iii, p. 361.

an axiom that no word is to be used without an idea. This principle is used by Berkeley in his essay *Of Infinites*,[1] and he owes it no doubt to Locke's repeated advice to lay aside the word, or at least to keep the word as a fixed sign of a definite idea. This principle had led Berkeley into elaborate speculations and indeed into an experiment about the solitary man,[2]—a case designed to do for words and ideas what the Molyneux problem had attempted for sight and touch. In the sketch demonstration of the Principle the same axiom (904) 'All significant words stand for ideas' stands first on the list of premises from which the New Principle is deduced. Yet before long we shall find it classed by Berkeley as a chief cause of the false doctrine of abstraction.

About the same time (541, 566) Berkeley turned his attention to essences and sorts. He writes that the distinction between real and nominal essence is fruitless. If a general idea be the unknown real essence, it is an unknown idea, a nothing. If it be the nominal essence, a man-made thing, clear as crystal, open to all to discuss and compare with personal experience, then call it 'denomination', but drop the obscurantist, scholastic term 'essence', Berkeley would say, for its label 'nominal' does not remove the tang of its cask.

The climax of the debate is reached in the notable series (566–72), entries which fixed, I believe, for life Berkeley's thought and to some extent his terminology. Here he selects his foe and decides his objective. He will oppose not general ideas, but abstract ideas, and the abstraction specified is that of Locke's *fourth* book, not as differing from the earlier books, but as carrying their teaching to the

[1] *Works*, vol. iii, p. 410.
[2] *C.P.B.* 571, 594, 598, 613, 657, 739 and Dft. *Int.* in *Works*, vol. iii, pp. 379–80; cf. *Hylas, Works*, vol. i, p. 467.

natural and logical outcome. Sharply distinguishing genera and species (the sorts) from abstract general ideas, he rejects the latter as including a contradiction in their nature, and he refers to the *Essay* (bk. iv. 7. 9 which is the famous passage about the abstract or general triangle). Berkeley tries to form the idea of the triangle according to Locke's recipe. He fails. He notes that Locke himself describes it as 'something imperfect that cannot exist'. If it cannot exist, it cannot, for Berkeley, be thought of. It is indeed 'made up of manifest staring contradictions' (*T.V.* § 125). The general idea had been to Berkeley the cause of confusion in mathematics. He sees now that it is a psychological absurdity, and the cause of Locke's sceptical tendencies. That which for Locke is the magnet of our thoughts, the currency of communication, the impulse of progress, is proved hollow, unreal, self-contradictory. From this point Berkeley never looked back. The impression made on him by this passage is well evidenced. This is 'the killing blow' (699), and the index letter in the margin 'I *etc*' is unique. Berkeley acted upon the 'etc'. The Lockian triangle figures largely in the *Theory of Vision* (§ 125) and in the Introduction (§ 13) to the *Principles*; a distant allusion to it occurs in the *Hylas* (*Works*, vol. i, pp. 403–4). Express references to it are in the *Alciphron*, Dial. vii, § 5, 1st ed., and in the *Defence of Free-Thinking in Math.* § 45, and a clear allusion in *Siris*, § 323.

The remainder of the *Commonplace Book* shows several of the consequences of this decisive change of view. Berkeley now takes a non-Lockian view of demonstration (592; cf. 220), which soon passes into a depreciation of demonstration.[1] He devotes attention to the doctrine of words (650–1, 668, 671, &c.). He has to seek other differentiae between man and beast (600) in lieu of Locke's 'perfect

[1] 870; cf. *Prin.*, § 107 'I do not say demonstrate'.

distinction'. The analysis of substance is made (712–13, 736–7), in which Locke is bracketed with the Schoolmen. Berkeley's razor is applied not only to extension, figures, motion, existence, substance, but to psychological entities like will and understanding; also to the scientific object, substantial forms, plastic virtue, Hylarchic Principle, and even to 'eternal and immutable' morality. He razes *judicium intellectus, indifferentia*, uneasiness; the *Aeternae Veritates* vanish (748), and the very faculty 'pure intellect', long supposed to deal with abstract ideas, is suspect, its occupation apparently gone (822).

Malebranche on Abstract Ideas

The evidence connecting Malebranche and Berkeley on this subject falls short of proof. We know that Berkeley examined Malebranche's teaching on the kindred subject of the 'sorts' (*C.P.B.* 296). And he repeatedly speaks as one familiar with the whole of Malebranche's system. He could hardly fail to see and ponder Malebranche's forceful attack on abstraction, at the time he was confronting his Goliath[1] and was in need of an ally.

The decisive passages in the *Search* are iii. 2. 8 and 9, vi. 2. 2 and 3, and the Illustration (i.e. excursus) on iii. 2. 8. In these passages Malebranche repeatedly warns his readers against 'general and abstract ideas'. The first of these (iii. 2. 8) is of special interest, because it follows close upon the exposition of the theory of seeing all things in God, and because matter is the point at issue. Malebranche distinguishes nine attributes of matter. He takes five of them away because they are separable. He isolates three as secondary though inseparable, and thus by a *reductio ad unum* he is left with extension as the essence of matter. Why then, he asks, do people persistently hanker after

[1] Locke, *v. C.P.B.* 689.

something else in matter? There may be in it, he admits, some unknown super-extensional quality, and if the Church so decides he will withdraw his contention. But at this point he offers a reason why men seek an occult quality in matter against the weight of evidence. The reason is a queer one, and not very lucidly expressed. From two passages in the *Principles* (§§ 17, 74) we can see that Berkeley's attention was drawn to it. Berkeley studies in 'the most accurate philosophers' the meaning of material substance. He finds it to be 'the general idea of Being'; and, again, he shows that the last resource of the beaten materialist is 'I know not what abstracted and indefinite notions of being or occasion'. Now Malebranche in the above passage abstracted from matter hardness, softness, fluidness, motion, rest, figure, divisibility, and impenetrability, and found that extension is the sole remainder. In the minds corrupted by false abstraction, he holds, the clear idea of extension blends with the general idea of being that accompanies all our thoughts and produces a refusal to admit that there is nothing in matter but extension. It is a curious doctrine, because the general idea of being which, for Malebranche, is the source and almost the fabric of the disorderly abstractions, flows directly, he says, from the mind's union with God. In fact he comes near representing the general idea of being, as blending our 'idea' of God with our idea of limitless extension. We make a bad use, he says, of the best things. His position is that the inescapable general idea of being makes mere abstractions impose upon us, by giving them an appearance of reality. He instances act, power, cause, effect, substantial forms, faculties, occult qualities, &c. These by themselves excite no determinate ideas in the mind. We should see their hollowness at a glance, but for the background of being in general.

Malebranche does not reject all abstract ideas, any more than he rejects matter by sapping the evidence for matter. But it is quite possible that in both cases he put into Berkeley's hands the weapon he himself forged but used half-heartedly. From 'idols are useless' to 'idols are nothing' is no far cry. The young iconoclast after reading Malebranche, assisted by Leclerc's systematic manuals of the New Logic, could hardly avoid the question, 'Can I truly form an abstract general idea?' If Malebranche does not reject the abstract general, at least he tirelessly recommends the concrete particular. He writes, in this chapter, 'If the vulgar philosophers . . . would give those men leave to be quiet who affix to these terms distinct and particular ideas, we should have nothing to reprehend in their conduct. But they set up themselves for the explaining nature by general and abstract ideas, as if Nature were herself abstract.' After instancing in the case of matter he concludes the chapter with the words, 'Real ideas will produce real science, but from general and logical (*de logique*, i.e. abstract) ideas can proceed nothing but a random superficial and a barren science. Wherefore we ought with serious reflection to attend to the distinct and particular ideas of things.'

Passing on to Book vi of the *Search* we find a striking development of the movement initiated by Bacon against pseudo-scientific objects masquerading as abstract ideas. In bk. vi. 2. 3 Malebranche argues that such abstract ideas are mere relics of animism; they are pagan deities usurping the rights of the one true God. Causality imputed to matter is what he has chiefly in view, but at times he goes further afield, and represents abstractions of the mind as a main obstacle in the pursuit of truth. He says: 'There are two things which I cannot too much mistrust (1) the impressions of my senses (2) my readiness to take abstracted natures and general ideas of logic for real particulars.'

Quotations to the same effect might be multiplied. Book vi in fact reaches this conclusion both from the study of method and from the study of causality. True method requires us to seek clear and distinct ideas, and to eschew abstractions as loose and obscure. His opinion of causality finds expression in the words, 'philosophers explain the effects of nature by some beings of which they have no particular idea . . . the mind is a pagan, whilst the heart is a Christian'.

If Berkeley's polemic against abstract ideas be unconnected with Malebranche's tremendous sayings on the subject, the coincidence is startling. It is just possible that the urge of his own immaterialism, combined with the obvious weakness in Locke's doctrine, may be sufficient explanation. Yet Malebranche's Illustration upon the eighth chapter of the second part of the third book greatly strengthens the evidence for connexion. Its aim is to enable readers 'to comprehend what I have said in some places, how that they give not the reasons of things who explain them by logical and general terms'. The gist of the argument is that such terms must signify being or mode of being, or they mean nothing. Consequently speakers and hearers must examine carefully their meanings, sticking closely to clear ideas. Then Malebranche goes on to say that we may and sometimes must (as when speaking of the soul) use significant words without distinct ideas. Still, whenever they are available we must give the preference to clear terms. For instance, we ought to say that God created the world by His Will, rather than by His Power. For Power is a term *de logique*, signifying no distinct and particular idea. Natural philosophy is the chief offender, and he mentions as offending terms— gravity, levity, nature, faculty, qualities.

Several of the elements in this argument are found in Berkeley's works. At the outset of the Introduction (§§ 7–9)

to the *Principles* Berkeley separates the cases of modes and
beings, and towards the end (§§ 18–24) in the use and
misuse of words he locates the origin of false abstraction.
Again, the proviso that sometimes words have to be used
without distinct ideas was a departure that became of decisive importance for Berkeley. As we saw above (p. 141)
during the writing of the *Commonplace Book* he reversed
his judgement on the point. With Malebranche's statement
in this connexion that we cannot always put the definition
in place of the defined we may compare Berkeley's change
of view about the definition of the soul.[1] Again, when one
thinks of the stress laid by Locke upon 'power' and the great
use that he makes of it, and notices that Berkeley made
similar use of it in the early part of the *Commonplace Book*
but dropped it towards the end (N.B. 495, 814) and marked
several of the 'power' entries with the obelus, it may be
legitimate to connect the change with Malebranche's con-
demnation of that term as a misleading abstraction.[2]

[1] Cf. *C.P.B.* 155–6 with 182.

[2] As stated above, p. 126, I have not laid stress on the possible
connection between Berkeley and Malebranche with regard to
abstract ideas. I have worked out the evidence for connection,
and must leave the reader to judge its value. The source of
Berkeley's doctrine of abstraction is a matter of literary interest.
The source of his doctrine of ideas is, if I mistake not, a matter
of practical moment.

VIII

THE ALLEGED WITHDRAWAL

THIS chapter calls for some apology; for it lies outside the direct scope of the title and sub-title of the book. Yet perhaps there is justification for including it. The chapter is an attempt to resist the disintegration of the Berkeleian philosophy. In a short time it will not matter to any one what Berkeley's sources were, or what the spirit of his philosophy, if our young students are taught that there were two, if not three Berkeleys, and that the challenging extracts from 'juvenile' writings they are required to read were answered in mature life by their author. To make a philosopher refute himself is the easiest and cheapest refutation. In Berkeley's case there may be legitimate lines of refutation. There are certainly legitimate lines of criticism. But the short way with him, which says that Bishop Berkeley ceased to be a Berkeleian, is not, I believe, legitimate.[1] One

[1] The supposed opposition between the teaching of Berkeley and that of Bishop Berkeley is graphically expressed by Dr. Kemp Smith (*Mind*, July 1933, p. 363), who asks, 'Do not nearly all Berkeley's second thoughts run counter to his first thoughts?' I should give the unexpected answer to that question. To me it is simply incredible that Berkeley 'ceased to be a Berkeleian'. Do bishops change their minds? Berkeley taught his early philosophy and presented his early books to Johnson and his other American friends, and corresponded with them and others on philosophy, *inter alia*, throughout the Cloyne years. I cannot recall a hint in his correspondence of any change of view. Surely the *De Motu* and the *Alciphron* contain Berkeley's early philosophy? He republished those works six months before his death. In case Bishop Berkeley suffered an unperceived conversion, the question deserves examination point by point. But mere differences of tone and emphasis in the *Siris* do not prove a conversion. For Berkeley in 1710, *esse* was *concipi* (by God) as well as *percipi* (by man). I believe the same to have been true in 1744.

way of showing the solidarity of Berkeley's thought is to trace through all his philosophical works his pivotal doctrine of abstraction. Accordingly this section will outline Berkeley's discussion of abstract ideas in the *Theory of Vision*, will proceed to a detailed analysis of the doctrine as it appears in the *Principles*, and will then briefly trace the subsequent history of the doctrine in Berkeley's other philosophical works.

A limited criticism of abstraction had been in the fashion for some time before Berkeley wrote. Newton's preface to his *Principia* mentions the passing of substantial forms and occult qualities. Cheyne opens his *Philosophical Principles of Natural Religion* (1705) with a rejection of the Universal Soul of Plato, of the Substantial Forms of Aristotle, of the Omniscient Radical Heat of Hippocrates, of the Plastic Virtue of Scaliger, of the Hylarchic Principle of Henry More. Berkeley recorded in the *Commonplace Book* (626) this charming gallery of ghosts, and reproduced it in the *Hylas* dialogue (*Works*, vol. i, p. 479). We have now to watch the steps by which this limited criticism of the pseudo-scientific abstraction was extended by Berkeley to the whole field of knowledge. Berkeley's studies of ideas and words had led him to see in the abstract idea the chief bar to the acceptance of the New Principle, and the chief buttress of atheism, scepticism, and materialism. He desired direct awareness, and rejected the abstract medium, which, plausible as a mediating function or operation of the mind, became a self-confessed figment and phantom, when he tried to give it shape and substance as Locke had done with his general triangle. If the geometrician is to be allowed to say that he can frame such an idea and that his science is built upon it, nothing can invalidate the titles of the abstract ideas of extension, of external existence, of matter. Berkeley is not simply attempting to discredit Locke. He had the greatest respect for Locke. But in fair fight for truth he takes Locke's triangle as the typical development of neo-scholasticism. The abstract triangle is typical. If it has to be 'all and none of these at once', so too has the abstract idea of colour. Abstract colour must be red, blue, and green, all and none of these at once. Probably Berkeley was correct in seeing the abstract idea in Locke's fourth book as the inevitable goal and grave of Lockian epistemology.

The New Theory of Vision—Abstract Ideas

Sections 122–5 look like an addition to the original design of the *Theory of Vision*.[1] They deal with the abstract idea of extension, as the supposed object of geometry, and the supposed idea common to both senses, sight and touch. They aptly round off the argument, and are in no way an inapposite addition. Only, when Berkeley began the *Commonplace Book* and soon afterwards planned the *Theory of Vision*, he still held the Lockian view of abstraction. Berkeley in §§ 122–5 deals explicitly with but one abstract idea, that of extension, but it is clear that when he wrote the passage he had already reached his final position, and was prepared to condemn *all* abstract ideas. At the end of § 125 he speaks of the source of the error (as to extension) as being also the source of errors in all parts of philosophy and science, and he hints at a fuller treatment of the vast and comprehensive subject. The remainder of the book is con-

---

[1] *v.* above p. 37, and note that the last two sentences of *T.V.*, § 124 must have been written after Nov. 29, 1708, on which day he wrote (*Works*, vol. iii, p. 368) of 'all knowledge is about universals', 'I could never bring myself to comprehend this doctrine', subsequently correcting to 'I can by no means see the necessity of this doctrine'. The guarded admission of the doctrine in *T.V.*, § 124 should be compared, but compared carefully, *v. infra*, p. 156, with the downright 'to which I fully agree' of *Intro. to Prin.*, § 15.

cerned with other matters, but it contains more than one reference to abstract extension as disproved and one striking mention of abstract motion, previously not named, as if all abstract ideas were already dead and buried (§ 137).

The formal disproof (§§ 122–3) of extension in abstract is simply an abbreviation of the disproof of abstract ideas. There is first the statement of what the term means. Abstract extension is extension stripped of all sensible qualities. The space that is to be both seen and touched must be a mass of paradoxes like Locke's triangle. It must be stripped of colour, of roughness or smoothness; otherwise it would be this concrete space. Yet it must have colour to be seen and tangible qualities to be touched. It must be thought to have colour in order to be thought to be seen, and so on. It must be stripped of figure and size; yet it must contain all figures and sizes, being the supposed object of geometry. After stating what the term means, Berkeley simply says he cannot answer for other folk, but for himself such an abstract idea is perfectly incomprehensible. He has tried and failed. He has tried 'all the ways'.[1] An empiricist must go by experience. This appeal to experience is decisive for Berkeley and recurrent in his works. We find it in the *Commonplace Book* (437) about the abstract idea of extension, just as in this passage from the *Theory of Vision*. We find it about all abstract ideas in the *Principles* (*Intro.*, § 10), and twenty years later (1730) writing to Johnson he says of the abstract idea of existence, 'I cannot find I have any such idea, and this is my reason against it'. He points out in passing that the universality required for general knowledge is not endangered by his rejection of abstract extension. He does not pursue the topic, but passes at once to

---

[1] He can neither perceive, imagine, nor any wise frame in his mind such an abstract idea. *T.V.*, § 123. The point is important because attempts have been made to limit Berkeley's *idea* to image.

the 'killing blow'—Locke's abstract idea of a triangle (§ 125). He gives more space to it in the *Principles*. But he is quite as effective here, perhaps more effective because here he quotes Locke against himself.[1]

Berkeley knew quite well that the problem of the sorts is bound up with the problem of abstraction. It is tantalizing to find him coming up to the problem of the sorts, and sheering off (§ 128). Light and colours are mentioned as a species or sort, and the terms, homogeneous, heterogeneous, specify, denominate, patterns, and kinds are prominent. The main theme in this part of the *Essay* is that of the two sorts, visible and tangible ideas. He says (§ 128), 'When, upon perception of an idea, I range it under this or that sort . . .' and there he seems to be on the point of giving his theory of sorts. Yet nothing clear issues, and the paragraph leaves the reader with the impression that the mind both makes the sorts and finds them. It would seem that when Berkeley was writing the last part of the *Theory of Vision* (probably in the autumn of 1708) he had already reached and stereotyped his attitude towards the Lockian abstract ideas, but that while interested in the sorts and assuming their reality, he had found no theory as to their relation to the particulars of sense.

The 'Principles' and Abstract Ideas—The Introduction and the Draft Introduction[2]

Locke (iv. 6. 13, 16) placed the sole source of general knowledge in the contemplation of our own abstract ideas.

[1] iii. 10. 33. The reference shows that Berkeley gave careful consideration to Locke's words in bk. iv. 7. 9, 'an idea wherein some parts of several different and inconsistent ideas are put together'
[2] The Draft Introduction is in autograph in the Chapman MS. note-book (D. 5. 17) in the T.C.D. Library. References to it here use the abbreviation Dft. Int., followed by the page-number of Fraser's vol. iii of the *Works* (1901) in which it is

Berkeley takes up the phrase 'contemplate abstract ideas' ironically in the *Commonplace Book* entry 761, and repeats that entry closely in the Draft Introduction (p. 371, *prima manu*). Noting also that the previous entry[1] expresses the spirit of the exordium of that Introduction and to a large extent its words,[2] we can see clearly the dominant thought in Berkeley's mind on November 15, 1708, on which day he began to draft his famous attack upon abstract ideas. The 'something in every drop of water, every grain of sand' is the *real essence* of scholastic philosophy. The Abstract Idea is the Lockian substitute, whose other name, 'nominal essence', betrays its parentage. Therefore 'the opinion that the mind hath a power of framing abstract ideas or notions of things' is the chief cause of perplexity in speculation, and of error in almost all parts of knowledge.

The plan of the Introduction is as follows:

§§ 1–5. Exordium, placing the problem in perspective.

§§ 6–10. Analysis of the alleged faculty of abstraction. Reason for rejection.

§§ 11–17. Criticism of Locke's arguments in favour of abstract ideas.

§§ 18–20. Language the source of the error.

§§ 21–25. Mainly about remedies.

In the analysis of the faculty, qualities or modes are first treated, then beings.[3] As regards qualities, two stages of the process are recognized. There is first the singling, i.e. the considering separately the qualities combined in a

printed. References to *sections* of the Draft are references to passages in the Draft which correspond to the sections of the Introduction.

[1] 760, like 761, marked in text and margin for Introduction.

[2] The opening paragraph of Dft. Int. contains the words 'Something they imagine to be in every drop of water, every grain of sand', which now appear in *Prin.*, § 101.

[3] *v. supra*, p. 146.

thing, as colour or extension. Then there is the framing
or putting together the common qualities of several things.
This second stage goes beyond the mere observation of a
quality in repeated instances. The mind is here not only
selective but constructive. It takes abstracts of abstractions
and frames them. The two stages are roughly abstraction
without the sorts and abstraction with the sorts. In the
case of *beings*, the mental separation is stated to be the same;
but here the singling is not so much in evidence, and the
stress falls on the putting together of the common qualities
of several beings, and thus forming abstract ideas as e.g.
man, animal, body. It would not seem that Berkeley mis-
represents or distorts Locke's account. But neither Locke
nor Berkeley gives crystal clear accounts, and indeed we
may say in excuse for the obscurity of two masters of plain
English, that, supposing Berkeley right, it must be hard to
give lucid accounts of how a nonentity is made.

Berkeley at once[1] denies that he has this faculty of
abstracting. He has something like it, constructive imagination, but that is not the same. He can single and imagina-
tively combine the separable. He cannot single the inseparable, nor work it up into a composite entity.[2]

Berkeley passes on to consider Locke's defence of abstraction. In the first place the alleged faculty puts a
perfect distinction between man and beast. In the *Com-*

[1] In the 1st ed., and it would be absurd to take the omission
of the words from the 2nd ed. 'I dare be confident I have it not'
as a withdrawal. Berkeley was fond of making small stylistic
omissions and insertions in later editions. Here the equivalent of
the words omitted is emphatically stated more than once in the
remainder of the paragraph (§ 10).

[2] 'The two proper acceptations of abstraction', *Int.*, § 10, should
be bracketed with the 'Twofold abstraction' of *Prin.*, § 99. This
latter passage gives, I think, Berkeley's clearest, if briefest, account
of the false abstraction; *v. supra*, p. 127–8.

monplace Book (766) Berkeley had taken this point seriously and had suggested an alternative differentia. Here he passes it off with a joke; he is entitled to do so because he is proceeding to discuss the connexion between speech and abstraction, which is Locke's real point.

The strongest argument is drawn from the use of words. There are general names; so there must be general ideas. Berkeley replies that the ideas signified by these names are not general, in the abstract sense of the word, but generalized. They are particular ideas deputizing for other particular ideas. He is careful to point out that he is not denying general ideas absolutely, but those framed by abstraction. Particulars become generals, he holds, not by abstraction, but by signification. They are made to signify other particulars. To illustrate further the meaning of abstraction he brings in again Locke's abstract triangle, and again administers 'the killing blow'. He then scores a few points off Locke with reference to the difficulty of abstracting. If abstract ideas are so difficult, why should they be so necessary for communication, easy and natural as it is? Again, neither youth nor maturity can be the age at which the difficult task is learned (§ 14).

Locke's contention that abstract ideas are necessary to the advancement of knowledge is considered next. Berkeley meets it by distinguishing the abstract from the universal. He denies that scientific knowledge is knowledge of the abstract idea. If that were true of any science it would be true of geometry,[1] and he proceeds to show that it is not true of geometry. When we prove of a triangle the equality of its angles to two right angles, we prove it not of the abstract triangle, but of a triangle which in fact may be right-angled or equilateral. In the proof such facts are not regarded, nor relied on. Hence the proof is universal, and

[1] Dft. Int. 368.

need not be repeated in other particular cases. A comparison of this section (15) with the corresponding passages in the Draft Introduction, p. 368, is of interest. In § 15 he speaks of 'a point much insisted on, that all knowledge and demonstration are about universal notions, to which I fully agree'. For these words the Draft *prima manu* reads 'a point much insisted on in the Schools, that all knowledge is about universals, yet I could never bring myself to comprehend this doctrine', the last words being corrected to 'I can by no means see the necessity of this doctrine'.[1]

At first sight it looks like a pronounced change of mind at short notice. But perhaps the change is rather of terminology than of doctrine. Are we to infer that Berkeley came round and accepted a scholastic tenet that he had previously rejected? Certainly the words 'to which I fully agree' should not be taken as an admission that knowledge of the particulars of sense is not knowledge. The addition of the 'and demonstration' is marked. Probably 'all knowledge and demonstration' is a hendiadys, whose real import is 'all demonstrative knowledge'; and if universal notions be taken in Berkeley's sense and not in Locke's then truly they are the goal of scientific knowledge. Universality, for Berkeley, is not the product of abstraction, nor does it consist in the 'absolute, positive nature or conception of anything, but in the relation it bears to the particulars signified or represented by it'. The universality of a geometrical demonstration does not argue the existence of abstract extension, but, on the contrary, the representative character of the particular. The section added in the second edition at the end of § 16 does not alter Berkeley's position at all.[2] It is due, no doubt, to philosophic balance, and the anxiety to avoid one-sidedness. The 'So far he may abstract' is a formula that occurs elsewhere, e.g. *Prin.*, § 5, *Alc.* vii, § 5.

[1] Cf. *T.V.*, § 124.　　　　　[2] See above p. 127 *n.*

The section (18–20) on language as the source of the
error about abstraction is given at much greater length
(pp. 371–80) in the Draft, and more convincingly. A few
months before he penned the Introduction, it had been
axiomatic to Berkeley that every significant word stands for
an idea. He had accepted the charge laid by Bacon, Locke,
and others upon the New Learning to 'lay aside the word'
and penetrate to the one true meaning and determinate
idea. At that stage of his thought the words *triangle, man*,
etc., seemed to postulate concrete universals, and his problem was to retain them, while giving up the abstract ideas
supposed to correspond to the words *extension, existence,
matter*. Further reflection showed him that he had been
confusing definition and idea. Where names are definable,
we must keep to the definition; but neither name nor definition guarantees the one idea. Names have other uses
besides that of evoking ideas. They determine action and
touch the chords of feeling. Often words are no more than
counters, having a potential but unrealized meaning. In
arithmetic and algebra long trains of reasoning can go on
and conclusions be reached by the aid of the symbol, without actual reference to the ideas symbolized.

In the Draft Berkeley puts more strongly the divorce
between word and idea. He there denies that words are
necessary for apprehending ideas, and states that every
appellative name has a diversity of meanings. He also expands the notion of speech as the algebra of thought. He
then gives an important analysis of propositional form and
the status of the predicate. His design is to show that its
two terms do not require or admit two corresponding ideas.
'Melampus is an animal' simply means, he says, 'Melampus
has a right to be called by the name animal'.[1] Try to make

[1] 'has a right to'. Perhaps a convenient Dublin idiom of
import baffling to logicians.

the proposition mean more, and it becomes either self-contradictory (Melampus is an abstract universal), or tautologous (Melampus is Melampus). Another very interesting passage which has completely disappeared in the revision is that on the solitary man in a world of particulars (pp. 379–80). This experimental conceit had been much in his mind, as we see from the *Commonplace Book* (571, etc., see above, p. 141). It does not appear in the *Principles* but is alluded to in the third *Hylas* dialogue (*Works*, p. 467).

The absence of any treatment of the sorts or species in the *Principles* is noteworthy. We know from the *Commonplace Book* that he saw the relevance and importance of the question, and had weighed the position of the sorts in the system of Malebranche (296). We saw him coming up to the problem in the *Theory of Vision* (§ 128). Is then the silence of the *Principles* the silence of embarrassment? 'He that knows he has no other than particular ideas' (*Int. Prin.*, § 24) would seem reducible, on the principle of *esse percipi*, to 'there are no other than particular ideas'. Does then Berkeley hold that sorts exist? A good deal can be learned of his views on the topic by comparing what he wrote in the Draft (pp. 365–6) with the corresponding sections of the Introduction as we now have it. Dealing with communication of ideas, he finds, as Locke did, that since there are so many ideas and so few words, one word has to stand for many particular ideas 'between which there is some likeness and which are said to be of the same sort'. He then wrote and *erased* the following judgement about the status of sorts. 'But then these sorts are not determin'd and set out by nature, as was thought by most philosophers. Nor yet are they limited by any precise abstract ideas settl'd in the mind, with the general name annexed to them, as is the opinion of the author of the *Essay*, nor do they in truth seem to me to have any precise

bounds or limits at all.' He adds that precise bounds to
the sorts are not necessary in ordinary speech, and that if
such there were, the sorting of particulars would not be
so much disputed as it is. On the opposite page we find
a note interesting as being one of the very few references
by Berkeley to nominalism. 'Every one's experience may
convince him that this is all that's meant by general names,
and that they do not stand either for universal natures distinct
from our conceptions as was held by the Peripatetics and
generality of the Schoolmen, nor yet for universal notions
or ideas as is the opinion of that sort of Schoolmen called
Nominals and of the author of the *Essay*.' I think it is
clear that Berkeley recognized nominalism (strict) and was
anxious to avoid it. Clearly also he held the fact of objective
similitude, and the 'existence' of the sorts, i.e. that some
things are alike because God made them 'after their kind'.
Opinions will differ as to why he cut the passage out. Perhaps the printer told him the Introduction was too long,
and he excised what was least to his main purpose. In any
case his belief in the sorts, as there expressed, seems quite
consistent with his rejection of abstract ideas. His silence
may be the silence of wisdom. He has a very sober, sensible, and, may we say it, an evolutionary view of what the
sorts are, but he knows that when they are much talked
about they become fetishes and worse, abstract ideas.

Other changes made by Berkeley in the Draft itself or
in subsequent revision may be briefly noticed. They turn
mainly on the sharp distinction between abstract and
general that Berkeley tried to establish, but failed to maintain in his terminology. In revising the Draft he makes
a point of substituting the word 'abstract' for 'general'.
Section 12 with its distinction between 'general' and
'abstract general' is mostly new. He erases from § 15
his earlier denial of universal notions, and from § 7 his

statement that abstract ideas, genera, species, universal notions 'all amount to the same thing'.

The use made in the main work of the position established in the Introduction is direct and indirect. Indirectly the rejection of abstract ideas induces the modern attitude of realism and fosters the habit of direct awareness. The direct use is to guillotine misleading concepts. Existence (§ 5), External world (§ 6), Matter (§ 11), Unity (§ 13), Being (§ 17), Presence (§ 68), Occasion (§ 74), Quiddity, Entity (§ 81), Time, Place, Motion (§ 97)—one after another they are brought to summary execution. The Cartesian paradoxes of matter are traced to a twofold abstraction (§ 99). Nor do ethical concepts escape. Happiness prescinded from particular pleasure, goodness prescinded from things that are good, abstract justice and virtue, these notions have marred the truth and usefulness of ethics (§ 100). Turning then to natural philosophy (§§ 101–2), he prefixes to the section the passage which formed the original opening of the Introduction (*v. supra*, p. 153). It is directed against the Lockian and neo-scholastic doctrine of the real essence which causes the properties and yet is unknowable. He classes together occult qualities, mechanical causes, and real essences. He pays especial attention to the *vis attractrix*,[1] 'the great mechanical principle now in vogue'. It is a general name for similar appearances, but is not an efficient cause. There is only one efficient cause of phenomena—the will of a spirit. Thus Berkeley in all but words says that the New Physics is built on the doctrine of abstract ideas. When he comes to mathematics (§ 118) he is quite explicit. The secret error in all branches of the science springs from the doctrines of abstract general ideas and external existence. In the case of arithmetic the opinion of the abstract idea of number has led to mysticism and idle speculation. Number is nothing apart from

[1] Cf. *C.P.B.* 488, 626–8.

numerable things. Glancing at arithmetic 'in its infancy', he finds that utility invented strokes and points, and the arabic notation. Numbers came into use in imitation of language. They are, like letters, symbols that dispose us for action. The existence of words with no particular meaning gave rise to the belief in abstract general ideas. Just so, neglect of the symbolic character of figures has led to belief in the abstract unit or collection of abstract units (§§ 121–2). The most obvious error in geometry, due to abstraction, is, he thinks, the doctrine of the infinite divisibility of finites. Men are ready to predicate of the mysterious abstract idea of extension what obviously does not belong to the concrete ideas of sense. He grants that the theorems and demonstrations of geometry are about universal ideas, but refers to the Introduction (§ 15) for the sense in which that term is to be understood. Again, he makes it quite clear that he recognizes the abstracting that issues in the generalized particular, deputizing for other similar particulars, but rejects the abstracting supposed to issue in the abstract general idea. Finally (§ 143) he notes the evil effect of the doctrine of abstract ideas in metaphysics and morality, instancing 'powers' and 'acts of the mind' as 'dark and ambiguous terms, presumed to stand for abstract notions'.

Three Dialogues between Hylas and Philonous[1]

In the first dialogue all the main features of Berkeley's doctrine of abstraction reappear. The Preface speaks of the abstractions that occur in the very entrance of the sciences, and echoes the opening of the Introduction to the *Principles* on real essences. The subject of the abstract idea is formally introduced on p. 403, where the usual distinctions are drawn and the usual refutation from experience

[1] N.B. References are to the pages in Fraser's ed. of the *Works* (1901), vol. i.

is given. The whole of the first part of the dialogue is an analysis of particular abstractions (colours, sounds, heat, pain, pleasure) singled and separated; Berkeley shows that, abstracted from the mind, they want reality. Passing to the primary qualities, he takes up in turn the wider abstractions, extension, figure, motion, denying that they can exist apart from the mind or from other sensible qualities. He shows the sense in which general ideas form the subject-matter of mathematics (403). In that context we find Berkeley's first published mention of 'pure intellect', the supposed faculty of abstract ideas. Berkeley does not deny 'pure intellect', but denies that it is the faculty of abstract ideas, and he gives it concrete 'spiritual objects, as virtue, reason, God'.

In the second dialogue (436) after the review of matter as object, substratum, cause, instrument and occasion, the final appeal is to matter as the general abstract idea of entity, which in its turn 'hath quite vanished out of sight'. In the third dialogue there are occasional references to the doctrine, such as 'unknown natures' and 'philosophical quiddities' (455), but nothing systematic on the topic, and nothing new, except the attempted solution of the problem of sameness, by reference to the abstract ideas of identity and diversity (467). It is interesting to see that the drama ends with a recognition by Hylas, that Unknown Natures and Absolute Existence are to be rejected as the fount of scepticism, and one might almost say that Berkeley has in the *Three Dialogues* dramatized the conversion of an abstractionist as well as the conversion of a materialist. The rejection of abstract ideas was to him no superficial or passing topic of interest, but one that had cut deep into his thoughts, and, in his view, was the corner stone of his philosophy.[1]

[1] The section added, p. 427, in the 3rd edition, 1734, on

De Motu

The *De Motu* was written in 1720 and published in 1721. Berkeley reprinted it in the *Miscellany* (1752), and in his letters to Johnson of 1730 he refers to it more than once, as an important and specific part of his philosophy. It was much more to him than an essay submitted for a prize offered by a French Academy. The *De Motu* does for motion what the *Principles* had done for matter. The *De Motu* was, we might say, Part III of the *Principles*, and there is evidence in the *Commonplace Book* that his original plan for that work was tripartite.[1] The *De Motu* discloses no substantial change of mind. The ideist terminology is kept in the background; he here speaks of 'things' where the earlier work spoke of 'ideas'. But his immaterialism stands, though naturally under the circumstances of the competition it is not stated aggressively. He says (§ 21) 'Duo sunt summa rerum genera—corpus et anima'. This statement is not a recognition of mind and matter, but is, in effect, a repetition of the 'spirit and ideas' of the *Principles*. For when he has spoken of *corpus* as *rem extensam* &c., he adds, 'Loquor de rebus cognitis: de incognitis enim disserere nil juvat'.

Berkeley's doctrine of abstraction, though not formally stated in the *De Motu*, is there assumed, and treated by implication as of capital importance. The essay opens with a warning against 'voces male intellectae', such as *nisus*, *vis*,

Malebranche's philosophy contains the rather severe judgement, 'He builds on the most abstract general ideas, which I entirely disclaim'.

[1] *C.P.B.* 589, 865, especially when the latter entry is taken along with the apparatus of marginal signs. *v.* Appendix, p. 184. Apparently the 'S. Mo' entries were designed mainly for Part II, and the 'N' entries for Part III ('our Principles of Natural Philosophy').

or *gravitas*, and on 'Voces generales et abstractae' definitely
states (§ 7) that they are not accommodated to the natures
of things, which are singular and concrete. They are indeed
useful to describe concrete *phenomena*. But they are not
realities, apprehensible by sense, imagination, or intellect.
As abstract ideas they are the false explanations that obscure our view of the causes and nature of motion, and hide
from us the *vera causa*, God. He instances the *impetus* of
Torricelli and the *vis activa* of Leibniz, and he says that
Newton did not adduce attraction as a physical quality but
as a mathematical hypothesis. The method of sound philosophy is to abstain as far as possible from abstract and
general notions; and of his three formally expressed principles (§ 66), the second is 'Cavere ab abstractionibus', the
other two being part and parcel of the same caution. The
result of observing these rules will be 'motus contemplatio
a mille minutiis, subtilitatibus, ideisque abstractis libera
evadet'. Those who place the principle of motion in bodies
are building on obscure and general terms, and those who
place it in mind are fortified by experience, and have behind them the authority of great thinkers from Anaxagoras
to Newton. Similarly with regard to the nature of motion,
if we take it as a 'simple and abstract idea' (§ 43) apart from
all that makes it sensible, we fall into the obscurities of
Aristotle and the Scholastics. Many sections of the *De
Motu* contain references to Berkeley's views on true and
false abstraction, and the whole work might be aptly styled
an appeal to 'vera natura' against 'abstracta mathesis' (§ 70).

Alciphron

The *Alciphron* was written in Rhode Island and was
published in 1732 (first and second editions) on his return
to London. Berkeley's travels on the Continent did not
alter his views on abstraction. Did crossing the Atlantic

affect them? No. In the first six dialogues abstract ideas receive little notice, the subjects treated scarcely permitting it. In the fourth dialogue the treatment of the Divine Visual Language involves a notice of semeiology which forms part of the explanation of general ideas. The ethical theories of Shaftesbury and Clarke, respectively, are in view in the phrases 'those heroic infidel inamoratos of abstracted beauty' (iii. 12), and 'abstract idea of moral fitness' (vi. 17). In the seventh dialogue the whole doctrine is formulated in the clearest possible manner. Each division of the subject receives specific and adequate treatment, and the whole is cunningly worked into the fabric of his defence of theism and Christianity. The doctrine of abstraction is prominent throughout the dialogue. Berkeley starts from a study of words as related to ideas, and, in the first two editions, he gives a set statement of the Lockian view, with a refutation which is the argument of the Introduction to the *Principles* in shortened and dramatized form. Semeiology receives close attention, and other signs besides words are instanced, which raise no determinate ideas. He states that the contrary opinion seems to have produced the doctrine of abstract ideas, and he draws his usual distinction between the true and the false abstraction. He studies closely and together the abstract ideas of force and grace, impugning the fairness of those who 'maintain the doctrine of force and reject that of grace; who shall admit the abstract idea of a triangle, and at the same time ridicule the Holy Trinity'. Practical faith or assent is contrasted with 'abstracted faith', i.e. the requirement of abstract precise distinct ideas of the nature of the Godhead, of the person of Christ, of original sin. These and other references to the 'wire-drawing' of abstract ideas show that his rejection of the abstract had entered into the fabric of his faith and into his outlook upon life.

Having to compare the bases of faith and science, he gives a clearer and more emphatic statement than he had as yet given of the place of signs in knowledge (§§ 11–14). Using the terms 'idea' and 'thing' indifferently, he asserts that general rules are not to be reached by mere consideration of the original ideas or particular things. The *activity* of the mind, he holds, lies in the realm of signs. 'It is not therefore, by mere contemplation of particular things, and much less of their abstract general ideas, that the mind makes her progress, but by an apposite choice and skilful management of signs.' He is here attempting a methodology that will avoid the errors of active abstraction and passive particularism. We see that his rejection of abstraction is no longer (perhaps it never was so) merely a polemic, but is a motive in a constructive methodology of signs. Applying it to arithmetic and algebra, he advances to the view that all sciences, 'so far as they are universal', are conversant about signs as their immediate object. The things we know are used as steps to the unknown. The lower faculty deputizes for the higher, sense for imagination, imagination for intellect. Turning to geometry he traces infinitesimals and other paradoxes to abstraction, and says that the supposition of abstract ideas creates difficulties throughout the several branches of human knowledge. He extends this view (§ 18) to the problem of freedom, and says that to make judgement, will, power, act, indifference, freedom, necessity, and the like into distinct abstract ideas seems to 'ensnare the mind into the same perplexities and errors which in all other instances, are observed to attend the doctrine of abstraction'.

Berkeley's two letters to Johnson, printed by Fraser in his Preface to the *Alciphron* (*Works*, 1901, vol. ii) belong like the *Alciphron* to the Rhode Island period. These letters should be read along with the two letters of Johnson that evoked them. All four are given in the Schneiders' *Samuel Johnson*, vol. ii, pp. 263 sqq. The Schneiders print the Johnson letters from copies kept by Johnson. I found the original[1] of Johnson's letter of February 5, 1730 in the Berkeley Papers in the British Museum. The fact that Berkeley kept this letter (or had a copy made), and that Johnson kept a copy too shows the value both sides set on the correspondence, which is indeed notable as being a very early sustained criticism of the Berkeleian philosophy by an acute mind, with Berkeley's systematic defence of it. In both letters, it will be noticed, Berkeley throws the weight of his defence upon what he has written in his books about abstraction. He regards it, as Hume did, as an original contribution to philosophy. He writes, 'Abstract general ideas was a notion that Mr. Locke held in common with the Schoolmen, and I think, all other philosophers; it runs through his whole book of Human Understanding', and he speaks of immaterialism as 'a principle or main point, from which, and from what I had laid down about abstract ideas, much may be deduced'.

Thus from the *Alciphron* and these almost contemporary letters, it is certain that Dean Berkeley in America still held to his early views on abstraction, and in one direction had pushed them further. He is more conscious than he was of the mischief caused by abstract ideas; at the same time he has become critical of the alternative. He sees the doctrine of abstract ideas as right in postulating mental activity in the sciences, as wrong in postulating the 'black hat that is not there'. He sees sense particularism as rightly standing out for apprehension of the actual, as wrong if requiring intellectual quiescence. Between these extremes Berkeley extends and deepens his own doctrine of signs, in which

[1] I presume it is the original, but the last page is lacking. See *Proc. R. Irish Acad.* xli, sec. C. 4. p. 142.

the higher faculties of mind are called into play by the concrete particulars of sense.

The changes made in dialogue vii in the third (1752) edition call for a special study. For on the strength of them the absurd legend has grown up that in mature life Bishop Berkeley sat loosely to his early doctrine of abstraction, and in 1752 made a death-bed recantation. I have already pointed out[1] how precarious inferences from Berkeley's corrections in the text may be. Those who argue from the 1752 textual omissions usually turn the blind eye upon the small but significant insertions of the same date, which point the other way, and, Berkeley's works being more written about than read, completely ignore those refutations of abstract ideas which stand unaltered in *all* editions of the *Alciphron*. The most striking change in the third edition of the *Alciphron* is the omission from dialogue vii of three complete sections, 5, 6, and 7, whose titles in the original table of contents were:

5. Abstract Ideas what and how made.
6. Abstract general Ideas impossible.
7. In what sense there may be general Ideas.

Fraser's first comment is very guarded (*Works*, vol. ii, p. 323). He writes 'the omission is significant if it means dissatisfaction with his former method of assailing "abstract ideas"'. In his vol. iii, p. 91, he gives the inconsistent and, I submit, misleading footnote, 'Note also Berkeley's reasonings in the first and second editions of *Alciphron* and his withdrawal in the third edition against abstract general ideas'. *A priori* such a withdrawal is highly improbable. A philosopher who published a tenet at the age of 25 might well at the age of 47 see fit to withdraw it. But if, as Berkeley did, he published it at the age of 25 and renewed it in an intensified form at the age of 47, reasserting it at the

[1] See above p. 154, *n*. 1.

age of 59 and later, a withdrawal at the age of 67 would be scarcely credible. In this case the tenet was no triviality, but one that, as we have seen, had entered into the deep of Berkeley's faith and attitude to life and into his outlook on science. If his intellect had wanted to withdraw it, would his heart have consented? And have we any solid reason for thinking that he wished to withdraw? The *De Motu* contains, indeed constitutes, a slashing attack upon abstract ideas. If Berkeley in 1752 wished to withdraw his polemic against abstract ideas, why did he republish the *De Motu* in that year? Lastly, had he become convinced that his early teaching was wrong, he was man enough to withdraw it openly. A clandestine withdrawal of so supreme a tenet is unthinkable in the case of one who had 'dedicated his age as well as youth at the altar of Truth'.

But hypothetical reasoning is unnecessary here. In point of hard fact the 1752 edition of the *Alciphron* does *not* withdraw Berkeley's doctrine of abstract ideas. It omits three sections that expounded the doctrine; but that is a different matter. Whatever the reason for the omission of the three sections the doctrine contained in them is not withdrawn. To withdraw that doctrine, Berkeley would have had to withdraw the bulk of the dialogue. Of its thirty-one sections, fourteen sections (those on which the weight of the argument falls) assert or assume the falsity of the abstract idea. In § 5 (1752) Alciphron asks 'Will you not allow then that the mind can abstract?' Euphranor replies, 'I do not deny it may abstract in a certain sense: inasmuch as those things that can really exist, or be really perceived asunder, may be conceived asunder, or abstracted one from the other; for instance, a man's head from his body, colour from motion, figure from weight. But it will not thence follow that the mind can frame abstract general ideas, which appear to be impossible. (See the *Principles of*

Human Knowledge, § 135, and the Introduction, § 20.)'
That question and answer with his formal reference to the
Principles seems proof positive that Berkeley's doctrine of
abstraction was the same in 1752 as it had been in 1710.
Further, far from withdrawing his line in old age, he con-
solidates it. In 1752 he inserts in §§ 12 and 14 sentences
that bring relations expressly under his doctrine of signs,
taking care to point out that 'these relations are not abstract general ideas'.

Why then did Berkeley omit these three sections? He
does not tell us, and we can only surmise. Perhaps he cut
them out because they are redundant and can easily be
spared. Perhaps because they argue a point that to his
mind was long ago settled and past argument. He did not
want to be flogging a dead horse. Most probably, I should
think, he cut them out in order to make his book more effective. He was not writing for metaphysicians. He was writing to convince folk of the truth of Christianity. These
sections occur at the climax of the whole work. The Free-
thinker has promised a demonstration that Christianity is
false (§ 1). The kernel of his 'demonstration' is that the
word 'grace' on which Christianity depends is a mere word,
and that no idea in the mind answers to it (§ 4). As we saw
above, Berkeley's discovery that there may be significant
words without ideas was epoch-making in his *Commonplace
Book* days, and gave a great impetus to his attack on abstract
ideas. So it was natural that as he wrote under the 'Hanging
Rocks' at Rhode Island, the old argument should remind
him of the old enemy, and that he should pen the three
sections, 5, 6 and 7, unfolding the refutation that had meant
so much to him twenty years before. But it was no less
natural that on revising the work amid the myrtles at Cloyne
in the last year of his life, he should regard the same three
sections as inartistic, and as breaking the continuity of the

main argument. The Free-thinker's argument is so telling that it calls for a speedy and a crushing retort. That retort is forthcoming in the fine *ad hominem* argument of §7, 'That which we admit with regard to *force*, upon what pretence can we deny concerning *grace*?' I suggest that Berkeley cut out the three sections in order to hurry to that 'killing blow'. The three sections give a technical exposition and a technical refutation of a metaphysical doctrine. They are 'cap and gown' philosophy. They are of 'that dry, formal, pedantic, stiff and clumsy style, which smells of the lamp and the college' (dial. v, § 20). They interrupt and delay the important argument about grace and force, and weaken its appeal to the average cultured reader. The dialogue reads better without them.

The Analyst (1734). *A Defence of Free-Thinking in Mathematics* (1735)

These mathematical works are more closely connected with Berkeley's metaphysic than appears at first glance. In both of them his doctrine of abstraction is decisive, if not prominent. The immediate purpose of the *Analyst* is pithily expressed in the words (§ 7) 'He who can digest a second or third fluxion, a second or third difference, need not be squeamish about any point in divinity'. But the scope of the work extends beyond that *argumentum ad hominem*. The *Analyst* does not mention immaterialism, but is in fact a continuation of his subtle defence of that doctrine, begun a quarter of a century previously. Its concluding section (50) connects it with the 'hints given to the public about twenty-five years ago', and all but says that he has here brought to fruition previous studies 'after so long an intermission'. The 'hints given to the public' were §§ 123 –32 of the *Principles* on the infinite divisibility, infinitesimals, and 'amusing geometrical paradoxes', a division of the work which ends with a promise of fuller treatment. The 'studies' intermitted must have been those of the *Commonplace Book* which centre round these mathematical problems. There are well over a hundred of these entries, on fluxions, infinitesimals, surds, angle of contact, quadrature of the circle, &c., a medley of topics, all dealing with the mathematicians' argument for the existence of matter.

There is indeed a personal link between the *Analyst* and those early studies which I have not seen noticed. The 'infidel mathematician' to whom the *Analyst* is addressed is Halley,[1] second only to Newton in fame. He is mentioned by name in the *Commonplace Book* (445), 'Halley's Doctrine about the proportion between Infinitely great quantities vanishes. When men speak of Infinite quantities, either they mean finite quantities, or else talk of (that whereof they have) no idea; both which are absurd.' Now when Berkeley was penning the sixty-seven Queries with which the *Analyst* concludes, he might have had the *Commonplace Book* open before him; for a score or more of them echo its entries; and it is interesting to see that the very first of these queries takes up the point of the entry which mentions Halley. The query is, 'Whether the object of geometry be not the proportions of assignable extensions? And whether there be any need of considering quantities either infinitely great or infinitely small?'

The *Analyst* aims at showing that the method of fluxions rests upon abstract ideas, impossible to conceive, because compounded of inconsistencies (§ 4). Berkeley instances 'velocity prescinded from time and space' (§ 30), 'nice abstractions and geometrical metaphysics', 'evanescent increments', and similar 'ghosts of departed quantities' (§ 35).

[1] I have assumed, perhaps rashly, the truth of the tradition, and should add that Professor Jessop (*A Bibliography of George Berkeley*, p. 10) has shown that a great part of Stock's story is unreliable.

We find in § 37 the usual appeal to personal experience as to the impossibility of forming an abstract idea (of velocity). Since the method of fluxions was held to be the key of geometry and therefore of Nature (§ 3), it is clear that Berkeley is dealing not only with a mathematical method, but with the nature of existence, and his early philosophy is present by implication in several of his concluding Queries, especially in No. 7, 'Whether it be possible to free geometry from insuperable difficulties and absurdities, so long as either the abstract general idea of extension, or absolute external extension be supposed its true object?'[1]

In *A Defence of Free-Thinking in Mathematics* (§ 12) the continuity of the *Analyst* with the *Principles* is clearly stated: 'My late publication of what had been hinted twenty-five years ago'. Its argument is for the most part narrowly controversial, and need not detain us. In two sections, 20 and 49, Berkeley lists the '*arcana* of the modern analysis'. He writes, 'Every reader . . . knows . . . what idea he frames or can frame of velocity without motion, or of motion without extension, of magnitude which is neither finite nor infinite, or of a quantity having no magnitude which is yet divisible, of a figure where there is no space, of proportion between nothings, or of a real product from nothing multiplied by something'. It is quite easy to recognize here a more pointed and practised use of the old weapon. Perhaps §§ 45–48 form the most interesting part of the tract; for they show us that his opponent, Dr. Jurin of Cambridge, recognized that the doctrine of abstract ideas was the real point at issue in the *Analyst* controversy, attacking Berkeley on that point of metaphysics. Accordingly Berkeley with great clearness restates his old doctrine, distinguishing between abstract general ideas and general

[1] *v.* also Nos. 8, 9, 14 and cf. *T.V.* § 124.

ideas, giving his reasons for rejecting the former, and elucidating his relation to the Lockian doctrine.[1]

Siris

Siris was first published in 1744. It contains no formal treatment of abstract ideas or kindred subjects. This need cause no surprise. The surprising thing would be if he had returned to labour an argument which he regarded as already established. The third (1752) edition of the *Alciphron* makes it clear that his early views on abstraction remained unchanged to the close of his life.[2] The *Siris* contains no suggestion of any such change. We find in it, indeed, explicit recognition of the doctrine of the Introduction to the *Principles*. Plato's ideas are distinguished from 'abstract ideas in the modern sense' (§ 335). Having to mention Plutarch's term for Deity, $\chi\omega\rho\iota\sigma\tau\grave{o}\nu\ \epsilon\tilde{\iota}\delta\sigma$, separated Form, Berkeley adds, 'not an abstract idea compounded of inconsistencies, and prescinded from all real things, as some moderns understand abstraction' (§ 323). The allusion to Locke's 'absurd triangle' is unmistakable. The *Siris* contains express approving references (§§ 249, 271) to the *De Motu* and the *Analyst*. Berkeley then in 1744 takes for granted the main results of his earlier work. An opinion to the contrary would have to maintain that in the *Siris* he has made substantial alterations in the doctrine of the *Principles*. It would be hard, if not impossible, to establish that contention. Certainly it is not the professed intention of the *Siris* to recant, correct, or even modify the teaching of his early works.

As to the merits of the book in general, the true estimate must lie somewhere between Fraser's judgement that it is the most profound of Berkeley's works (*Works*, vol. iii, p. 117) and its author's own statement that it is a 'rude

[1] *v. supra*, pp. 130–2.   [2] *v. supra*, pp. 168–71.

essay' (§ 297). It is certainly not designed as the exposition of a new metaphysic or of any metaphysic. It is a treatise on tar-water combined with a meditation, whose one unfaltering purpose is to show that God worketh, if not all, at least in all. No doubt on that account Berkeley does not trouble to make clear his position as regards the authors he quotes. Like a bee among flowers he lays antiquity under tribute, and wherever he can suck the honey of the universe —its unity in God—thither he flits.

The abstractions of physics, the elastic ether, gravity, and force, are attacked in *Siris* just as they were in the *De Motu*, and are coupled with 'hamate atoms', as explaining *ignotum per ignotius*. The particular *phenomenon* is still the reality (§ 231). Knowledge is still the interpretation of signs (§ 253). Absolute space and absolute motion are still phantoms (§ 271). The idea-things are still there in all but name, part of the cosmic chain, but not receiving emphasis disproportionate to their value. Opposing Cudworth's statement that 'The Democritic hypothesis doth much more handsomely and intelligibly solve[1] the phenomena, than that of Aristotle and Plato', he states that all phenomena are appearances in the mind, and denies that external bodies, figures, or motions can produce an appearance in the mind (§ 251). Berkeley has simply substituted the Latin 'appearance' for the Greek 'idea'. In § 292 he says of these 'appearances' just what he had said of 'ideas' in the *Principles*. 'They are such as we see and perceive them. Their real and objective[2] natures are, therefore, the same: passive without anything active; fluent and changing without anything permanent in them.' This passage is in the nature of a climax; for Berkeley passes at once to the contemplation of a new

---

[1] *Sic*. Cudworth has 'salve', i.e. σώζειν.

[2] 'objective' here means perceived. It is almost equivalent to subjective in modern usage.

and distinct class of objects, 'the Mind her acts and faculties'.

What Berkeley says in *Siris* about the human mind is not extensive or profound or very clear. He says at least as much in the *Principles*, and writes there certainly more systematically about it. It is more than doubtful if he accepts the 'native inbred notions of the Platonic philosophy.'[1] In Berkeley's last public pronouncement that remains, a sermon on the Will of God,[2] we find a remarkable passage on innate ideas. This passage is modelled on, and, in part, reproduces *Alciphron*, dial. i, § 14, and echoes certain thoughts and phrases from the sections of *Siris* to which we have just now referred. There Berkeley, expressly in the draft copy of the sermon, by implication in the British Museum fair copy, rejects actual original notions in the mind, and substitutes 'natural inbred dispositions' for the 'native inbred notions' of *Siris*.

In the final sections of *Siris* Berkeley soon passes from the psychology of the human mind into 'remote inquiries and speculations'. Here too there is nothing advanced as his own, inconsistent with his earlier writings. Plato was to him the prince of ancient philosophers.[3] But Berkeley was no Platonist. He no more accepts the Platonic Ideas, because he expounds them appreciatively, than he accepts Plato's doctrine of matter, or Aristotle's, because he expounds them with obvious relish and a degree of sympathy intelligible in an immaterialist. Berkeley finds an 'imperfect notion' of the Holy Trinity in Plato and Plotinus. He no more understood the Church's tenet in a Platonist sense,

---

[1] *Siris*, §§ 308–9. N.B. 'Some perhaps may think. . . .'
[2] Preached Whitsunday 1751, published *Hermathena*, vol. xxii, 1932; *v.* especially pp. 9, 10, 30–1.
[3] N.B. 'whose hoary maxims scattered in this Essay are not proposed as principles, but barely as hints', § 350.

than he attributed efficacy, force, or material extension to tar, when, speaking with the vulgar, he claims that tar-water cures diseases.

The closing problem of *Siris* is the nature of the Supreme Being. Making 'the best of those glimpses within our reach', Berkeley conceives that 'God may be said to be All in divers senses'. He tentatively discusses the relations of the Persons in terms of τὸ Ἕν and Νοῦς. But the stress falls on his unwavering conviction that the Substance of Deity is 'the cause and origin of all beings . . . the same which comprehends and orders and sustains the whole mundane system' (§ 328). The argument of this section and, in fact, of the *whole* of *Siris* expresses and, some may think, justifies the intuition that inspired his youth. In his last book Berkeley delineates, in the light of enriched experience and with some colours of sunset, his early vision of all things in God,

'That Spring of Life which this great World pervades,
 The Spirit that moves, the Intellect that guides,
 Th' eternal One that o'er the Whole presides.'[1]

As a young man in Trinity College Berkeley read much, thought much, saw clearly, and wrote as for far off future days. In the quiet of Cloyne he read much, thought much, learned much, but unlearned little or nothing. He was in the year 1744, as he had been in the year 1710, and as he remained till the closing scene at Oxford, an unrepentant immaterialist, anti-abstractionist, theist, and Trinitarian.

[1] From verses prefixed to some copies of *Siris*, 2nd ed., Dublin 1744, found by Professor Jessop, and reprinted in *Proc. R. Irish Acad.*, 1933, vol. xli, sec. *C*. 4, p. 159.

APPENDIX I [1]

BERKELEY'S *COMMONPLACE BOOK* [2]

THE date, the purpose, the structure and the marginal signs of the *Commonplace Book* are closely connected subjects. The argument as to date turns largely upon the structure and purpose of the work. The apparatus of marginal signs, which, for its own sake, deserves more attention than it has yet received, can also throw much light upon the questions of structure and purpose.

If the *Commonplace Book* be a book, that is a purposeful composition,[3] a fairly precise date for it is a *desideratum*. If otherwise, if, that is, Add. MS. 39305 be merely a pair of old note-books filled with random jottings, its date would not matter much, and the accepted date, 1705–8, would be near enough for current uses. At present, writers take quotations from the *Commonplace Book* to adorn their tale, much as theologians of the old school used quotations from Scripture. A serious use of the work in a study of the sources and the growth of Berkeley's system is nearly impossible while its date remains uncertain and its purpose obscure.

Dr. G. A. Johnston and Professor R. I. Aaron have published valuable studies, to which I am indebted: but with a new angle of approach and some new evidence, we may perhaps carry the solution of these problems somewhat beyond the point they reached.

The Purpose

The Times has styled the *Commonplace Book* 'Berkeley's

---

[1] Reprinted by permission without substantial alteration from *Hermathena*, vol. xxii, 1932.

[2] Johnston's numbering of the entries is followed in this Appendix.

[3] Among the definitions of 'composition' the *Oxford Eng. Dict.* gives (21 b) 'A train of ideas put into words'. In that sense the term is, I think, a just description of the *C.P.B.*, and one needed to correct the first impression left on the mind by the apparent discontinuity of the entries.

Scrap-book'. That term seems to represent the prevailing view. In a similar vein, commentators describe the entries as 'jottings' or 'aphorisms'. Now there is systematic purpose in the book, in a higher degree than these terms would suggest. Misconceptions arise partly from overlooking the purpose, partly from assigning the wrong purpose. It has been supposed that the work could be accounted for, partly as a desultory companion to Berkeley's private reading, and partly as a record of subjects debated in his College Society. This debating Society has clouded the issue. It is a red herring across the trail. Berkeley has written a good deal in Add. MS. 39305 that has no claim to inclusion in the *Commonplace Book* proper. To draw the line between relevant and irrelevant material is an essential preliminary. We must know precisely what we are trying to date before we date it. I have given reasons elsewhere[1] for thinking it improbable that there was any real connexion between the work of the Society and the *Commonplace Book*. It is surely a mere accident that 'That the Junior begin the Conference' and 'Time a sensation, therefore onely in ye mind' occur on successive pages. One has only to look at page 103 of the manuscript, to read what is there and, if I may say so, what is not there, to be convinced that after December 7, 1706, the note-book ceased to be a Society rule-book. The *Commonplace Book*, in the accepted meaning of the term, begins on page 104, and to suppose that it or any of the pages that follow were filled in before page 103, while the note-book was a Society book, would be a gratuitous assumption.

If one leaves the College Society out of account, the inadequacy of the scrap-book hypothesis is manifest. The entries were not casually made; they are not 'jottings'. For Berkeley they were sections. He calls them so on one occasion (208). The *Commonplace Book* externally is a very formal work.[2] The original entries are for the most part confined to the right-hand page, the opposite page being reserved for later comments and corrections. A definite margin is left throughout. The beginning and end of each entry are clearly marked by capitals and spacings. Though the handwriting is, for the most part, impetuous, there are scarcely two cases of serious doubt as to whether entries are separate or continuous. Of course some diarists keep their log with great care. But if one considers this sustained attention to external form, along with the nature of the entries, and the fact that scores of them reappear in Berkeley's published works, in some cases *verbatim*, one must conclude that the sole and adequate purpose of the *Commonplace Book* was authorship. Even those few entries that seem trivial and personal have some bearing upon his writing. The entries seem disjointed at first sight: but familiarity and close study will often bring to light the connexion of thought and the latent argument. Berkeley modified his literary intentions as the work progressed, but 41, 49, 60 are indications that right from the start he had publication in view. The *Commonplace Book*, in my view, was a definite piece of work, undertaken by Berkeley as a preliminary stage in working out the argument of the *Theory of Vision* and of the *Principles*, just as, apparently, he wrote another *Commonplace Book* as a prelude to the *Querist* (Fraser, *Works*, vol. iv, p. 567, note).

The Marginal Signs

Of this thesis, which is not new, the apparatus of marginal signs furnishes new proof. As a whole, this apparatus has received little attention. Signs set against some hundreds of the entries have never yet been printed. For reference I tabulate them at the end of this sketch. They might be difficult to print in the text, and I do not wish to exaggerate their importance. But is an edition of the *Commonplace Book* complete without them? The marginal letters are in the printed texts: but they look lost and lonely, because detached from the rest of the apparatus. Few readers know that in the manuscript the letters form part of a system in which practically every entry has a marginal sign, and some have more than one. Over 500 entries are marked with a letter, some 300 are marked ×, and nearly 200 are marked +. Berkeley has left an index of the letters. I give below my view as to the meaning of the other symbols and their variations.[1]

Before dealing with the details of the system, I wish to point out that the mere fact that the apparatus is there shows that the *Commonplace Book* is no rag-bag of philosophical odds and ends. The 950 entries must have been written under the control of some design, or they could never have been brought within the compass of so simple a system. Further, the apparatus shows that Berkeley made a definite, careful, and calculated use of the *Commonplace Book* when it was written. The *Commonplace Book* was not only his storehouse, but his workshop. The initiated reader, if he understands the sign system, can often tell in the case of a given entry, merely by looking at its sign, whereabouts in the published works to find it, or at least where *not* to look for it. Most paragraphs of the *Theory of Vision* and of the *Principles* still show the influence of the *Commonplace Book*. The same influence is most marked in the case of the original (draft) Introduction to the *Principles*.[2] And it is natural to infer that the lost Part II[3] of the *Principles* made use of the large group of entries dealing with morals and psychology.

Again, apart from what the marginal apparatus meant for Berkeley, it serves us a good turn. It provides an objective criterion as to what constitutes the *Commonplace Book* proper. There is a good deal of material in one of the note-books that has obviously no connexion with the metaphysical entries.

---

[1] Most of them are shown on the photograph of MS., p. 118, which forms the frontispiece of this book.   [2] See below, p. 202.

[3] The Preface to *Hylas*, which mentions Part II, adds point to this suggestion. This Preface has made clear use of the six entries on p. 4 Add. MS. 39304, which Fraser published as part of the *Commonplace Book* (*Works*, vol. i, p. 92). Four of these appear in substance, the first almost in terms. For 'Giant and Dwarf' cf. 689. The third dialogue in several places shows the influence of the *Commonplace Book*: e.g., *Works*, vol. i, p. 479, 'substantial forms, hylarchic principles, plastic natures . . . possibility of Matter's thinking': cf. 626, 707.

There is some border-line material. And editors have been somewhat subjective in forming their canon. I suggest that no material to which Berkeley has not applied the marginal apparatus should be regarded as part of the *Commonplace Book*. This test would exclude two sections that Johnston includes: (1) The 'Queries'.[1] These are simply odd notes on Locke's *Essay*. They occupy page 102 of the manuscript, recto and verso. This was a blank page between the two codes of Rules. The 'Queries' were written *after* December 7, 1706: for page 103, which contains the statutes of that date, has subsequently been used as a blotting-pad for the verso of 102, which contains part of the 'Queries'. Probably they were written before the *Commonplace Book* was begun: but in any case the absence of marginal signs shows them not to be part of the *Commonplace Book*. (2) The same applies to 946–53. 951 has been brought into the *Commonplace Book* as 151, and is there duly indexed S. Mo. These entries too are merely notes on Locke's *Essay*. Fraser did not include them. They have little claim to inclusion. They occur on p. 164, verso: but they could not have been written or read continuously with the main body of entries: for they are upside down.

Thus the apparatus of marginal signs supplies a useful criterion. It serves to distinguish the *Commonplace Book* proper from the other contents of the famous note-books. It confirms the view that Berkeley wrote it as a prelude to his published works. Now to keep such a book and to invent such an apparatus might naturally occur to any author. But if there is no consequence, it is a curious coincidence that shortly before he began his *Commonplace Book* (Fraser gave it that name) Berkeley came across John Locke's *New Method of a Commonplace-Book*. Locke says that he had himself used the method for five and twenty years. It is a highly elaborate system of entries and index signs. The tract is the last item in the *Posthumous Works of Mr. John Locke* (1706). Berkeley names this work at the end of his *De Ludo Algebraico*, published early in 1707, and praises it, or parts of it, highly.

[1] Numbered i–xxiv by Johnston.

The marginal sign system falls into two divisions, approximately equal: letters of the alphabet and mathematical symbols. As regards the letters, I can be brief. The system is self-explanatory. Berkeley has prefixed a table, showing the meaning of each letter, to the second of the two note-books (page 3 of the manuscript). The sign system brings out the distinction between the two note-books, and I shall have occasion to refer to them separately. So I here note that, following Johnston, I designate as A the note-book now appearing as the first (MS., pp. 3–95), and as B the other note-book (pp. 96–180). The index of letters is in its proper place: for the existing letter system is clearly original in A, and has been extended to B, and one might perhaps argue that the mathematical symbols were original in B, and have been extended to A.

The distribution of index letters shows the distribution of subject-matter, so the following table may be of some interest:

		No. of Entries	
	Index Letter	*Note-book A*	*Note-book B*
I.	Introduction . . .	58	4
	(i.e., to the *Principles*).		
M.	Matter	66	62
P.	Primary and Secondary Qualities	18	17
E.	Existence	29	..
T.	Time	3	11
S.	Soul—Spirit . . .	120	15
G.	God	15	4
Mo.	Moral Philosophy . . .	44	5
N.	Natural Philosophy . .	26	8

The line between T. and S. is Berkeley's. It would seem to mark off the subjects of *Principles*, Part I, from those of the projected Part II (and Part III?). It will be seen that the only 'lettered' topic at all equally represented in both note-books is matter (and its qualities). There is an interesting vestige of an earlier sign system in B. S., which now means Soul or Spirit, originally in B meant Space. There are over 40 cases in B of

S. stroked out,[1] and for the most part M., sometimes P., has been substituted. In a few cases, e.g. 98, 123, the original S. has been left standing: for Berkeley has omitted to stroke it out. But any one can see that these entries have nothing to do with Soul or Spirit.

In addition to the 58 shown in the table, about 25 more entries in A were originally designed for the Introduction. The I. has been stroked out,[2] and for the most part S. Mo. substituted. Abstract ideas now monopolize the Introduction, but this theme came gradually to Berkeley in the course of his *Commonplace Book* construction. He first planned to give in the Introduction a theory of demonstration (592), truth, knowledge, and certainty (687). It is interesting to note that there are no cases of E. (Existence) in B. The meaning and nature of Existence *was* the New Principle, or the most positive form of it, which he discovered with exultation when he was three-quarters of the way through note-book B, and which he proceeds to develop in the new note-book A. Very few, if any, of the 'lettered' entries appear in, or are represented in, the *Theory of Vision*, and as the letters belong primarily to note-book A, it is clear that B was a preliminary to the *Theory of Vision*, and A a preliminary to the *Principles*. This is only a broad generalization as to ground plan. It cannot be pressed in the case of particular entries. For instance, the group on Time with which B opens is represented in the *Principles*, § 111, and the very first entry in A is embodied in the *Theory of Vision*, § 145.

I come now to the two mathematical symbols. I found the clue to the meaning of × in the entries 687 and 865.

687. N. Mo. ×. Truth, three sorts thereof—natural, mathematical, & moral.

865. N. Mo. ×. Three sorts of useful knowledge: that of coexistence to be treated of in our Principles of Natural Philosophy, that of relation in Mathematiques, that of definition, or inclusion, or Words . . . in Morality.

It is quite clear that × was originally the mark for one of his three primary divisions of subject-matter. It is the symbol

[1] See frontispiece.   [2] See below, pp. 202–3, note.

for mathematics in the widest sense, covering geometry, extension, and all pure quantity. There are over 300 entries so
marked, and they all come under this broad heading. Possibly
the little note on the back of page 9, '× this belongs to
geometry',[1] is Berkeley's own note of the meaning of the symbol.

From these 300 'mathematical entries' Berkeley then proceeded[2] to select those with a bearing on the themes of his
first book. He did so, I suggest, by two stages[3]; (1) Against the
selected entries he set the figure 1, for the most part in an angle
of the × (he also set the 1 opposite some of the M. entries).
(2) He then distributed those so selected between the three
main sections in the original plan of the *Theory of Vision*,
marking them respectively 1, 2, 3 in an angle of the ×. The
meanings thus are—

$^1×^1$ Distance—*T.V.* §§ 1–51;

$^1×^2$ Magnitude—*T.V.* §§ 52–87;

$^1×^3$ Heterogeneity of sight and touch—*T.V.* §§ 121–46.

The present third section (§§ 88–120) is in the nature of an
afterthought. Nominally it is on 'situation': but in fact it is
monopolized by the problem of the inverted retinal image.
The marginal signs bear out this view. There is a clearly
marked group of seven entries[4] dealing with this problem, of
which 235–6 are remarkable for their close correspondence with
T.V. §§ 103, 108. All the seven, and they only, have the special
sign, $^1_a×^3$. It would seem that Berkeley became aware of the
capital importance of this problem as the *Commonplace Book*
progressed. Years after, in his *Theory of Vision Vindicated*, he
writes (§ 52): 'The solution of this knot about inverted images
seems the principal point in the whole Optic Theory . . . the
surest way to lead the mind into a thorough knowledge of the
true nature of Vision'. It is worth noting that the pages of

---

[1] Printed as part of 438.

[2] I am presuming that he did not insert the signs as he went
along. The letters certainly seem subsequent to the entries, a
few of which are marked Int., Introd., Pre., &c.

[3] I speak with less confidence about the first stage.

[4] e.g. 128, shown on frontispiece.

the *Commonplace Book* most charged with the joy of discovery
are those which come immediately after his intensive study of
this problem. The problem, I suppose, supplied him with the
clearest proof from fact that we do not properly see what we
think we see.

Reference to the table on page 204 will show that $\times^2$ Magnitude and $\times^3$ Heterogeneity are definitely earmarked for their re-
spective subjects. $\times^1$ Distance is not so unmistakable. Yet there
are enough instances to establish the meaning, e.g. 172, 504 (the
Barrovian case, *T.V.* § 29, &c.); 306 (see *T.V.* §§ 26, 34). Of
those marked $\times^+$ several deal with distance, and I suggest that
in these cases the original 1 has been stroked through by
Berkeley, possibly because of the confusion caused by the
figure 1 doing double duty (if my conjecture is sound) for the
first book and for the first section.

Several entries are marked for two sections. 240 is interesting. It is marked for all three sections, and its principle, i.e.
'unlike signs', occurs in all three sections of the *Theory of Vision*
(§§ 9, 23, 65, 143–5).

The asterisk * which occurs occasionally I have not treated
as part of the apparatus. It is always, I think, merely a reference to a qualifying entry on the opposite page.

I turn now to the symbol $+$. It occurs against 123 entries
in note-book B, and against 65 in A. In the last quarter of A
it is rare. My suggestion is that Berkeley used it as we might
use a minus sign, as a mark of omission. Cajori[1] shows that
the usage of these signs was not fixed in the seventeenth century. In any case arbitrary symbolism would appeal to Berkeley.
At one time I thought it might be '–' subsequently stroked
through. I see now that that explanation is unnecessary, and
in most cases evidently not true to fact. It is clear[2] that
Berkeley would need some sign to set against those entries
which represented positions tentatively occupied and subse-

----

[1] *History of Mathem. Notations*, vol. i, §§ 208 sqq. Note that
$+$ and $\times$ and six other 'operationum logisticarum symbola'
appear in the *Tabula Lusoria*: Fraser, *Works*, vol. iv, pp. 55–7.

[2] e.g. 'I must cancell', 870.

quently abandoned in the course of further thought, or against entries which for any other reason he decided not to use. This sign + is as good as any other for that purpose. Over against 486 he has written the caution, 'this I do not altogether approve of', and over against 473 we find the flat contradiction 474. Both 473 and 486 are marked +, and it is clear that in the majority of cases the symbol is neater and more efficient than such verbal cautions and contradictions.

I do not pretend that this conclusion is established. Those who have patience to look through the list of entries so marked (pp. 204–5) may find a better explanation. I will only say I have had it in mind during several months' close examination of the entries, and have not found a clear case of breakdown. Trivial, personal, irrelevant, or merely unsuitable entries are marked +. The sign in fact seems proper to all those entries which would be of no service to him in writing his books. This view is not inconsistent with the view advanced above as to the purpose of the whole work. Material amassed by an author often proves unsuitable as the work progresses. I draw attention to 424. It provides, on my theory, an instructive instance of the working of Berkeley's mind and pen. Beside the M. appears ⊕ in the manuscript, and the reader must remember that the second half of the entry is a later comment written on the opposite page, and marked M. Berkeley when he first made the entry wrote boldly, but consistently with the Principle. On later revision he is afraid of his own courage, and marks the entry +. Subsequently he reflects upon the distinction between mediate and immediate object. Courage returns. He recants his recantation by ringing the +, adds the opposite page entry, and marks both entries M.

The groups 143–6, 158–62 (?163) are marked +. I suggest that the reason for the sign here is prudence. All these entries, in my view, were made in direct criticism of W. King's *De Origine Mali*. The 'A.B.' of 144 and 161 is King,[1] the powerful

---

[1] I am interested to hear from M. Maheu that this explanation of A.B. occurred independently to him, and that he observed,

Archbishop of Dublin, who was subsequently to pass the severe censures on the *Theory of Vision* answered by Berkeley in the appendix to the second edition (see Berkeley's Letter to Percival, March 1, 1710), and to demonstrate the imprudence of giving 'the least handle of offence to the Church or Churchmen' (727) by citing Berkeley before his ecclesiastical court on the charge of receiving illegal ordination.[1]

If my explanation of + is correct, the symbol is the most important part of the marginal apparatus for students of the development of Berkeley's thought. For the large group of entries so marked will constitute a 'Black List' of metaphysical positions tentatively held and definitely rejected. Of these the most important are—

The Soul knowable—25, 44, 156, 182.
Simple Ideas—53, 135–6, and 14 others.
Doctrine of Powers—41, 52, and 7 others.
All Ideas from without—330, 906.
No word without ideas—371, 904, and 5 others.
No soul apart from ideas—583, 585–7, 631, 646.

The much quoted 'Mind is a congeries of perceptions' is on the Black List. So too are most of the tasteless and unworthy references to mathematicians—facts which illustrate the unfairness of indiscriminate and uninformed quotation from the *Commonplace Book*.

Biography and the Date

This mass of detail must seem, I fear, trivial and unimportant, but it all goes to build up a view of the *Commonplace Book*, essential perhaps to a sound judgement on those larger questions of date and structure to which I now turn. The *Commonplace Book* is thus shown to be no day-book, no journal for jottings, no scrap-book, nor collection of philosophical bric-à-

as I did, the 'A.B. of Cashel' in the Chapman MS. which proves Berkeley's use of A.B. as abbreviation for 'Archbishop'.

[1] See Berkeley's autograph letter to King preserved in T.C.D. Library.

brac. It is on the face of it a composition with a defined purpose, undertaken and carried through as the scaffolding of Berkeley's published works.

The composition of the *Commonplace Book* must, then, have required serious attention, and a sustained labour of the intellect. I do not see its author, arm-chaired, opening his note-book just before going to bed, and jotting down in it casual reflections upon his reading. He surely gave the best working hours of his day to it. I see him sitting up to the table, with the immortal note-book in front of him, and Locke, Malebranche, Molyneux, and all the other books piled around, the books being companion to the note-book, rather than it to them.

Now at what period of his life could Berkeley have given the requisite time and pains? And what length of time would one expect the work to occupy? Can we find a period in which Berkeley was free from the pressure of other work, with mind untroubled by fear of want or by anxiety about his career? I think we can. I think there is a period that fits all the facts; a period not too long and not too short; a suitable period of some twelve or thirteen months. The traditional two or three years is, to my mind, too long: for then it is not so easy to account for the underlying unity of the work and its continuity of thought and interest. If, on the other hand, we compress the period unduly, say, to six months, we do not allow sufficient time for the real and substantial development shown in course of the work, nor even for the mere marshalling of the host of authorities consulted by this mind—encyclopaedic, critical, well-educated, mature, and scholarly.

Now the Fellowship Examination seems to me to be an important and neglected factor in the question of date. I could not be positive in the matter, but it seems to me unlikely that Berkeley could begin to write the *Commonplace Book* with that ordeal hanging over his head. Stock, in his *Life*, says: 'He was admitted fellow of that College June 9, 1707, having previously sustained with honour the very trying examination which the candidates for that preferment are by the statutes required to

undergo.' The examination was 'trying', because it was on a
wide course, competitive, open practically to all comers, and
occasional. If held, it was held by statute, as at present,
immediately previous to Trinity Monday. If no Fellowships
were vacant, it was not held. Some years three or four Fellowships might be thus filled: then there might be no examination
for three or four years. Death, resignation, and, especially,
preferment by 'going out on a College living', made the vacan-
cies, if any. I have searched in vain for early records of the actual
examinations. Nor can I find any details as to courses read.
The statute prescribes: 'Quattuor diebus praecedentibus elec-
tionis diem, ab hora octava antemeridiana ad decimam, et ab
hora secunda pomeridiana ad quartam, omnes electores dili-
genter exquirant . . . primo die, in dialectica, et mathematicis:
secundo, in philosophia tum naturali, tum morali; tertio, in
linguarum peritia, in historiis, et poetis, et in toto genere
humanioris literaturae: quarto, in scribendo de themate aliquo,
et versibus componendis.'

This statute must have been the controlling factor in
Berkeley's reading after his graduation in 1704. One can read
its conception of the *scibile* even in the ground-plan of the
Commonplace Book.

Interesting sidelights upon the working of the Fellowship
Examination system are to be had in the Locke-Molyneux
correspondence.[1] Molyneux had undertaken to secure a young
Trinity scholar to translate Locke's *Essay* into Latin. He
secured a Fellowship candidate. He writes, on May 7, 1695:
'As to the translation that is going on here, tis undertaken by
one Mr Wm Mullart. He proposes to finish it in half a year
or nine months at farthest: for he cannot wholly disengage
himself from some other studies.' And again of Mullart:
'Aug. 24th, 1695. I formerly told you how he designed for a
Fellowship, had any at that time hapen'd vacant, as there did
none. But very lately there are 2 fellowships become void and
a 3rd like to be so before the time which is next June 1696 &

he tells me plainly he must endeavour to get one of them &
that there will be at least 5 competitors if not six & therefore
he must use his utmost diligence application and study in
the intermediate time to fit himself for the examination they
undergo; and this, he says, will take up so much of his time that
he knows not whether he shall have any to spare for the
translation.'

This Mr. Mullart just touches Berkeley's life. So I will
briefly give the relevant facts. Mullart's 'diligence, application
and study' were rewarded. On June 8, 1696, he was elected
to the third of the four Fellowships filled on that day. In the
College Register we may read Mr. Mullart's appointment to
various lectureships in almost each succeeding year till we reach
the following important entry:

'1706 Sep 24th The living of Clinish in ye Diocese of
Clogher being void by ye death of Mr Robert Smyth,
Mr Mullart was nominated to it.'

Clearly it was Wm. Mullart's 'going out' that let George
Berkeley in.

Let us reconstruct the situation. Berkeley coming up for
Michaelmas Term, which opens on October 1, 1706, is met
by the news that there will be an election to Fellowship on
Trinity Monday, 1707 (the sole election for six years). There
has been no election since 1704, and, as it proved, the next
election after 1707 was in 1710. He has eight months for intensive preparation. He cannot afford to take chances. He is a
brilliant student, but he has brilliant and hard-working friends,
like Synge[1] and Madden,[2] who no doubt were his rivals, because
they were subsequently his colleagues. Berkeley was a comparatively poor man, an Erasmus Smith Exhibitioner. True,
there were poorer men in his College set (574). But there is
only one vacancy, for which the best men of three academic
years are competing. Clearly, Berkeley had every reason for

---

[1] Mentioned in Chapman MS. *N.B.* 'tristem in musaeo solitu-
dinem, duramque eorum qui vulgo audiunt *Pumps* vitam': *De
Lud. Alg. Works*, vol. iv, p. 59. The context explains the colloquialism *Pumps*.   [2] *C.P.B.* 574.

concentrating on the Fellowship Examination of 1707. His career may depend on winning that one vacant Fellowship. He has now little time to devote to his Society, with its cast-iron rules. One piece of literary work must be done at once. The *Arithmetica and Miscellanea Mathematica*, which has been on the stocks for nearly three years, is finished off, and prepared for the press. Early in 1707 these 'first-fruits' are published, as a Fellowship thesis, conciliating influential opinion, indirectly and diplomatically, by the dedications, answering damaging rumours (as that he hated mathematics), showing off his powers of composition in the Latin tongue, indicating his absorption in sterner disciplines, and holding out the promise of greater things.

Once he had won a Fellowship, his career was safe, his position secure. For the first year or two a Junior Fellow's College duties would not be exacting. Here, then, is a golden opportunity for settling down to authorship. He can now *solutiore animo* examine, arrange, express those high thoughts which have long been beckoning. I submit then that the biographical facts point to June–July, 1707,[1] as a probable date for the beginning of the *Commonplace Book*, and that they make an earlier date next door to impossible, especially during the eight months immediately preceding the Fellowship Examination of 1707.

The Structure of the 'Commonplace Book'.

Before discussing the internal evidence as to the date, I must deal with the question of structure. While doubt remains as to which is the first page and which the last, we cannot draw any conclusion about the date which would be precise enough for purposes of scholarship. Here I have something new to say: but as, in the main, it provides new support for old belief, I can be brief.

[1] He proceeded M.A. July 15. The Long Vacation began July 9. It is important to realize that the immaterial hypothesis (19) was clear-cut in his mind *before* he began to write the *C.P.B.*

Lorenz was the first to show that the *Commonplace Book* is composite. It consists of two note-books bound together. The fact is visible and palpable. Lorenz further argues that the note-books have been accidentally bound together in wrong order. His view is generally accepted. I do not dispute the substantial fact. At the same time, in justice to precision and to the book-trade, it should be pointed out that the time-order of writing is not necessarily the right order for binding. It is not impossible that Berkeley himself had the books bound.[1] Probably, however, the *present* binding of the *Commonplace Book* is after Berkeley's time. It is uniform with 39304 and 39313 in the Berkeley Papers, and with those only. 39313 is inscribed, 'Hugh James Rose 1828'. On the flyleaf is written, apparently in Rose's hand: 'These MS. sermons and charges of Bishop Benson were found among the papers of Dr. George Berkeley, son of the celebrated Bishop Berkeley. They probably came into his possession through his friendship with Mrs. and Miss Talbot, with the former of whom Bishop Benson's sister resided till her marriage with Archbishop Secker.' One might infer that either to Berkeley's son or to H. J. Rose we owe the present binding of the *Commonplace Book*. However that may be, the present front page (page 3) has been a front page for a long time. Father and son have recognized it as such. It may be that 'G: B: Coll: Trin: Dub: alum'[2] is the father's signature, and I am sure that the signature half-way down the page is that of George Berkeley, Jr., in his young days, at least before he took his M.A. (1759). He has inscribed himself with ornamental flourishes, displaying his Bachelor's Degree and his Oxford College.[3] So there is no proof that the work came to Berkeley, Jr., or to Rose in the form

[1] Since writing this, I came across an indication that Berkeley may have used the *C.P.B.* later in life. See above p. 172.

[2] Or did the son matriculate at T.C.D., April 25, 1752, on his way to Oxford (June 4)?

[3] The A.B. is disguised by flourishes and the *ex aed. Xti* is microscopic; but I happened to notice the son's 'A.M. ex aed. Xti' elsewhere in the Berkeley papers. On comparison I do not

of two detached note-books. Even if Bishop Berkeley left them so, still even he might not consider the present manuscript order 'wrong'. It is at least as 'right' as that of some printed editions.

To return to the question of the time-order. Lorenz and Johnston put note-book B before A. In the main I agree with them; but I wish to advance a new reason for agreeing with them in the main, which is also a reason for differing from them in certain not unimportant details. The evidence as presented by Johnston is not convincing. He writes:[1] 'A contains the date August 28th, 1708. B contains the dates January 10, 1705–6, and December 7, 1706. There is no doubt as to these dates, consequently A must be later than B. This is absolutely conclusive.' The dates *per se* will not bear this stress. The dates in B occur in matter unconnected with the *Commonplace Book* proper. The same *might* hold of the date in A (but see below, p. 201). When Dr. Johnston says that he has read the *Commonplace Book* for years, and considers the order to be B A and not A B, he gives an argument morally conclusive, and one to which all Berkeleian scholars will defer. But, none the less, there is need for an objective argument such as the following, which seems to me to be absolutely conclusive.

The Orthography of 'Idea'.

I noticed that during the course of writing the *Commonplace Book* Berkeley has made a marked change in the orthography of the pivotal word of his philosophy. I will tabulate the facts shortly. In outline the change is this. In the first third he

think there can be any doubt as to this signature which has puzzled readers of page 3.

[1] *Development of Berkeley's Philosophy*, p. 22. Subsidiary arguments are unconvincing, e.g. Fraser on Newton's knighthood. In a private note-book where Newton occurs *passim*, 'Sir Isaac' and 'Mr. Newton' are equal and opposite accidents. Take a parallel case such as 'Eddington' in a 1932 note-book!

writes 'idea' invariably. In the central third he writes 'idea'
and 'Idea' indifferently. In the last third he writes 'Idea'
consistently. That the change of practice was from small
to capital, and not *vice versa*, needs proving. I do so along
three lines: the evidence of the *Commonplace Book* itself,
the evidence of his published works, and the evidence of
his other writings of the period. If the change were from
capital to small, the order of note-books could not be B A, for
B opens with 40 pages of unbroken 'idea'. But no more could
the order be A B. For, if so, we should have to suppose that
Berkeley first wrote 'idea' and 'Idea' indifferently, then fixed
on 'Idea', then changed abruptly to a steady 'idea', then
reverted to his original indifference. Whereas if the order be
B A, and the change be from small to capital, a simple, natural,
and accountable change occurred. He first wrote 'idea' uniformly. When he discovered the Principle, idea takes on a new
meaning, and the word a new importance. He is out to 'change
ideas into things' (*Hylas, Works*, p. 463). He studied the nature
of the idea. It became concrete and objective. He decides to
show to the eye of his readers this added importance. Such a
change is not to be made all at once. So we find a transition
period, in which both styles compete, the capital gradually
superseding the small letter. Finally, perhaps under the influence of preparing the *Theory of Vision* for the press,[1] 'Idea'
became the fixed orthography.

The evidence of his other writings, both unpublished and
published, points beyond a doubt to the same conclusion. The
following table analyses all the occurrences of the word in the
Berkeley manuscripts of the period. Not much survives prior
to the *Commonplace Book*; but the two essays that do survive,
it is worth noting, are formal, representative writings, carefully revised, and preserved in the Molyneux Papers. This
table proves, I think, that the orthographical change was

---

[1] I think that a good portion of the *Theory of Vision* was
written, no doubt, in draft, before the completion of the *Commonplace Book*, but I do not express a final opinion. Surely 754
refers to the Dedication to Percival?

deliberate, purposive, and in the direction idea–Idea, not vice versa:

Date	Manuscript	idea	Idea
Jan. 1706	The Cave of Dunmore Essay (Dublin Copy A) .	1	none
probably 1706–7	Of Infinites . . .	13	none
probably 1706–7	The Queries and MS. page 164 (946–953), verso .	9	none[1]
Jan. 11, 1708	Sermon on Life and Immortality . . .	3	none
1707–8	Commonplace Book, Notebook B . . .	120	6
	Commonplace Book, Notebook A . . .	69	211
Nov. 15–Dec. 18, 1708	Draft Introduction to the Principles . . .	none	over 200
	Draft of Principles, §§ 85–145	none	89

I pass to the evidence of the publications. 'Idea (spelt with a capital) in *Siris* is very different from idea in the earlier works.' So Johnston writes.[2] It would not be fair to take this casual remark *au pied de la lettre*. Still, the remark is unfortunately phrased. For the orthographical facts are the other way about. The earlier works—*Theory of Vision*, *Principles*, *Passive Obedience*, *Dialogues*, also the *Analyst* and *Alciphron*—print with capital. *Siris* prints 'idea' (even of Plato's),[3] and it is, I think, the only major publication to do so. A closer scrutiny of the books of the early period shows that Berkeley at that time took great pains in the matter. It should be remembered that he would find both usages in the books he read. Now, here is a curious fact. In the *Theory of Vision* (1709) he prints the word invariably in italics with initial capital—*Idea*. In the *Principles* (1710), retaining the capital, Idea, he drops the italics in the

---

[1] 953 has 'Ideas', but as it begins the entry, it does not enter into account. All entries begin with capitals.

[2] *Development*, p. 256.

[3] The only 'Idea' I have noticed is in Table of Contents.

case of realities; he retains the italics (with capital), however, in the cases of abstract, unreal, or otherwise suspect ideas. In view of these facts we cannot regard the marked orthographical change that occurs in the *Commonplace Book* as undesigned or insignificant. It is, surely, an outward and visible sign of an abiding change of intellectual orientation.

To show graphically the bearing of these facts upon the questions of structure, I must inflict yet another table upon the reader. It pursues the analysis straight ahead through the pages of the manuscript in the B A order. Its page divisions at 143, 28, and 57 are more or less arbitrary, and struck in the interests of my argument. To a reader of the manuscript the broad fact is objective and independent of such arrangement. But I arrange the details thus to assist those who have not the advantage of reading the manuscript, and to enable them to visualize the three periods—the 'idea' period at the outset, the 'Idea' period at the close, and the middle or transition period, during which the new practice comes in gradually, competes with the old, and finally ousts it.

Entries			*idea*	*Idea*
1–276	Note-book B, pp. 104–43		72	none (excluding 1 on verso, obviously a later addition, 179).
{277–395 903–45	ditto	pp. 144–64	48	5 (+2 on verso).
396–524	Note-Book A, pp. 4–28		46	6
525–681	ditto	pp. 29–57	18	96
682–902	ditto	pp. 58–95	5	107

I submit that the above analysis constitutes an independent, new, and objective proof that note-book B is, in general, prior to A. It may be said that this is a laborious proof of a proposition that nobody doubts. I do not fear that reproach. For there are doubters, and will be. Moreover, this line of proof, if sound, corrects the prevailing opinion on certain points, and thereby facilitates a much needed restoration. Thus we may reach a clear view of the structure of the *Commonplace Book* as a whole.

I have claimed for B priority *in general*. Strictly, what is proved is that the first part of B was written before the last part of A. I have not yet met any argument that compels us to think that Berkeley finished B before he began A. And there are indications that towards the middle of the period he had the two note-books in use simultaneously.[1]

A is not simply a continuation of B. B begins—may we say it?—with a 'try-out' of the 'immaterialist hypothesis'; A begins with a 'try-out' of the New Principle. I grant that the very first entry of A (396) links to B and the *Theory of Vision*. But the entries 397–411—i.e. the first three pages of A—do not look back to B. They look ahead. They reveal the author on a peak in Darien, descrying new territory, and mapping its main features, or, in prose, show us Berkeley taking stock of the position reached in his previous study and projecting the Introduction and scope of the *Principles*. There is further proof that A does not continue just where B left off. It seems to me that when he was on page 6 of A he was also on page 158 of B. For at that point in both books we have a duplicated series of eight or nine entries;[2] not identical, but very close indeed; cf. 365–73 with 411–20. These entries, with the exception of the last two in each group, concern Infinitesimals, and are closely related to, probably copied in from, the essay *Of Infinites*. If A were a simple continuation of B, a double transcription of such length and so close in time would surely be a blunder hard to explain. Whereas, if at that stage he were filling both note-books simultaneously, we have the easy solution that he entered them in both note-books because he had not then decided whether to use them for the *Theory of Vision* or for the *Principles*, or for both.

The orthography of 'idea' towards the end of B and the

[1] Locke, *New Method of a Common-Place-Book*, p. 321, advocates two or more note-books.

[2] An occasional entry is duplicated. This is the only case of a duplicated series.

beginning of A is that of the transition or middle period. He makes such entries as 392: 'By thing I either mean Ideas or that which has ideas.' From 904 to 923 'idea' predominates: but 923 has 'neither our Ideas nor anything like our ideas'. We must, therefore, keep entries 903–53 in their manuscript position (relative). Johnston,[1] 'in agreement with Lorenz, Erdmann, Rossi, and Hecht', takes them out of B and prints them after A. This unnatural surgery is indefensible. These entries record several positions[2] that Berkeley had held, but definitely abandoned, weeks before he finished A. The section is ludicrously isolated when transposed to the end of A, as in Johnston's text. Moreover, it is very much wanted at the end of B. For the demonstration of the Principle *more geometrico* (903–24) is the decisive factor in the structure[3] of this part, and forms the transition to the theme of A. Finally, the argument from orthography given above clinches the matter.

My view as to the structure of the *Commonplace Book* can be expressed shortly in terms of the pages of the manuscript and in terms of Johnston's numbering of the entries. With the proviso that probably the closing pages of B and the opening pages of A overlap in point of time-order, my view is this: the *Commonplace Book* proper consists of MS. pages 104–164 (recto) and pages 3–95, and was written approximately in that order. I would, therefore, 'top and tail' Johnston's text, relegating the 'Queries' and entries 946–53 to an appendix. I would re-transpose entries 903–45 to their original place after 395. Thus, 900 would be the concluding entry, with 901 and 902 as Berkeley's flyleaf finale. Immediately before 396 I would insert Berkeley's own index-table of the marginal letters. I would restore the apparatus of marginal signs throughout, and I believe we should have the *Commonplace Book* substantially as

---

[1] *Berkeley's Commonplace Book*, p. xxi *n.*

[2] e.g. 904, 906, 908, 911, 916 (all marked +).

[3] The compression at end of B is explained, if, at foot of p. 159 (378), he went ahead to p. 161 and sketched out 'my Principle with a demonstration', subsequently filling all adjacent blank pages.

Berkeley wrote it, and with as close an approximation to the original time-order as we need or can attain.

The Date

I have indicated above my view as to the nature and precise contents of what we are trying to date. We are trying to date a purposeful homogeneous composition, of determined structure, continuously written, and systematically used by Berkeley. The whole work is contained in the two note-books which now constitute B.M. Add. MS. 39305. Our problem, then, is two-fold: (*a*) to determine the date of the opening page of the work (104 of that manuscript); (*b*) to determine the date of the closing page (94 of the manuscript).

(*a*) The *Commonplace Book* could not have been begun before December 7, 1706. That is the one precise and certain fact. Page 103 is headed with that date, very formally written out *in extenso* to fix an agreement. Therefore, page 104 was not written before that date. This argument seems to me conclusive. I cannot conceive any circumstances under which Berkeley would have first made the tremendous entries on page 104 and sqq. and then gone back to page 103, supposed blank, and used it as a record of a trivial agreement, not completed, about a debating society.[1]

As to the further question, 'How long after December 7, 1706, was page 104 written?' there is evidence, but, I think, no rigorous proof. Whatever may have been the reason why the 'underwritten persons' did not subscribe on page 103, it is natural to think that Berkeley would thereupon, after a decent interval of time, convert the Society rule-book to his private purposes. I have given biographical reasons above for thinking it highly improbable that Berkeley could have undertaken the *Commonplace Book* till after the Fellowship Examination.

---

[1] It will be noted that I now regard both codes of rules as in Berkeley's handwriting: see *Hermathena*, vol. xxii, p. 7. The curious spelling 'buisiness' is found in both sets of rules (pp. 97, 103), and also in the sermon of Jan. 11, 1708.

There are indications that during the early months of 1707 Berkeley used this note-book occasionally for rough notes; several pages have been torn out at the far end; pp. 168–9 certainly contain rough work for the *De Ludo Algebraico*,[1] which he was preparing for the press early in 1707. On page 165 there are odd notes for the sermon of January 11, 1708. On page 166 laws of motion are listed, apparently from Keill's *Introductio*. On page 164 there are rough notes on Locke's *Essay*, which, with the Queries, look like 'tip' questions for the Fellowship Examination. The Queries themselves (page 102) were almost certainly written in this period (see above, page 182). The Cave of Dunmore Essay, an inaugural address, is proper to the Society rule-book period, and it occurs right at the far end; but most of the casual entries mentioned above must belong to the interval between December 7, 1706, and the opening date of the *Commonplace Book*. Once that work began, the note-book would be kept, and clearly has been kept, for the one purpose. All these facts make it very probable that page 104 was not written till June or July, 1707. If we consider the minimum period needed for the composition, and work backwards from the autumn of 1708, by which time the last page was certainly written, we should infer that the work was begun in or soon after June, 1707.

(*b*) As to the date of the conclusion of the *Commonplace Book* we can be fairly precise within a small margin. Professor Aaron has noticed that a book published in 1708 is quoted in the last quarter of the work[2]; but that fact does not carry us far, as Professor Aaron shows. The decisive factors seem to me to be: (1) the date on page 95; (2) the draft Introduction to the *Principles*. Of these two, the latter gives the only evidence that can stand alone as virtual proof.

(1) I incline to the opinion that Aug. 28, 1708, at the top of page 95, is Berkeley's dating of the completion of the *Commonplace Book*. But I admit that it and 'The Adventure of the [Shirt]', which seems to go with it, may have no more

---

[1] So Fraser, *Works*, iv, p. 54, note.

[2] 721, Locke, *Some Familiar Letters*.

significance for us than the small sum which Berkeley has scribbled at the foot of the same page.

The latter half of page 94 is crowded with entries, written small, yet neatly. The writer has not allowed himself to over-flow into either of the adjacent verso pages, as he did at the close of his other note-book. Outwardly page 94 (889–900) has all the appearance of a deliberate conclusion—it contains twelve entries, while page 95 simply contains 901, 902. Upon 902, I think, no-thing turns. It may have been written immediately after page 94, or before it, or much later. It may be a quotation or Berkeley's own reflection. The sentiment is of the type to be found in the early correspondence with Percival. It forms a fitting epilogue to a work by a young, ambitious author with lofty ideals.

901 may, of course, be merely the remembered date of some holiday adventure.[1] Yet the entry is put prominently at the head of a page, and the month is written out in full. In the autumn of 1708 Berkeley had some reason (if only habit), no doubt literary, for dating his writings precisely. In the Draft Introduction to the *Principles*, which he began on November 15, 1708, and finished on December 18, 1708, he has entered in the margin not only those days, but almost all the days in between. He has put the date at the end of each day's work in November–December. He might have had the same reason for doing so a couple of months earlier.

(2) If August 28, 1708, be not the actual date we seek, it must be near it. I know no reason for putting the date of completion earlier. The draft Introduction prevents us from making it much later. This draft, begun on November 15, 1708, must have been based on a previous draft. For in parts it is written out fair, as if for the press, the long quotations from Locke being actually penned in italics. So the original composition of the Introduction to the *Principles* must be put back to the early autumn of 1708. Subsequent revisions have obscured the dependence of the Introduction upon the *Commonplace Book*. But originally the Introduction embodied whole entries

[1] I do not think that 'shirt' is the correct reading; but I have puzzled in vain to find a better. It is nearly 'ship', but not quite.

verbatim, as well as taking over from it and developing the experimental conceit of the 'Solitary Man', who was to do for the *Principles* what Molyneux's 'Blind Man' had done for the *Theory of Vision*. I select the most striking instances of dependence, adding in brackets the pages of Fraser's *Works*, vol. iii, where the entries may be found. These are: 310 (383), 606 (380), 651 (380), 750 (380), 760 (357), 761 (371). This is evidence and, I think, proof, that the *Commonplace Book* up to 761 was written before he began to draft the Introduction to the *Principles*. Now entries marked for the Introduction run on to the last page but two (872). In fact, it is only at 870 that he finally abandons his original intention of including a theory of Demonstration in the Introduction (592), and for which, no doubt, he had prepared a specimen 'Demonstration' months before (903–24). It is, therefore, certain that the first 761 entries, and almost certain that the remaining entries, were written before the Introduction to the *Principles* was begun,[1] that is, before the early autumn of 1708.

We may, I think, regard it as established that the *Commonplace Book* proper was not begun before December 7, 1706, and that it was finished before November, 1708: and there are good grounds for holding that Berkeley began the *Commonplace Book* proper shortly after his election to a Fellowship (June 9, 1707), and completed it on August 28, 1708.

Note.—This paper is based on a first-hand study of the actual manuscript. My brother, Mr. F. M. Luce, has kindly checked a good deal of the detail for me.

[1] 870, 'I must cancell all passages.' It would be possible to take this of passages in an Introduction actually written. But then would he not take up pen and cancel them, instead of recording his intentions? It seems to me more natural to interpret it of passages in the *Commonplace Book*. Some twenty-six entries have the marginal sign 'I' (= Introduction) cancelled. The great majority of these concern Demonstration and Certainty, e.g. 537, 554, 556, 590, 592, 710, 731, 740–7, 752–3, 763. 770 with 'I' cancelled shows another change of plan. In 870, after 'pretend', B. at first wrote 'at least near the beginning'.

CLASSIFICATION OF ENTRIES MARKED WITH MATHEMATICAL SYMBOLS ($\times\ +$)

N.B.—(1) In a few cases the symbols are combined with letters; for the letters see Johnston's edition.

(2) Some of those marked $\times^{+}$ appear to have been originally $\times^{1}$ = Distance.

(3) The position of the numbers in the angles is not consistent. They may even be at a little distance from the symbol.

$\times$ 21, 26, 31, 55, 61, 72, 75, 88, 103, 106–7, 110 (?), 119, 121–3, 170, 226, 244–7, 251, 256–63, 267–70, 272–3, 276, 284, 295, 300, 317, 319–20, 324–6, 328, 331–6, 340–50, 352–9, 365–70, 375, 377, 382–3, 385, 387, 410–17, 423, 425, 429, 435–7, 442–3, 445, 447, 456–7, 459, 461–3, 465, 468–70, 475, 482–5, 489, 494, 503, 512–14, 517–19, 523–4, 529, 531–6, 545, 550, 556, 559, 562–3, 579–80, 611, 620–1 (?), 642, 657, 687–8, 710, 734, 742–3, 745–7, 752, 763, 771–81, 783–5, 791, 815–16, 846–7, 849, 858, 865, 880, 885, 889, 892–3, 895, 925–30, 933–4, 939–41.

$^{1}\times$ 56, 609, 738.

$^{1}\times^{1}$ 58, 172, 306, 313, 453, 504.

$\times^{+}$ 97, 99, 173–4, 186, 223, 225, 386, 391, 444, 458.

$^{1}\times^{2}$ 11, 90, 118, 124, 127, 142, 152, 171, 176–7, 185, 194, 201–5, 209–10, 212–13, 216, 218–19, 221–2, 227–8, 238, 241–2, 253, 265–6, 277, 281–3, 285, 312, 314, 762.

$^{1}\times^{3}$ 27–8, 32, 35, 43, 49 (4 times), 54, 59, 69–70, 79, 102, 108, 116, 126, 139–40, 229, 249–50, 252, 271, 305, 307, 396, 439–40, 722.

$^{1}\times^{3}$ 104, 128, 150, 233–6, 255, 286, 318.

$^{11}\times^{2}$ 291–2 (may be $^{1}\times^{2}$), 438.

$^{1}\times^{123}$240.

$^{1}\times^{23}$ 93, 105, 881.

$+$ 1, 2, 5–8, 10, 12, 14–16, 24–5, 29, 33, 38, 41–2, 44, 52–3 (?), 62–3, 65–6, 73, 77, 83–4, 86, 89, 95–6, 98, 101, 109, 112–13, 125, 131–2, 134–6, 141, 143–6, 149, 153–6, 158–64, 166–7, 169, 182, 184, 187, 191–3, 195–7, 199, 206–8, 215, 217, 220, 230, 248, 254, 264, 290, 293–4, 302–4, 321, 330, 337, 339, 362–3, 371, 373, 381, 384, 389–90, 392–4, 398, 403, 405–6, 409, 418, 420, 422, 430, 433, 448, 451, 460, 464, 473, 486–7, 490–1,

495-9, 505-9, 530, 548, 551, 564, 567, 570, 573, 575, 583, 585-7, 601, 604, 614, 628, 631-4, 646-8, 669, 672, 674, 723, 733, 754, 904, 906, 908, 911, 916-17, 931, 942-5.

The Arithmetica and Miscellanea Mathematica

Hone and Rossi, *Bishop Berkeley*, p. 14, note, speak of 771 as written about the same time as the *Arithmetica* (written from 1704, published early in 1707). If they are right, my view as to the date of the *C.P.B.* is clearly wrong. I do not think they are right. The series 771-83 is preparatory for the treatment of Mathematics in the *Principles* (§§ 120-25). Possibly 410 and 929 show recollection of what he had hoped to do for Arithmetic and Algebra by his first publication: but he had similar hopes with regard to the *Theory of Vision* and the *Principles* (see title-page, &c.). I have examined the *Arithmetica* carefully, and can find in it no trace of evidence for the above suggestion made by Hone and Rossi. All the evidence points the other way. In the *C.P.B.* Berkeley outlines a study of the nature of number and the philosophy of the numerical sciences. His outlook is mature. In the *Arithmetica* his aim and objects are much humbler, and his outlook is 'juvenile' (to use Fraser's damning and often misplaced epithet). Contrast his early rhapsodies about Algebra in his *De Ludo Alg.*, e.g. 'Ars magna mirabilis, supremus cognitionis humanae apex', with 779-81. Arithmetic and Algebra 'are sciences purely Verbal & entirely useless but for Practise in Societys of Men. No speculative knowledge, no comparing of Ideas in them'. Surely years of thought and his doctrine of abstract ideas separate the two works.

My view that the *Arithmetica* was an *ad hoc* publication hurried through the press in view of the Fellowship election is supported by the following facts. Three copies are in the T.C.D. Library—one marked 'ex dono authoris,' another with pen and ink corrections, I think, by Berkeley's hand. This latter (oo. g. 55) differs from the other two in the following points. The impression is much clearer. It is without the Tabula Lusoria. It is without the table of *Errata* and *Addenda*, which Fraser's text incorporates, and the *ne quis* note (*Works*, vol. iv, p. 72). It looks like an advance presentation copy: for it has a crimson ornamental end-paper. The page containing the *Errata* and

Addenda has been slipped into the other copies at a later date.
It is headed: 'Quae potissimum prae absentia Authoris irrepse-
runt sic corrigantur.'

THE TEXT

The manuscript is perishing, in parts rapidly. So it is a matter
of urgency to fix the text now. Already we are dependent, for
a few readings, upon Fraser's work of sixty years ago. Professor
Aaron has published in *Mind* (October, 1931, April, 1932) lists
correcting Johnston's text. I venture to add the following corrections and textual notes, giving the MS. page and the entry
number.

MS. Entry.

102 back xvi *for* 'we names' perhaps *read* 'we've names'.

112 78 *for* 'S. 61, 65, 66' *read* 'S. 1, S. 5, S. 6'.

113 88 *for* 'general' *read* 'severall'.

134 225 *for* 'thought' *read* 'thoughts'.

141 262 *for* 'make' *read* 'made'.

145 287 N.B.—after 'witchcraft to see' occurs, lightly
penned through, 'we know nothing but our
thoughts or w^t these (?) think'.

150 309 *for* 'say I' *read* 'says I'—a colloquialism.

4 399 *omit* '[Natural]'.

7 414 *for* 'lato' *read* 'dato'.

8 421 N.B.—on verso against 420.

12 451 *for* 'sin' *read* 'sic'.

15 461 *after* 'arguing' *insert* 'against'.

18 471 *for* 'discussed' *read* 'discors'd'.

474 the second 'rationis' is abbreviated 'rōnis'.

20 482 *for* 'sensible' *read* 'sensibile'.

23 494 *for* 'intended' *read* 'intimated'.

29 525 *for* 'a fool' *read* 'afoot'.

30 533 *for* 'difficulty truly' *read* 'difficulties'.

31 538 probably one entry.

33 547 The MS. here is much perished: but I prefer
'Principle' to 'principles', and 'understanding'
to 'considering'.

34 550 I prefer 'Relations' to 'relation'.

36 561 *before* 'none' *insert* 'few or'.

38 569 *for* 'Barrow's' *read* 'Bacon's'. This is quite certain.

MS. Entry.

41   587   *for* 'and empty words with us' *read* 'empty sounds without a meaning'.

48   626   *for* 'form' *read* 'forms': *for* 'Hylaschic' *read* 'Hylarchic'.

       628   *for* 'attractivae' *read* 'attractrix' (used by Berkeley in *De Aestu Aeris*).

54   664   *for* 'viz' *read* 'v.g.' (so also in 671, and in 683 and 699 *for* 'e.g.').

56   676   *for* 'abstract general' *read* 'general'.

       677   *for* 'really' *read* 'on't'.

65   729   *for* '2nd & 4th' *read* '2 1st'.

66   730   *for* 'words' *read* 'beards' (cf. Locke, iv. 10. 9).

66   732   *for* 'fact' *read* 'Text'.

70   757   *for* 'Both' *read* 'Res' (Respondeo; cf. *Misc. Math. Works*, vol. iv, pp. 17, 44, and Resp., p. 32, ib.).

71   761   *for* 'information' probably *read* 'informations' (so Draft Intr., *Works*, vol. iii, p. 371).

       762   *for* 'systems' probably *read* 'spheres'.

74   782   'severest' is doubtful. 'Gospels' is quite illegible now.

75   784   *omit* '[b. 4, c. 8]'.

       788   N.B.—after 'imaginable' B. wrote and erased 'thing or intelligible thing'.

78   801   *before* 'volitions' *insert* 'the'.

80   813   *after* 'bodies' *insert* '&'. Note capital 'Our', as often for emphasis.

87   845   *for* 'seeing' *read* 'being' (the same archaism occurs in 672 and in B.'s letter to Percival, Jan. 19, 1711).

89   859   *for* "'we', our 'selves', our 'mind'" *read* 'we or selves or mind'.

92   871   *for* 'cavil' *read* 'covet'.

       872   *for* 'diseases' *read* 'discovery'.

APPENDIX II
THE PROBLEM OF BERKELEY'S VISITS TO MALEBRANCHE

THE following are the data:

(*a*) On November 24, 1713, Berkeley wrote to Percival, 'Today he (l'abbé d'Aubigne) is to introduce me to Father Mallebranche, a famous philosopher in this city.' (Rand, op. cit. p. 129).

(*b*) On November 25, 1713, Berkeley wrote to T. Prior, 'Tomorrow I intend to visit Father Malebranche, and discourse him on certain points.' (*L.L.* p. 67).

(*c*) Stock's *Life* (1776) contains the following account: 'At Paris, having now more leisure than when he first passed through that city, Mr. Berkeley took care to pay his respects to his rival in metaphysical sagacity, the illustrious Père Malebranche. He found this ingenious father in his cell, cooking in a small pipkin a medicine for a disorder with which he was then troubled, an inflammation on the lungs. The conversation naturally turned on our author's system, of which the other had received some knowledge from a translation just published. But the issue of this debate proved tragical to poor Malebranche. In the heat of disputation he raised his voice so high, and gave way so freely to the natural impetuosity of a man of parts and a Frenchman, that he brought on himself a violent increase of his disorder, which carried him off a few days after.'

(*d*) Berkeley arrived in Paris for the first time on November 17, 1713 (Rand, pp. 128–31) and stayed there about a month, expecting 'every minute' the arrival of Lord Peterborough, whom he was to attend as Chaplain. On the homeward journey, Berkeley reached Paris about July 10, 1714. He gives no record of his doings on that visit. He appears to have stayed there about ten days, and to have reached England, via Brussels, in August. (Rand, p. 138).

Inference from these data is tempting, but precarious. All we know for certain is that Berkeley twice, namely, on November

24 and 25, 1713, had the intention of visiting Malebranche, and was on the point of doing so. We cannot be sure that the philosophers met, nor that they did not meet. If we are to consider the probabilities, there is room for difference of opinion. On the one hand it could be argued, firstly, that the proposal on the 25th of a visit for the 26th is an indication that the introduction proposed for the 24th did not take place, and, secondly, that Berkeley's subsequent silence is an indication that even the interview proposed for the 26th did not come about. On the other hand, it may be reasonably asked, 'How could so polite and punctilious a man as Berkeley propose to call on Malebranche, apparently by himself, on the 26th, unless an introduction had already been effected, and how could he state positively that he was going to discuss 'certain points', unless the subject had been broached and an appointment made?' The objection from Berkeley's silence might be met by pointing out that no letters of his survive for the latter fortnight of the stay in Paris,[1] that the silence cannot be proved, and that in any case it could be explained, e.g. by a disagreement at the interview.

The story (c) in Stock's *Life*, as it stands, is unreliable, and possibly it should be regarded as entirely worthless. Malebranche died in October 1715. Berkeley was then in England, and had been there all that anxious summer and autumn (Rand pp. 139–54). His second continental tour did not begin till the early autumn of 1716. So there is no foundation for the witticism that he was 'the occasional cause of Malebranche's death'. Does the story raise any presumption that the philosophers met? Dr. Robert Berkeley, the Bishop's brother and Vicar-General, supplied Stock with most of the particulars for the *Life*. If we could be sure that this story came from that source, we might reasonably say that it looks like an oral account given by Berkeley of a meeting either in November 1713, or, rather, as the opening words would suggest, in July 1714, the story being embroidered later by the London wits. On the other hand, as Professor Jessop points out to me, the story is

[1] After the letter of Nov. 25 to Prior the next extant letter is that to Percival dated Dec. 28, 1713 from Lyons.

full of improbabilities and errors other than the date. According to Lyon (*L'idéalisme en Angleterre au XVIIIᵉ siècle*, 1888,
p. 136), Malebranche did not like oral discussions, and his last
illness was slow and painful. Again, no translation of Berkeley's
works had been made at the time. Readers may like to be
reminded that De Quincey, in his essay, *Murder considered as
one of the Fine Arts*, gives a version of Stock's story.

INDEX

TITLES IN THIS SERIES

7. Samuel Bailey, *A Review of Berkeley's Theory of Vision, Designed to Show the Unsoundness of That Celebrated Speculation*, London: James Ridgway, Piccadilly, 1842.

James F. Ferrier, "Berkeley and Idealism," London: *Blackwood's Magazine* (June 1842).

John Stuart Mill, "Bailey on Berkeley's Theory of Vision," London: *Westminster Review*, 38 (1842).

Samuel Bailey, *A Letter to a Philosopher in Reply to Some Recent Attempts to Vindicate Berkeley's Theory of Vision, and in Further Elucidation of its Unsoundness*, London: James Ridgway, Piccadilly, 1843.

James F. Ferrier, "Mr. Bailey's Reply to an Article in Blackwood's Magazine," Edinburgh and London: *Blackwood's Magazine* (June 1843).

John Stuart Mill, "Rejoinder to Mr. Bailey's Reply," London: *Westminster Review*, 39 (1843).

8. George Berkeley, *Philosophical Commentaries, Transcribed from the Manuscript and Edited, with an Introduction and Index by George H. Thomas: Explanatory Notes by A. A. Luce*, printed by Mount Union College, 1976.

9. A. C. Crombie, *George Berkeley's Bicentenary, The British Journal for the Philosophy of Science*, Vol. IV, No. 13(May 1953). Edinburgh and London: Thomas Nelson and Sons Ltd.

10. Alexander Campbell Fraser, *Life and Letters of George Berkeley. With Many Writings of Bishop Berkeley Hitherto Unpublished*, Oxford, At the Clarendon Press, 1871.

11. G. Dawes Hicks, *Berkeley*, New York: Russell & Russell, 1932.

12. G. A. Johnston, *The Development of Berkeley's Philosophy*, London: Macmillan and Co., 1923.

13. A. A. Luce, *Berkeley and Malebranche: A Study in the Origins of Berkeley's Thought*, Oxford, At the Clarendon Press, 1934.

14. C. B. Martin and D. M. Armstrong, eds., *Berkeley: A Collection of Critical Essays. The Articles on Berkeley from "Locke and Berkeley: A Collection of Critical Essays,"* Garden City, New York: Anchor Books, Doubleday & Company, Inc., 1968.

15. I. C. Tipton, *Berkeley: The Philosophy of Immaterialism*, London: Methuen & Co. Ltd., 1974.